GREEK & ROMAN PLAYS

FOR THE INTERMEDIATE GRADES

Dr. Albert Cullum

FEARON TEACHER AIDS

A Paramount Communications Company

Editorial Director: Virginia L. Murphy
Editor: Carolea Williams
Copyeditor: Kristin Eclov
Cover Design: Lucyna Green
Cover Illustration: Helen Kunze
Inside Illustration: Helen Kunze
Inside Design: Diann Abbott

ISBN 0-86653-941-7

Printed in the United States of America
1. 9 8 7 6 5 4 3 2 1

CONTENTS

INTRODUCTION

Walter Schirra, one of the Apollo 7 astronauts, once commented he was pleased that his children came home from school with much innovative math and science, but wondered why they didn't come home more often with a poetic verse or a line from a play. Has our fascination with the technology of education caused us to overlook the values of a lyrical phrase, a musical theme, a painting, or the emotions of tragic and comic plays? The benefits of drama in the classroom are many.

Greek & Roman Plays for the Intermediate Grades incorporates the classic comedies and tragedies of Sophocles, Euripides, Aeschylus, and Plautus. Several of the plays are similar in subject matter, but the authors have told the stories from different points of view.

The plays are organized by author, not chronologically. This provides an opportuntity for students to research background information about the different plays, such as the circumstances leading up to the events, explanations about the main characters and general Greek or Roman mythology.

SELF DISCOVERY

Students who are given opportunities to participate in classroom theater will gain a greater understanding of themselves and others. Through drama, students can place themselves in an imaginary world. In this world, students can identify with heroic deeds and silly laughter. They can discuss the weaknesses of mortals and the power of the gods. Students can begin to express opinions without having to prove what they feel. Drama in the classroom is not intended to prepare children for professional acting careers, but simply to give them an opportunity to express and experience genuine human emotions. Hughes Mearns in his book *Creative Power* (Dover, 1959) states the case for classroom dramatics persuasively:

> "A higher appreciation of art always follows dramatiza-
> tion whether it be of literature or history or geography.
> A child who feels the wind in his limbs, soars as a bird,
> and whose body opens as a bursting flower experiences

these events with a deeper meaning. And those children who danced and sang in the imaginary valley all their days will feel the nearness of those mountains which have once been themselves, and they will be better for it!"

LITERATURE APPRECIATION

In addition to fostering emotional growth, classroom drama can serve as an excellent introduction to great literature. Two of the reasons classical literature has lasted for centuries are that it deals with universal human themes and it can be interpreted on many intellectual and emotional levels. There is absolutely no reason to fear the classics. Children are perfectly able to grasp the conflicts, passions, moral issues, and vocabulary of good literature. Young students can understand what truly creative giants of any period are saying. I will always remember the distinguished character actress Mildred Dunnock's comment about her favorite Electra. Before she became an actress, Miss Dunnock was an elementary school teacher. At an American National Theatre and Academy meeting in New York City, she once stated that her favorite Electra had been a sixth-grade girl!

CURRICULUM INTEGRATION

Classical dramatic literature also supports many areas of the curriculum. Use the plays provided here as a means of extending vocabulary. In the Greek tragedies and Roman comedies presented in this resource, words are often repeated from play to play. Students will have opportunities for "instant review" or "instant replay" as they meet the same words in a variety of situations. Developing vocabulary in this manner is a meaningful learning experience. After reading and discussing the Greek tragedies and the Roman comedies, students could easily add several hundred words to their vocabulary.

Reading a Greek tragedy or a Roman comedy can be a delightful change of pace. Classical literature brings out many parallels with contemporary problems. In the Greek tragedies, the playwrights forcibly express the fact that evil doers suffer consequences, that people make great sacrifices, and that the horrors of war are many. In the Roman comedies, the playwright Plautus points out the generation gap of the times, severe class distinctions, and the frivolity of Roman social life. After reading one of the plays together as a class, invite students to share and discuss their opinions. If given the opportunity, students will amaze you with their depth of understanding of tragic and comic situations.

Stories of the Greek and Roman gods fascinate most students. The gods were an integral part of Greek and Roman culture, so use the plays to teach the attributes, powers, and foibles of the gods in an exciting social-studies unit. Students will become involved with these immortals and will want to know more about them. Encourage students to delve into independent research and to arrive at their own conclusions. Suggest that students organize a Zeus Committee, an Apollo Committee, or an Artemis Committee. Through independent research, children can explore libraries, attics, basements, and local bookstores for all types of information about their particular immortal god. Students may even become interested in writing their own plays based on data collected.

CREATING POSITIVE EXPERIENCES

- When introducing a new play, write the names of the characters on the chalkboard and pronounce each name with the students until it no longer seems strange or unfamiliar.

- Ask for volunteers to read each part. Never assign roles. There are two kinds of children—the ones who want the leading roles and the ones who are too sensitive or too shy to try out for the leading roles. Drama is not only for the obviously extroverted children, but also for the very shy quiet ones. The Greek chorus provides an opportunity for all to participate. In the Greek chorus, shy children can begin to take a step forward and discover their strengths. Here is a place where children are not exposed alone, but have the security of working in unison with others. The Greek chorus provides an easy way to find a place in the sun for every member of the class.

- Limit props. To present a Greek tragedy, all you need are a few platforms. In a Roman comedy, all you need are materials to represent the doors to two or three houses. The doors can be authentic or simply cloth or paper hangings with cut-out openings. Hang signs bearing the names of the owners over the doorways to help the audience identify whose house is whose.

- Keep staging simple. There need not be a change of scenery. The curtain opens once and closes only once. You can be creative in manipulating the Greek chorus. Possibilities are limitless. Try arranging the chorus in formal rows (kneeling or standing), in two separate groups, or scattered randomly about the stage. Chorus members can walk about the auditorium or sit in the first row of the audience.

- Keep in mind that Greek chorus members always speak in unison, clearly and slowly. This is challenging and difficult, but soon students will begin to develop this ability. Even more importantly, the Greek chorus needs to know how vital they are to the success of the play. A Greek play is incomplete without a chorus commenting on the action.

- Keep the action of Roman comedies moving at a swift pace. Timing is important.

- Encourage students to create their own handmade costumes. In my classroom, Creon in Antigone arranged the folds of his large piece of white cloth exactly to his liking. My numerous Electras planned and chose carefully the costumes they wore. All of my royal characters from Queen Clytemnestra to Athena hunted and searched for appropriate pieces of purple or gold to make them look more regal.

- Respect student input and ideas. Presenting plays in the classroom can be a highly creative experience if the approach is student-oriented. Don't concentrate on the final product as much as the process of getting there.

- Provide encouragement. Not only do you have the privilege of introducing great literature to young imaginative minds, but you have the priceless opportunity of giving children the gift of believing in themselves.

ELECTRA

By Sophocles

INTRODUCTION

The Greek tragedy *Electra* is a play about revenge and murder, not ordinary revenge, for it was wished for and planned for many years. Ever since her mother, Queen Clytemnestra, killed her father, King Agamemnon, after his victory in the Trojan War, Electra was tormented by a desire for revenge. She waited years for her brother, Orestes, to grow up and return to his native land to avenge their father's death. Although she was powerless and ill-treated by her mother and stepfather, she continued to be haunted with dreams of revenge—in fact, this dream sustained her in her misery until Orestes finally did return.

Another of the great Greek dramatists, Aeschylus, used the story of Electra and Orestes' revenge in his tragedy *The Libation Bearers*, and centuries later, the German composer, Richard Strauss, wrote his opera *Electra* on the same theme. In the summer of 1969, Sophocles' version of the legend was produced by Joseph Papp and his New York Shakespeare Festival actors. Twenty-five free performances were given on the streets of New York City, and all were enthusiastically attended by both children and adults.

STAGING

In staging *Electra*, only one platform is needed. It should be located in the center of the stage and have steps leading up to it and more steps in back so that the characters can enter the palace. The entrance to the palace is the focal point, and the drama builds up to a crescendo as Electra comes closer and closer to fulfilling her mission. The Greek chorus never enters the palace. They enter and exit from stage right and stage left.

COSTUMES

Everyone can wear floor-length pieces of cloth of a solid color, except Electra. It can be effective to have Queen Clytemnestra and King Aegisthus bedecked with costume jewelry. Electra is dressed in rags and her hair is wild. She spends much of the play wailing on the ground, as her obsession with revenge has almost turned her into an animal.

VOCABULARY

account
accustomed
advised
affairs
afflictions
alas
altar
amends
ancient
anguish
artifice
avenge
axle
bearer
befriend
beseech
birthright
boldly
bondage
brazenly
brink
burden
calamity
canopy
caution
cease
censure
champion
chariot
chastisement
cling
comfort
compensate
condemns
confident
consent
delight
despise
determined
dirge
discord
disgraceful

dishonor
dismay
divulge
dungeon
enforce
entangled
enterprise
entrusted
exile
faithful
fanciful
fatal
fate
forged
foul
frustrate
goddess
greetings
grief
grieve
headlong
human
inflict
inform
insolence
joyous
jubilation
justice
lament
launched
liberty
lock
longing
lurks
luxuries
manhood
manner
memory
meteor
misery
mocking
moderation

mourn
occasion
offerings
oracle
original
persuade
pillar
pity
positive
possessions
prudence
prudent
purge
purify
purpose
rashly
reawakens
recklessness
recognize
remedy
respect
restored
restrain
retribution
robes
sacrificed
scepter
shaft
shameful
shed
shrill
slain
sneer
sorrows
stifles
sufferings
suspect
sustain
thankless
threats
thunderbolts
tidings

tirades   unison   venture
tribute   unjust   wailing
trinkets   urn   wandering
triumphant   utter   warnings
tutor   vengeance   woes
undertake

CHARACTERS

Orestes, only son of Agamemnon and Clytemnestra
Pylades, Orestes' friend
Tutor, Orestes' servant and teacher
Electra, Orestes' sister
Chrysothemis, Orestes' sister
Clytemnestra, Orestes' mother, the Queen
Aegisthus, Orestes' stepfather, the King
Chorus Leader
Chorus
Servants

ELECTRA

Tutor: Now Orestes, son of Agamemnon, how many years have you been longing to see this place, where you are standing now? Here is the place where your sister Electra saved you as a baby when your mother and uncle ended your father, Agamemnon's, life. It was I who carried you away at your sister's orders on the day your father died! I took you to safety, looked after you all these years, and brought you up to manhood. Now you must avenge your father's death!

Orestes: Faithful old friend and servant, your devotion to me is beyond question. Listen, I'll tell you what I have decided to do, and as you listen, make amends to whatever seems amiss. When I went to the oracle to discover how I might best avenge my father's death, the gods answered, "Give those who kill an equal share of their just desserts." My plan is for you to enter the palace to discover the present state of things among those who live here. Their eyes will not recognize you, for the years have wrinkled your face and shaded your hair with much silver. Spin a tale about Orestes having been killed and give your oath that it is true. I am confident that from a forged death I shall rise again like a new meteor to dazzle my enemies. Hear my prayer, oh gods! House of my fathers, receive me with your blessings. I have come to purify and purge. Give me my birthright. Give me my possessions. Let me rebuild my father's fallen house! No more words, for such is my prayer. My friend and teacher, go to your task for now is the time, and time is the umpire in all human affairs.

Electra: (From within the palace.)
Ah me! Alas!

Tutor: Listen, Orestes, a cry of bitter grief.

Orestes: The voice reawakens my memory. Could it be the cry of my sister Electra? Let us wait to hear again.

Greek & Roman Plays for the Intermediate Grades © 1993 Fearon Teacher Aids

Tutor: No! Let us not delay our leave. Let us follow our original plan lest we meet ruin.

(Exit Orestes, the Tutor, and Pylades. Enter Electra.)

Electra: Oh sky that is earth's canopy, each night that dies with dawn I bring my sad songs here. You count how many tears I shed for my lost father. Oh my father! My poor father! My mother and her new husband Aegisthus have taken you from me. I alone, father, mourn your death. Never will I cease from dirge and sad lament. Never! Never! Oh ye gods who see all things, come to my aid! Send my brother Orestes back to me for I can no longer sustain this grief alone.

(Enter the Greek chorus.)

Chorus: Electra, child of a sinful mother, why are you wasting your life in unceasing despair? Your father, Agamemnon, died long ago.

Electra: Oh gentle-hearted women, I know you come to comfort me in my sorrow, but I cannot change or cease to mourn for my father. Leave me and let me weep.

Chorus: You cannot call him back from the hands of death. Must you still cling to misery?

Electra: Unfeeling the mind and hard the heart of one who could forget a father slain.

Chorus: Your heavy burden of grief is not carried alone. Your sister Chrysothemis lives within the palace in peace and is not tired of life. And your brother Orestes, though in exile, awaits his triumphant return to the land of Argos.

Electra: Year after year I wait for him. He wants to come, I know he wants to come, but only disappointment arrives for me.

Greek & Roman Plays for the Intermediate Grades © 1993 Fearon Teacher Aids

Greek & Roman Plays for the Intermediate Grades © 1993 Fearon Teacher Aids

Chorus: Zeus, the king in the heavens, sees all, Electra. Take comfort. Time has power to heal all wounds.

Electra: Half my life is wasted away in hopeless waiting. I am alone, and my strength will soon be gone. Oh gods who rule heaven and earth, make retribution fall upon my mother, Clytemnestra, and her new husband, Aegisthus!

Chorus: Be wise, Electra, and say no more.

Electra: Leave me! Leave me! My ills are past remedy. Never shall I heal my wounds of tears and lamentation.

Chorus: Do not make, my child, trouble on top of trouble.

Electra: Is there moderation in what I suffer? Can it be right for me to neglect the death of my father? If they who killed him do not suffer death in return, then fear of the gods and respect for men have vanished for all mankind.

Chorus: We shall always be here if you call.

Electra: I am sorry to be always complaining. Forgive me. But what woman would not cry to heaven if she saw a father suffering such outrage. My mother has become my bitterest enemy! What happiness do you think I feel when I see Aegisthus sitting upon my father's throne and wearing my father's robes? My cry is for Orestes to come and put an end to all this.

Chorus Leader: Is Aegisthus gone from home that you speak so boldly?

Electra: I would not dare venture out if he were near. He is visiting another city.

Chorus Leader: Then perhaps I might be bold myself and speak with you more freely.

Electra: Aegisthus is not here. Say what you will.

Chorus: What news about your brother Orestes? Is he coming or do we wait in vain?

Electra:	He promises, but his promises come to nothing.
Chorus Leader:	So great an enterprise is not done quickly.
Electra:	Yet I was quick enough when I saved him.
Chorus:	Take heart, Electra. He's a good man and brave. He will not desert you.
Electra:	If I did not believe so, I would have died long ago.
Chorus:	Hush. Say no more. Chrysothemis, your sister, comes.

(Enter Chrysothemis.)

Chrysothemis:	Electra! Why have you again come outside the house spreading your talk? Have you not learned to restrain your useless anger? My sorrow is as deep as yours, but I choose to bow before the storm of my mother and stepfather, for I am powerless. Oh yes, what you think is right, and yet I submit or lose all liberty.
Electra:	To forget your slain father and take your mother's part is shameful. Shameful! I will not yield to them for all the trinkets, luxuries, and delicate food that give you such pleasure. It is enough for me to eat the garbage they fling at me. You might be known as Agamemnon's child, but the world calls you Clytemnestra's daughter. Everyone knows you for what you are—a traitor to the memory of your father!
Chorus:	Do not quarrel. Each of you can help the other.
Chrysothemis:	I am well accustomed to her tirades. But I speak to warn my sister of the danger close to her. They plan to end her long complaints.
Electra:	What punishment can they inflict upon me worse than the pain I have now?

Greek & Roman Plays for the Intermediate Grades © 1993 Fearon Teacher Aids

Electra

Chrysothemis:	I'll tell you everything I know. They have determined to place you in a dark dungeon if you do not cease your wailing, a dungeon so deep that you will never see the sun again. So think on this and be prudent.
Electra:	Is this decided then?
Chrysothemis:	It is decided the moment Aegisthus returns.
Electra:	Let them do what they will.
Chrysothemis:	Are you mad? Do you choose to suffer so?
Electra:	Yes, to escape from the sight of all of you!
Chrysothemis:	Will you not listen and let me persuade you?
Electra:	Never!
Chrysothemis:	Then I speak no more. I leave you now and continue with my errand.
Electra:	Where are you going with those offerings?
Chrysothemis:	I am to lay them on our father's tomb. Our mother sent me.
Electra:	She who killed him is making offerings to him?
Chrysothemis:	She had a dream that frightened her.
Electra:	Oh, gods, gods of our fathers, hear you this?
Chrysothemis	Do you find cause of hope in her bad dream?
Electra:	Fate often hangs upon a word or two. Speak your tale.
Chrysothemis:	In her dream, our mother saw our father return to life and stand beside her. She saw him take the scepter from Aegisthus and plant it on the altar where it burst into a leafy bloom, casting a shadow upon the house.

Greek & Roman Plays for the Intermediate Grades © 1993 Fearon Teacher Aids

Electra: None of her offerings must touch the tomb. Cast them away! How can you think our father could accept such a tribute from the fiend who killed him? Instead, give the memory of our poor father a lock of hair for token, one of yours and one of mine. Kneel to him and pray that he himself will come from the dead to befriend us.

Chorus: Your sister speaks from the heart. Follow her bidding.

Chrysothemis: Do it I will! But keep it secret this that I undertake. If Clytemnestra hears of this, I shall pay dearly for this enterprise.

(Exit Chrysothemis to Agamemnon's grave.)

Chorus: This dream perhaps speaks with the voice of justice. Oh gods, smile upon this house that has seen so many years of shame and misery.

Chorus Leader: Be quiet. Here comes Queen Clytemnestra.

(Enter Clytemnestra with a servant on each side.)

Clytemnestra: Wandering at your own sweet will, Electra, now that Aegisthus is away? You spread evil tales about me, saying I am cruel and unjust. You say I caused your father's death. This I do not deny! But do you ever ask why? Why? Ask me why! This father of yours whom you are always mourning sacrificed a child of mine, a sister of yours. He sacrificed my child to the gods. Who gave him that right to sacrifice a daughter of mine? Yes, I killed your father, and if you think me wrong, correct your own mistakes before you censure mine.

Electra: Could you admit anything more foul than the killing of my father? It was with great anguish that he sacrificed his daughter to the goddess Artemis. Remember his reason for doing so. Artemis was annoyed that father had killed a stag in the sacred forest and she controlled the winds so that father's fleet could not sail to Troy and back home again. Against father's will and with much resistance on his part, he made the painful sacrifice. But what right had you to kill him? Under

Greek & Roman Plays for the Intermediate Grades © 1993 Pearon Teacher Aids

what law? You and your new husband, Aegisthus, thus enforce upon me a life of misery because I never let your consciences sleep. Go! Denounce me in public, call me what you will. Call me vile, brutal, unfilial, impudent. If I am all these things, then I am your true daughter!

Chorus: Electra is so furious that she is beyond all caring whether she be right or wrong.

Clytemnestra: Look how she so brazenly insults her mother. Is there anything she will not stoop to? She has no shame at all!

Electra: I am ashamed at what I do. But your wickedness sets the example for me. Evil in one breeds evil in another!

Clytemnestra: I swear by the goddess Artemis that when Aegisthus returns, you will be punished for this insolence!

Electra: Make your offerings to the gods. My words shall trouble you no longer.

Clytemnestra: (To her servants.)
Lift up the fruit offerings to the god Apollo as I pray. Oh god, Apollo, if there be any who plot in secret to wrest from me the wealth I now enjoy, frustrate them. Let me have royal power until I die. Save me from harm. God Apollo, graciously grant me all my desires. Such is my prayer.

(The Tutor enters.)

Tutor: Is this the house of King Aegisthus?

Chorus Leader: You have made no error. This is it.

Tutor: And this lady is the wife of the King?

Chorus: She is indeed the Queen.

Tutor: Greetings to your majesty. I am the bearer of joyous tidings for you and King Aegisthus.

Greek & Roman Plays for the Intermediate Grades © 1993 Pearon Teacher Aids

Clytemnestra: If the news is joyous, then the message will be friendly. Speak.

Tutor: It is a brief message. Orestes is dead!

Electra: Oh no! This is death to me!

Clytemnestra: What sir? Take no account of her.

Tutor: As I said, Orestes is dead.

Electra: Orestes dead? This is the end for me!

Clytemnestra: Be silent! What was the manner of his death, stranger?

Tutor: I will tell you all. Orestes was in Delphi to compete in the Olympic Games as a chariot driver. To begin with all went well with every chariot. And how they cheered him on as his horse and chariot took the lead. The crowd sensed he was to be the victor and in unison screamed, "Orestes, son of Agamemnon, Orestes, Orestes, Orestes!" But then in a fatal moment his left chariot wheel grazed a pillar, the axle shaft snapped, and Orestes was flung headlong and entangled in the reins. Two men will soon deliver to you an urn filled with his ashes. Such is my sad story.

Chorus: The name of Orestes is blotted out forever! The ancient line of Argive kings has reached its end in calamity!

Clytemnestra: Oh Zeus! Is this news happy or bitter? What bitterness if I must lose a son to save my life.

Tutor: I did not think you would grieve so much at the hearing of my news.

Clytemnestra: A mother never truly hates her child.

Tutor: I see my message was a thankless one.

Clytemnestra: No, not thankless. You have brought me positive proof that he is dead. Now I am free . . . free from all fear of him. Since he left this house, he has charged me with

Greek & Roman Plays for the Intermediate Grades © 1993 Fearon Teacher Aids

his father's death, and each hour that passed, cast over me the shadow of my death. But now I am free of his threats, and without Orestes, Electra's threats are harmless. No longer will her shrill voice utter ugly warnings. I can now live in peace.

Electra: Oh my poor brother! Your unnatural mother exulting in your death. Can this be justice?

Clytemnestra: Justice is done to him, but not yet to you.

Electra: Goddess of vengeance, hear me!

Clytemnestra: She has heard already and has spoken.

Electra: Your hour will come!

Clyemnestra: Who will silence me? You and Orestes?

Tutor: Then I may return to my city now that all is settled?

Clytemnestra: Back home? No. Come inside as our guest and leave this one to wail her sorrows and her brother's, too!

(Exit Clytemnestra and the Tutor into the palace.)

Electra: Orestes, my darling brother, you are dead, but your mother laughs. A sneer she left for you. I now have no father, no brother . . . alone. Where can I turn to, my beloved champion, Orestes? Alas, I must return into bondage to those whom I most hate, those who killed my father. Can this be justice? No! I will never set foot into their palace. Let them come and kill me, for that would be a kindness. I want to die!

(She sinks to the ground.)

Chorus Leader: Oh Zeus! Mighty Zeus! Where are your thunderbolts to destroy the evil that ensnares this house?

Chorus: My daughter, do not weep!

Electra: Who can now avenge Agamemnon, my father? There is no comfort. Let me be!

Chorus: Your fate is hard and cruel!

Electra: Year after year of bitter grief.

Chorus: We have seen your tears!

(Enter Chrysothemis.)

Chrysothemis: I come in great haste to bring you sweet news. Good news! Joyful news! My news will cure all your woes and sorrows.

Electra: What possible cure could you have to remedy my afflictions? They have grown past remedy.

Chrysothemis: Orestes has returned! Truly, beyond a doubt he is here!

Electra: Are you mad? Are you so cruel as to make fun of my calamity?

Chrysothemis: I am not mocking you. By our father's memory, I swear that Orestes is here!

Electra: Leave me!

Chrysothemis: Listen, Electra, I implore you. When I came near father's tomb, I saw a lock of hair upon it . . . freshly cut hair! At once my heart was filled with the thought of our beloved Orestes. Who else would place this tribute on father's grave, but he or you or I? It was not I, and you had not been there. Who else would make such an offering, but Orestes, our brother? Fate has been hard on us, but today may be the beginning of great happiness for us.

Electra: I can only pity you. How little you know!

Chrysothemis: Is this not the best of news I bring you?

Greek & Roman Plays for the Intermediate Grades © 1993 Fearon Teacher Aids

Electra: You are living in a dream world, my sister. The truth is very different from your fanciful thinking.

Chrysothemis: I saw the freshly cut lock of Orestes' hair!

Electra: Poor Chrysothemis. Orestes is dead! Think no more of him.

Chrysothemis: This cannot be true!

Electra: A messenger told us all. He is being made welcome by our mother who smiles.

Chrysothemis: This fills me with dismay.

Electra: We two are left alone. Chrysothemis, let us stand together. Listen to my plan. Together we could be brave enough to take revenge on Aegisthus, the one who brought doom to our father! Give your consent, sister. Stand by me. Let us put an end to our life of dishonor. A life of shameful suffering is disgraceful!

Chrysothemis: What can you be thinking of? Such utter recklessness. How weak we are, how strong our foes. Keep your rage in check before you bring destruction upon both of us. Without Orestes, we must yield to those in power.

Chorus: Prudence and caution are things worth having in this life.

Electra: Then I must do the deed myself! I admire your caution, but I despise your spirit. Away with you! You are no help to me at all. Now go and tell our mother everything you have heard.

Chrysothemis: Give up this folly. Be advised by me.

Electra: No! There is nothing worse than bad advice.

Chrysothemis: Can I say nothing you will accept?

Electra: Go, for your ways can never be mine!

Greek & Roman Plays for the Intermediate Grades © 1993 Fearon Teacher Aids

(Exit Chrysothemis.)

Chorus: Discord within, dividing sister from sister. Electra bathed in an ocean of tears. She is like a bird in the night that cries in inconsolable grief.

(Enter Orestes and Pylades. Pylades is carrying an urn.)

Orestes: Ladies, can you tell me where I can find the house of Aegisthus?

Chorus: You have found it.

Orestes: Would you kindly inform them within the house that we have come.

Chorus Leader: She (the chorus points to Electra) might best do such an errand, for she is nearest of kin.

Orestes: Tell them we come with the ashes of Orestes.

Electra: It is what I feared. Small weight for you, but heavy grief for me!

Orestes: You weep, I know, for what has happened to Orestes.

Electra: I want to hold the urn in my hands and weep. Weep over his dust. Give it to me to hold.

Orestes: Bring it to her and let her hold it. No doubt she is a friend and member of the family.

(Pylades hands urn to Electra.)

Electra: Orestes, my brother, you have come to this! A little dust. Here is all that is left of my beloved. Your death is death to me, but joy to our enemies. Our mother, if she is a mother, dances in delight. Our mother monster runs mad with joy! Oh my dearest brother, I can live no longer without you. Take me with you. Let us be one and share a common grave. Let me die and become a dusty shadow with you.

Greek & Roman Plays for the Intermediate Grades © 1993 Fearon Teacher Aids

Chorus Leader:	Your father, Agamemnon, died. So has Orestes, your brother. So shall we all.
Chorus:	Remember, Electra, all that is mortal dies.
Orestes:	My silence stifles me. What can I say?
Electra:	Why do you speak so strangely?
Orestes:	Are you the princess? Can you be Electra?
Electra:	To my sorrow, I am.
Orestes:	Treated so harshly and with such dishonor?
Electra:	Sir, why do you gaze at me and speak so sadly?
Orestes:	The sight of all your suffering.
Electra:	What you see is nothing. Compared to what evil lurks within that house, my suffering is nothing!
Orestes:	I am one who truly shares your sorrow.
Electra:	The one I had is dead. In this urn are his ashes.
Orestes:	(Pointing to the chorus.) Are these our friends? May I speak so their ears hear?
Electra:	They will not betray you.
Orestes:	Give me the urn and I will divulge all.
Electra:	No! No! Do not be so cruel as to take my beloved from me!
Orestes:	I cannot let you keep it. I insist you hand me the urn.
Electra:	Oh my dear Orestes, how cruel life is. I may not even bury you.
Orestes:	You speak too rashly. This is no time to talk of funerals.

Greek & Roman Plays for the Intermediate Grades © 1993 Fearon Teacher Aids

Electra: Is it wrong to mourn my brother's death?

Orestes: Those are not the ashes of your brother.

Electra: What are you saying?

Orestes: I am saying the truth!

Electra: He lives?

Orestes: As I live!

Electra: You? You are Orestes?

Orestes: Look . . . father's signet! Do you believe me now?

Electra: Oh light of heaven, what joy! Oh day of happiness!

Orestes: It is indeed!

Electra: Women of Argos, look! Look upon Orestes, my brother. Dead only by artifice, and by that artifice restored to me!

Chorus: We see Electra! And to see your happiness brings tears of joy to our eyes!

Electra: Orestes is here, alive! Oh son of Agamemnon, at last you have found me. You have come to your sister!

Orestes: Contain your joy in silence, for they may overhear us within the house. Say little until the occasion gives you leave.

Electra: Who could be silent at your homecoming?

Orestes: We must be prudent. There is danger in too much happiness.

Electra: How can I restrain my joy? Oh women of Argos, Orestes has come home!

Greek & Roman Plays for the Intermediate Grades © 1993 Pearon Teacher Aids

(Enter the Tutor from the palace.)

Tutor: You reckless fools! Can you not see you are standing on the brink of deadly danger? Your plans might well come into the palace before you. Stop your jubilation. Delay now is fatal!

Electra: Who is this man, Orestes?

Orestes: You entrusted me into his arms many years ago. Remember him now?

Electra: Dear friend, to you the House of Agamemnon owes a great deal. You were the only one remaining loyal after our father's death. I call you father, for to me you are a father.

Tutor: Say no more, I beseech you. There will be many days and nights when you may tell all. One word with you, Orestes and Pylades. This is your moment. She is alone. There are no guards near her. Do not delay!

Orestes: Pylades, the hour has come! The gods have opened the door to the House of Agamemnon to avenge his death!

(Drawing his sword, Orestes and Pylades, followed by the Tutor, rush into the palace.)

Electra: Oh Apollo, hear my prayers!
I beseech you Apollo to give us your favor. Help our purpose! Show mankind what chastisement the gods can inflict upon those who practice wickedness!

(Exit Electra into the palace.)

Chorus: There go the hunters into the palace. They are hounds on the trail of the evil doers. Soon there will be a fulfillment.

(Enter Electra from the palace.)

Electra: Listen, oh women! Listen! Soon Orestes will do it. Soon. Listen in silence, oh women!

Greek & Roman Plays for the Intermediate Grades © 1993 Fearon Teacher Aids

Chorus Leader:	Why have you come out, Electra?
Electra:	To give a warning if Aegisthus arrives.
	(A long silence ensues. Electra and chorus freeze as statues.)
Clytemnestra:	(From within the palace.) Help! Death is upon me!!! Aegisthus, where are you? Help! Help!
Electra:	Do you hear? Do you hear?
	(Another loud scream from within, followed by a long silence.)
Chorus:	The cry for vengeance is at work.
Chorus Leader:	Here they come after having taken their revenge. And who condemns?
	(Enter Orestes and Pylades.)
Chorus:	Not I! Not I!
Orestes:	The gods have spoken. No longer will you feel your mother's cruelty!
Chorus Leader:	Beware! Aegisthus is returning!
Chorus:	Back to the house quickly!
Electra:	Leave all to me!
	(Exit Orestes and Pylades into the palace.)
Chorus:	Great him in a friendly manner so that he will not suspect the retribution that awaits him.
	(Enter Aegisthus.)

Greek & Roman Plays for the Intermediate Grades © 1993 Fearon Teacher Aids

Aegisthus: They tell me that some visitors have arrived with the news of the death of Orestes. You must know something about the matter. Speak! What have you heard?

Electra: Of course I know. I loved Orestes! How can I make so little of his death!

Aegisthus: Where are these visitors to be found?

Electra: In the palace. They won their way to Clytemnestra's heart.

Aegisthus: Is the body of Orestes to be seen?

Electra: You will see his body.

Aegisthus: Let the doors of the palace be opened. Let all the people see his body. (Enter Orestes and Pylades carrying the shrouded body of Clytemnestra.) People of Argos, look! Look upon this body and realize that I am master of this state. Turn back the shroud and let me see the face of Orestes.

Orestes: You should lift the veil and make your last farewell.

Aegisthus: So I will. Call Clytemnestra to come witness my final words to Orestes.

Orestes: She will arrive soon.

(Aegisthus removes the cloth covering the face.)

Aegisthus: Oh gods! What is this? What trap have you set for me?

Orestes: You cannot tell the living from the dead?

Aegisthus: You! You are Orestes! No! You have come to kill me! Let me speak!

Electra: Let him say nothing. Nothing less than his life will compensate for all the evil he has done!

Orestes: Come into the palace.

Aegisthus: Why must I go in there?

Orestes: I give the orders. Your life shall end on the spot where you killed my father!

Aegisthus: Must this palace see more sorrow? Death upon death?

Orestes: This palace shall see your death! Time is passing. Enter!

Aegisthus: Lead the way.

Orestes: You go first.

Aegisthus: Afraid I'll cheat you?

Orestes: Lawless men must pay with their lives!

(Aegisthus enters the house, followed by Orestes, Pylades, and Electra. Aegisthus then screams.)

Chorus: Children of Agamemnon, your sufferings are ended at last. Once again the House of Agamemnon is free!

(The chorus exits slowly. The curtain slowly closes on an empty stage.)

Greek & Roman Plays for the Intermediate Grades © 1993 Fearon Teacher Aids

ANTIGONE

By Sophocles

INTRODUCTION

Even though Sophocles wrote this Greek tragedy centuries ago, it is still relevant and vital today. *Antigone* deals with the power and evil of dictatorship and the courage of people who dare to defy it. Many countries throughout the world have been controlled by the iron fists of dictators. The people were told what to do, what to think, and what to read. We are often critical of people who do not fight against their dictators, but this is easier said than done.

Antigone is a play that will live forever. Through the heroine, Sophocles depicts the inner courage of an individual, the strength of the human spirit, and the power of one person. Antigone, a young woman, dares to speak up against the cruel and inhumane decree of Creon, the dictator King.

STAGING

There are three vital factors within the play—Creon (the royal power), the individuals who oppose him, and the Greek chorus. Designate these three factions by using three platforms. A striking contrast in the height of the platforms will make your stage setting most effective. It will be even better to have a set of two or three steps leading up to the highest platform. The royal power has the highest platform and is in the center. The people who speak to him in opposition are on a lower platform to the right, and the Greek chorus is on a still lower platform to the left of center. The platforms will eliminate the confusion of staging. Of course, it is not necessary for the actors to stay on their respective platforms all the time.

COSTUMES

Use large pieces of solid-colored cloth with a hole cut out for the head. Anyone designating royalty can have a tinge of yellow or gold around the edges of his or her robe. The soldiers can wear shorter tunics that come to the knees. The wider the material, the more folds the costumes will have.

VOCABULARY

abhorrence
accusations
advice
advise
amends
appointed
approve
arrogant
authority
avengers
banished
behold
borne
bribed
brief
burial
calamity
cease
chariot
claim
concerns
confirm
confronts
content
convince
decreed
defiant
desperate
destruction
disaster
disgrace
dishonor
dismays
disobedience
distinct
doom
edict

embraced
ensnare
enterprise
entombed
evident
exile
fetch
folly
forbidden
government
grief
guilt
hence
honor
intolerable
issued
judgment
kinship
lament
lamentations
launch
loathsome
lurking
misery
mourn
muttering
necessity
ordained
outrage
override
penalty
perilous
perplexed
possess
proclaim
proclamation
profit

prophesied
prophet
rage
reckless
rejected
remorse
resist
resolved
resource
restrain
rite
royal
sacred
scorn
senseless
sentinel
serpent
shrill
shudder
slain
solemn
suffice
summoned
swerved
temperate
tomb
traitor
tyranny
unnatural
vile
villain
wearisome
will
wisdom
yield

CHARACTERS

Creon, King of Thebes
Eurydice, Creon's wife
Haemon, Creon's son
Antigone, Creon's niece
Ismene, Creon's niece
Teiresias, a blind prophet
Messenger
Sentinels
Chorus Leader
Chorus
A Boy

ANTIGONE

Antigone: Oh sister Ismene! Unhappiness, calamity, disgrace, and dishonor have fallen upon us. Our brothers are dead, and now King Creon has issued a proclamation to all the city. Do you understand? Or, do you not know what outrage threatens one of those we love?

Ismene: Antigone, I have heard nothing . . . nothing since our two brothers were killed in battle.

Antigone: I sensed as much, and that is why I have brought you outside the palace to tell you secretly.

Ismene: There's trouble in your looks, Antigone. What is it? Some dark shadow is upon you.

Antigone: It concerns our brothers' burials. King Creon has ordained honor for one and disdain for the other. Eteocles is to be entombed with every solemn rite and ceremony to do him honor, but as for Polyneices, King Creon has ordered that none shall bury him or mourn for him. Polyneices must be left to lie unwept and unburied. So King Creon has decreed to all the citizens and to you and to me. The person who disobeys King Creon shall be put to death. Will you join hands with me and share my task?

Ismene: What dangerous enterprise have you in mind?

Antigone: To lift his body! Will you join me?

Ismene: Would you dare bury him against Creon's law?

Antigone: My brother I will bury, and no one shall say I failed.

Ismene: You are too bold! King Creon has forbidden it.

Antigone: He has no right to keep me from burying my own brother.

Ismene: Antigone, please remember that we are not trained to fight. I yield to those who have the authority.

Greek & Roman Plays for the Intermediate Grades © 1993 Fearon Teacher Aids

Antigone: I will not attempt to convince you, but I shall bury him. If I have to die for this pure crime, I am content, for I shall rest beside him. But you, if you so choose, may scorn the sacred laws of burial that heaven holds in honor.

Ismene: Nay, I do not scorn, but against King Creon's will I am too weak.

Antigone: Make that your excuse. I go to heap earth upon the brother I love.

Ismene: I fear for you. I tremble for your life.

Antigone: Look to yourself, but do not fear for me!

Ismene: Your heart is full with fever.

Antigone: I know I please whom most I ought to please.

Ismene: But what you intend to do is impossible!

Antigone: When my strength fails me, then shall I cease.

Ismene: But why attempt this hopeless task at all?

Antigone: I will face the danger that so dismays you, for it cannot be so dreadful as to die a coward's death.

Ismene: Then go if you must. Your task is senseless and blind folly, but remember that I love you dearly, sister Antigone.

(Exit Antigone and Ismene in opposite directions. Enter the chorus.)

Chorus: Here comes Creon, the new King of Thebes. Why has he called this gathering?

Creon: By royal edict, I have summoned you here. Upon a single day, two brothers, Eteocles and Polyneices, killed each other. I now possess the throne and royal power by right of nearest kinship with the dead. For the two brothers who died in battle, I proclaim the following edict. Eteocles, none more valiant than he who fought

Greek & Roman Plays for the Intermediate Grades © 1993 Fearon Teacher Aids

Antigone

gloriously for his country and so laid down his life, shall be entombed with every grace and honor. But Polyneices, who returned from exile to fight against us, shall be left unburied. Such is my will!

Chorus: Such is your will, my lord.

Creon: Look to it then and see that you defend the law now made. I have appointed guards to watch the unburied body.

Chorus: What further orders do you lay on us?

Creon: That you resist whoever disobeys!

Chorus: None are so foolish as to long for death.

Creon: Death is indeed the price!

(Enter a sentinel.)

Sentinel: Creon, my King, I am out of breath with running. I am here to tell you all. It may be nothing, still I'll tell you. I can suffer nothing more than what is my fate.

Creon: Is your news unpleasant?

Sentinel: Aye, and fear makes a man pause long.

Creon: Make an end to it. Tell your story and be gone.

Sentinel: Then here it is. The body, the unburied body of Polyneices, has been sprinkled with dust and given the sacred rites!

Chorus: Who has dared a deed so rash?

Sentinel: I know not. There was no sign of digging, the earth was hard, dry, and undisturbed. There was no track of chariot wheels. The person who had done such a deed left no trace at all.

Chorus: Perhaps this deed was ordered by the gods?

Greek & Roman Plays for the Intermediate Grades © 1993 Fearon Teacher Aids

Creon: Silence! Cease your chatter or my wrath will fall upon you. I know that a person could be bribed to do this act. Of all vile things on earth, none is so vile as money. I speak to you plainly and confirm it with this oath—unless you find the author of this burial rite, mere death shall not suffice for you.

Sentinel: I am not the one who did it!

Creon: Then bring forth the person who did!

Sentinel: May the gods grant that the guilty one be found!

(Exit Creon to the palace and the sentinel to the burial grounds.)

Chorus: Many are the wonders of the world, and none so wonderful as human beings. Full of resource against all that comes to harm them. Against death alone is a human being left with no defense.

(Enter sentinel with Antigone.)

Chorus Leader: What strange sight is this? I doubt my eyes!

Chorus: Antigone! Antigone! What have you done? Unlucky daughter of an unlucky father. It cannot be you who disobeyed King Creon?

Sentinel: We caught her in the act of burying her brother! Where is King Creon?

(Enter Creon.)

Chorus: Back from the palace in good time he comes.

Creon: Why do you bring this girl? Where was she taken?

Sentinel: Burying her brother we captured her! All was evident.

Creon: Is this the truth?

Sentinel: I saw her burying the body you had forbidden to be touched. Is that distinct and clear?

Greek & Roman Plays for the Intermediate Grades © 1993 Fearon Teacher Aids

Creon: Speak you who look down at the earth. Are these accusations true or false?

Antigone: I admit to all. I do not deny it!

Creon: Sentinel, you may go. (Exit sentinel.) But tell me, and let your speech be brief, had you not heard of my edict forbidding such a deed?

Antigone: I heard and knew.

Creon: And you dared to disobey my law?

Antigone: It was not Zeus who issued this decree, nor did I believe that you Creon, a man, could override the laws of heaven!

Chorus: Antigone shows her father's temperament, fierce and defiant. She will not yield to any storm!

Creon: Those who are most obstinate suffer the greatest fall. I have seen the wildest horses tamed and only by a tiny bit. This girl is insolent, and she boasts of what she did. Even though she may be my niece, she shall not escape the direct penalty, and neither shall her sister.

(A sentinel exits to fetch Ismene.)

Antigone: Would you do more than simply take and kill me?

Creon: I desire no more.

Antigone: Why do you delay? I have no pleasure in hearing you speak. What greater glory could I have presented to heaven than to bury a brother!

Creon: You are the only one in the city to think so.

Antigone: The people think as I do, but hold their breath for fear of you.

Creon: You honored a traitor.

Antigone: It was a brother who died, not a servant.

Greek & Roman Plays for the Intermediate Grades © 1993 Fearon Teacher Aids

Creon:	Down then to death! No one while I live shall master me.
Chorus Leader:	See, here comes Ismene.
	(Enter sentinels holding Ismene.)
Creon:	You, lurking like a serpent in my house, do you confess you shared this burial or will you swear you had no knowledge of such a deed?
Ismene:	I share the blame and do not shrink.
Antigone:	No! Justice forbids your claim. You refused, and I gave you no part of it!
Ismene:	I am glad to share your danger at your side.
Antigone:	I love not those who love in words alone.
Ismene:	Sister, let me die with you.
Antigone:	Leave me to die alone. Remember, you would not help me. You cannot claim as yours what you rejected.
Ismene:	What joy have I to live when you are gone?
Antigone:	Ask Creon. It was Creon whom you cared for!
Ismene:	Oh mighty Creon! Antigone is Haemon's bride. Can you kill her, the bride of your son?
Creon:	Are there no women in the world but she? An evil wife I like not for my son.
Antigone:	Oh Haemon, hear not your father's scorn.
Creon:	You, Antigone, have become wearisome to me!
Ismene:	Oh mighty King, he is your son! How can you take her from him?
Creon:	It is not I, but death, that stops this wedding.
Chorus:	It seems then, oh Creon, that you are resolved that she must die?

Greek & Roman Plays for the Intermediate Grades © 1993 Fearon Teacher Aids

Creon:	Delay no more! Take them away!
	(Sentinels drag out Antigone and Ismene.)
Chorus:	Thrice happy are those who have never known disaster!
Chorus Leader:	See! Here comes Haemon, your son.
Creon:	Do you come in anger, Haemon, or are you still my loyal son, whatever I may do?
Haemon:	Father, I am your son, and may your wise judgment rule me.
Creon:	In all things be guided by your father. All men pray that they will have obedient children. So, think this woman Antigone your enemy. There is no greater curse than disobedience. This brings destruction upon a city.
Haemon:	Father, it is the gods who give us wisdom, but it is my duty as your son to report to you what the people of the city are saying. The city mourns this girl, and they are saying that she does not deserve death for burying a brother. They say she deserves a crown of gold. Such is the muttering that spreads everywhere. Father, the man who thinks that he alone is wise, is often proven to be empty. There's no disgrace in learning more and knowing when to yield, even if one is king. Oh father King, let your anger cool and profit from the wisdom of another.
Chorus:	Oh King, your son has not spoken foolishly. You can learn wisdom from another.
Creon:	I, King of Thebes, should take a lesson from a boy?
Haemon:	Think of what should be done and not of my age.
Creon:	To honor disobedience? Is that what should be done?
Haemon:	This is not government by tyranny!
Creon:	Villain! Do you oppose your father's will?
Haemon:	Only because you are opposing justice.

Greek & Roman Plays for the Intermediate Grades © 1993 Fearon Teacher Aids

Creon: You shall be sorry for this talk! Bring out that loath-some creature named Antigone, that abhorrence, that she may die before Haemon's very eyes!

Haemon: You shall from this hour not look again upon my face!

(Haemon exits.)

Chorus: In anger he has gone, my lord. The young, when they are greatly hurt, grow desperate.

Creon: He shall not save these women from their doom.

Chorus: Are you prepared to destroy both sisters?

Creon: Not Ismene, for she has not sinned against me.

Chorus Leader: What of the other? How is she to be slain?

Creon: Into a deserted cave she will be thrust. There let her pray for death!

(Creon exits.)

Chorus: Behold! They bring Antigone here. We cannot keep back our tears, which rise like a flood.

(Enter sentinels holding Antigone.)

Antigone: Friends and my countrymen, now do I make my last journey, now do I see the last sun that ever I shall behold. Never another! Ah, cruel doom to be banished from earth.

Chorus: You were too bold, too reckless. Now kingly power takes terrible vengeance!

Antigone: Unwept and unfriended, cheered by no song, they drag me to death! Never again shall I see the sun in the heavens.

(Enter Creon.)

Creon: Enough of this! Hence with her! Into her tomb prison as I commanded. She shall live no more among the living.

Greek & Roman Plays for the Intermediate Grades © 1993 Fearon Teacher Aids

Antigone: Why should I look to heaven for help if this is what the gods approve?

Creon: Your end has arrived. The sentence is passed. I have no comfort to give you!

(Sentinels drag out Antigone.)

Chorus: Behold! Teiresias, blind but seeing all men, enters our land.

(Enter Teiresias guided by a boy.)

Teiresias: My lord, King of Thebes, my journey is shared with this lad, for the blind need someone to guide their steps.

Creon: What tidings, old Teiresias, do you bring?

Teiresias: Hear then the prophet. You will do well to listen.

Creon: Have I ever from your wisdom swerved?

Teiresias: You now tread the razor's edge.

Creon: Your words make me shudder. Speak more.

Teiresias: Before the sun has set, you will give a child of your own body to make amends for murder. The gods are aroused against you. They are avengers, and they lie in your path to ensnare you. Not many hours will pass before your house moans loudly with lamentations. Hatred for you is moving in the city. These are the arrows that I launch at you! But now, lad, lead me home that he many vent his rage on younger men, that he may learn to keep a tongue more temperate and find more understanding within himself.

(The boy leads Teiresias out.)

Chorus: Teiresias has prophesied dread things, oh Creon! Every prophecy he has spoken has been fulfilled.

Creon: Yes, this I know and am perplexed.

Chorus: Oh mighty Creon, listen to his advice.

Greek & Roman Plays for the Intermediate Grades © 1993 Fearon Teacher Aids

Creon:	Advise me and I will listen. What shall I do?
Chorus Leader:	Release Antigone from the cave of death and lay the unburied Polyneices in a tomb.
Creon:	You would have me yield?
Chorus:	We would and quickly. The gods are ready to punish the foolishness of men.
Creon:	How difficult it is to yield, and yet I cannot fight against necessity. Yes, I will yield!
Chorus Leader:	Quickly, go then and do it. Leave not this task to others.
Creon:	Sentinels, make quick your speed and release Antigone from her tomb of death.

(Sentinels run out, followed by Creon. Enter a messenger.)

Messenger:	Listen, you people of Thebes. All is lost! Nothing is firm. You have no happiness.
Chorus:	What is the weight of this heavy news you bring?
Messenger:	I bring you death!
Chorus Leader:	Death? Who is dead?
Messenger:	Haemon is dead!
Chorus Leader:	Slain by himself or by his father's hand?
Messenger:	He killed himself.
Chorus:	Oh Teiresias, how your prophecy comes true!
Chorus Leader:	But look, Eurydice, the Queen, comes forth from the palace. Has she heard about her son?

(Enter Eurydice.)

Eurydice:	Good people, all, I heard. But tell it to me once more, for I am no stranger to bad news.

Greek & Roman Plays for the Intermediate Grades © 1993 Fearon Teacher Aids

Antigone

Messenger: Dear mistress, I will tell you what I saw. I went with Creon up the hill to where Polyneices' body still lay, and we gave it holy washing and prayed to the gods that they would restrain their anger and be merciful. Then from the cave we heard a shrill lament! We rushed to the cave and saw the body of Antigone hanging in death. But Antigone was not alone in that cave of death, for Haemon was there, too. In remorse, we saw him lean on his sword and drive half its length into his body. He embraced Antigone, spilling his royal blood upon her. Dead with the dead he lies!

(Exit Eurydice into the palace.)

Chorus: What can we think of this? The Queen, without a word, has gone hence.

Messenger: It is strange.

Chorus Leader: Her silence seems perilous.

Messenger: It is most unnatural. I'll follow her. (Follows Eurydice into the palace.)

Chorus: Look! Creon comes!

(Enter Creon.)

Creon: Behold, people of Thebes, the slayer of his very own son. My own stubborn ways have borne bitter fruit. My son is dead. Haemon torn from me so young. The fault is mine!

Chorus: Oh, how too late you discern the truth!

(Messenger enters from the palace.)

Messenger: Oh King, more sorrow upon your head! Within your house a second store of misery confronts you.

Creon: What? More? What worse evil yet remains?

Messenger: Queen Eurydice, your wife and true mother of Haemon, is dead! In grief, she plunged a blade into her heart.

Creon: In one fell swoop my son and my wife! Oh gods, are you merciless?

(Sentinels carry in the body of Eurydice.)

Chorus: Behold and see. There is her lifeless body!

Creon: Where will it end? What else can fate hold in store for me? Is there no one here who with one deadly thrust will end my life? My grief crushes me.

Messenger: The Queen cursed you as she died!

Creon: The guilt of slaying my wife and my son is mine alone. Even though I touched them not, I killed them both. Come night with no dawn. I pray for death.

Chorus: Then pray no more. You cannot escape your suffering as decreed by the gods.

Creon: I know not which way to look. All things are crooked that I handle. My life has become intolerable.

(Creon exits into the palace. Sentinels follow with Eurydice.)

Chorus: Proud words of arrogant men in the end meet punishment. Old age learns too late to be wise.

(Chorus exits slowly.)

Greek & Roman Plays for the Intermediate Grades © 1993 Fearon Teacher Aids

Antigone

IPHIGENIA IN AULIS

By Euripides

INTRODUCTION

This play presents a perfect example of how the Greek gods supposedly exerted control over human beings. Sometimes the gods went so far as to demand a sacrifice to appease their displeasure, and citizens were forced to obey, no matter how much they personally objected. This is the case in Euripides' moving drama.

Before the play opens, Agamemnon, King of Greece, had killed a stag in a forest sacred to Artemis, the goddess of hunting. To punish him, Artemis decreed that he must sacrifice his eldest daughter, Iphigenia, before the winds would blow again. Agamemnon's fleet was thus becalmed at the island of Aulis, and his army, anxious to set off for the Trojan War, was about to revolt against his leadership. Despite his love for his daughter, Agamemnon was eventually compelled to do as Artemis commanded.

There are several versions of the myth about Iphigenia, all of which have inspired later poets, musicians, and dramatists to retell her story. In some of these, Artemis relents at the last moment and transports Iphigenia to a distant land to be a priestess. In Euripides' play, however, Iphigenia accepts her fate. Her mother, Clytemnestra, is less understanding. She never forgives her husband for sacrificing their daughter, and the family is cursed with a later history of revenge and murder as dramatized by Sophocles in *Electra* and Aeschylus in his *Oresteian Trilogy*.

STAGING

One small high platform with steps leading up to it will be sufficient. This platform, center stage, is the place where the sacrifice takes place. It can be dramatic to have no character use the platform except Iphigenia at the end of the play. The Greek chorus can huddle around it, and other leading characters can stand near it.

COSTUMES

All characters wear floor-length flowing robes of a solid color, with the exceptions of the soldiers and servants. Their tunics should come only to the knees.

VOCABULARY

abominable
accompany
affairs
altar
appease
aware
beseech
betrayed
boldly
brawl
brink
brutality
cease
clamor
comforted
commit
conceived
confounded
conscience
conspirator
counsel
countenance
crazed
curse
custom
decent
deception
decreed
deed
delight
demigod
desperately

despise
devastate
disaster
divine
doom
eager
envy
escorted
evil
fatal
gaze
greet
groan
hardship
hesitate
honor
horror
humiliated
hymn
ignored
implore
inflicted
intention
loathsome
loyalty
lutes
misery
misfortune
mocking
mortal
mourn
omen

overwhelmed
peril
plot
possess
precious
predicted
pretext
prophet
protest
reasonable
repent
reproach
righteousness
royal
sacrifice
savior
seized
sentinel
slain
sobs
spineless
treacherous
treason
various
verge
victim
vile
vowed
will
witless
woe
worthy

CHARACTERS

Agamemnon, King and leader of the Greek Army
Menelaus, Agamemnon's brother
Clytemnestra, Agamemnon's wife, the Queen
Iphigenia, Agamemnon's eldest daughter
Orestes, Agamemnon's son
Achilles, Greek Army officer and demigod
Old Servant
Chorus Leader
Chorus
Servants
Messenger

IPHIGENIA IN AULIS

Agamemnon: Old man, where are you? Come here instantly.

(Old servant enters.)

Old Servant: My lord Agamemnon, what do you command of me? (Agamemnon paces back and forth without comment.) What new plan do you have in mind?

Agamemnon: Listen to the silence. Not a bird sings, the waves are still, and the winds are hushed.

Old Servant: Why do you worry so? The guards are quiet.

Agamemnon: I envy you, old man. I am jealous of men who live their lives without worry and who do not sense peril.

Old Servant: The letter in your hand you have written many times. You seal the letter and then rip the seal open. Over and over you repeat this act. I have watched you, and often tears stream from your eyes. My lord Agamemnon, at times you seem to be on the verge of madness. I am a loyal servant. Share your agony with me.

Agamemnon: Listen to the silence, old man, and then listen carefully to my story. The prophet Calchas spoke to me about this frightening calm. He predicted that we would not be able to set sail and overthrow the land of Troy unless I made a sacrifice to the goddess Artemis. There would be utter ruin for me and my army unless I made this sacrifice. Listen carefully, old man, listen! The goddess Artemis will make the winds blow if I sacrifice my daughter, Iphigenia, and victory will be mine. I will gain a great victory over Troy, if I agree, but I would never have the cruel strength to kill my own daughter! And yet, after hearing my brother Menelaus advise me to commit this horror, I wrote a letter to my wife, Clytemnestra, asking her to bring Iphigenia to this camp. I contrived the deception that Iphigenia was to marry Achilles, one of my officers, and that it would be a happy marriage for her. Now I know I did great

Greek & Roman Plays for the Intermediate Grades © 1993 Fearon Teacher Aids

wrong to have sent such a letter, and in my hand, I have the truth telling them not to come.

Old Servant: What does this letter say?

Agamemnon: (Reading.)
Clytemnestra, this letter brings you a different message. Do not send Iphigenia to me! Her marriage to Achilles has been postponed.

Old Servant: But will not Achilles be angry at having to postpone his wedding?

Agamemnon: Achilles knows nothing of the marriage. I conceived the plan alone. Forget that your legs are old and quickly deliver this new letter to Clytemnestra before it is too late.

Old Servant: I will run all the way, my lord.

Agamemnon: If you meet them on their way, convince them to turn back. Make them go back!

Old Servant: Yes, my lord.

Agamemnon: Go. Run. Help me out of my agony! (Old servant runs out.) My heart stands close to the brink of grief!

(Exits. Enter the chorus.)

Chorus: The shore and the waves do not speak. All is still. The birds have flown away, leaving behind silent air. Nothing moves on this day.

(Enter Menelaus, shoving the old servant to the ground.)

Old Servant: Menelaus, what you are doing goes against all conscience!

Menelaus: Remember that you are but a servant.

Old Servant: You had no right to stop me and open the letter.

Menelaus: The letter you carried brings evil and disaster upon Greece.

Greek & Roman Plays for the Intermediate Grades © 1993 Fearon Teacher Aids

Iphigenia in Aulis

Old Servant:	Give me the letter!
Menelaus:	Beware, servant, you speak too boldly.
Old Servant:	I will not give up my right to that letter.
Menelaus:	If you do not cease your chatter, you will feel the pain of this stick.
Old Servant:	To die for my lord Agamemnon would be a good death.
Menelaus:	Old man you talk too much.
	(Enter Agamemnon.)
Old Servant:	Lord Agamemnon, Menelaus took the letter from my hand by force and opened it. I could not stop him.
Agamemnon:	What is this brawl?
Menelaus:	I certainly have the right to speak before you listen to a servant.
Agamemnon:	Why do you strike my servant?
Menelaus:	Look into my eyes, Agamemnon.
Agememnon:	Do you think that I, Agamemnon, shrink from the gaze of your eyes?
Menelaus:	This letter that I hold in my hand carries the seeds of treason.
Agamemnon:	I order you to give me the letter.
Menelaus:	No! Not until every Greek has read it.
Agamemnon:	You broke the royal seal, which you had no right to do.
Menelaus:	For this secret plot you will suffer.
Agamemnon:	Have you no shame to pry into my affairs?
Menelaus:	None, for your mind is constantly shifting. Your plans change from day to day. Your mind is treacherous.
Agamemnon:	How I despise your smooth tongue!

Greek & Roman Plays for the Intermediate Grades © 1993 Pearon Teacher Aids

Menelaus: Remember how eager you were to lead the Greek army against the City of Troy? Remember? Remember how you asked for my counsel? I encouraged you to follow the advice of the prophet Calchas to sacrifice Iphigenia to the goddess Artemis so that the Greek ships could sail. You agreed! Remember? In pretext you arranged for her to marry Achilles. Remember? Now your story is that you will not play a hand in your daughter's death! I groan for Greece that she has a ruler so weak and spineless!

Chorus: Brother versus brother is a sad tale to tell. These ugly words are painful to hear.

Agamemnon: You may choose madness, but I will keep my life decent and with honor.

Menelaus: Am I not your brother?

Agamemnon: You are my brother only when you speak like a sane man.

Menelaus: Greece is in trouble. Agamemnon, listen to the silence about you. The gods need and demand the sacrifice. As ruler, you should bear some of the hardship.

Agamemnon: Some god has driven you mad.

Menelaus: To some you are the King of Greece, but to me you are a traitor.

(Enter a messenger.)

Messenger: Oh commander of all the armies of Greece, I run ahead of the others to bring you the news. Your daughter, Iphigenia, and her mother, Clytemnestra, have arrived, and with them is your baby son, Orestes. I know that delight will fill your heart to see them once again. Rumors are spreading about that perhaps a wedding has been arranged for Iphigenia? People wonder who will be the bridegroom. Shall I announce the lutes to be played and the dancing to commence? Will you and Menelaus begin the bridal hymn? Shall I fetch the bridegroom?

Greek & Roman Plays for the Intermediate Grades © 1993 Fearon Teacher Aids

Agamemnon: We are grateful for their safe arrival. Now go get some rest. (Exit messenger.) This is the beginning of my disaster. Look at me, brother Menelaus, and see my face weep. What countenance can I present to my wife, Clytemnestra? She will soon discover that I am an author of evil. Iphigenia will cry out asking why her father is sending her to her death. Even the infant child, Orestes, will utter sounds that are meaningless in protest. I have fallen into a pit out of which there is no escape.

Chorus: We grieve over the King's misfortune.

Agamemnon: You have won, Menelaus.

Menelaus: No! I withdraw all the words I said to you. My words were witless. It is an outrageous thought to sacrifice a daughter! My thoughts have changed, and again we are brothers.

Chorus: A worthy speech, Menelaus.

Agamemnon: My thanks reach out to you, brother. You have spoken worthy of yourself. Quarrels between brothers are loathsome. But I'm afraid we have reached a fatal place, and there is no point of return.

Menelaus: I don't understand your words. No one can force you to sacrifice your daughter.

Agamemnon: I could secretly return them home, but I doubt if I can keep the secret from the whole army.

Menelaus: You do wrong to fear the mob so desperately. The army need not know.

Agamemnon: The prophet Calchas will see that everyone knows of the intended sacrifice. These prophets are the curse of the earth. I feel myself quite helpless. Menelaus, take all precaution that Clytemnestra not discover my plan to sacrifice Iphigenia. (Speaking to the chorus.) And you, guard my plans well!

(Exit Agamemnon and Menelaus.)

Chorus: Many are the natures of man, various their manners of living, yet a straight path is always the right one.

Greek & Roman Plays for the Intermediate Grades © 1993 Fearon Teacher Aids

Chorus Leader:	Behold here comes Clytemnestra, the Queen, with her princess daughter, Iphigenia, holding her baby brother, Orestes.
Chorus:	Let us prepare to receive them.
	(Enter Clytemnestra, Iphigenia, and Orestes.)
Clytemnestra:	Noble family of Agamemnon, welcome.
Chorus:	Gently and without clamor we greet you.
Clytemnestra:	It is a good omen to be greeted so kindly. I am here to lead my daughter into a blessed marriage. And this is Orestes, Agamemnon's young son.
Chorus:	Agamemnon comes!
	(Enter Agamemnon.)
Clytemnestra:	Most honored lord, we arrive at your command.
Iphigenia:	Seeing you again, dear father, I am happy.
Agamemnon:	You speak for both of us, Iphigenia, beloved daughter.
Iphigenia:	It was a wonderful thing you did bringing us here. Your brow is worried, your eyes have no quiet within them . . . they are full of tears. Are you not glad to see us?
Agamemnon:	Soon, Iphigenia, there will be a long parting to come for both of us.
Iphigenia:	You speak in riddles, father. We just arrived. What is this long parting you speak of?
Agamemnon:	Iphigenia, you will be leaving me to go on a long journey.
Iphigenia:	Shall I go on this long journey alone, or will my mother and young brother accompany me?
Agamemnon:	You will go alone, daughter.
Iphigenia:	Where will my new home be, beloved father?
Agamemnon:	You ask too many questions. Now go to get some rest. (Exit Iphigenia.) Forgive my self-pity, but giving my child to Achilles in marriage makes my heart sad. Yes, there is also happiness, but it is still giving a daughter away.

Greek & Roman Plays for the Intermediate Grades © 1993 Pearon Teacher Aids

Clytemnestra: I, too, am not unfeeling. When will the marriage to Achilles take place?

Agamemnon: To bring them good luck, we shall wait until the moon is shining at its fullest. And I would like to add that I shall give Iphigenia away.

Clytemnestra: Where shall I stay?

Agamemnon: You will return home to take good care of Electra and Chrysothemis, our two younger daughters.

Clytemnestra: It is against all custom that the mother not lift the wedding torch for her daughter.

Agamemnon: I say it is wrong for you to stay.

Clytemnestra: It is a mother's right to be at her daughter's wedding.

Agamemnon: It is wrong of a mother to leave two unattended daughters at home.

Clytemnestra: You are very aware that they are well guarded and most safe.

Agamemnon: My final words to you are to go!

Clytemnestra: No! You do your part at the wedding, and I shall stay to do my part! (Exits in anger.)

Agamemnon: I have become a conspirator against my own loved ones. I am confounded! Yes, I must go to the prophet Calchas to ask him what would please the goddess Artemis the most, even though her wish might spell my doom. (Exits.)

Chorus: Behold, here comes Achilles.

(Enter Achilles.)

Achilles: Where is Agamemnon? Tell him I am here. Tell him that all of Greece is ready to attack Troy.

(Enter Clytemnestra.)

Clytemnestra: I heard your voice, Achilles, and I greet you with much pleasure.

Achilles: I do not know you.

Clytemnestra:	Agamemnon is my husband, and soon you will marry our daughter, Iphigenia.
Achilles:	I do not understand your words, my lady. What marriage do you speak of? I have never courted your daughter, and neither has Agamemnon spoken to me of this planned marriage.
Clytemnestra:	Now, I do not understand you. Your words amaze me!
Achilles:	Let us try to solve this riddle together. Perhaps we both speak the truth.
Clytemnestra:	I think the whole marriage has been a lie! I am covered with shame in speaking to you.
Achilles:	Do not be overly concerned. It is but a light matter. Perhaps the gods are mocking us.
Clytemnestra:	I am humiliated by this deception. Farewell. My eyes are too embarrassed to look upon your countenance.
Achilles:	I, too, say farewell and go to seek Agamemnon.

(Enter the old servant.)

Old Servant:	Do I have permission to speak?
Clytemnestra:	Speak.
Old Servant:	You remember my loyalty, my lady? I have been loyal to you and to your children.
Clytemnestra:	Yes, your loyalty has never been questioned. You have been a servant in our palace for many, many years.
Old Servant:	I am more loyal to you, Queen Clytemnestra, than to King Agamemnon.
Clytemnestra:	Do not hesitate to present me with this mystery that you are guarding.
Old Servant:	I tell you directly that King Agamemnon plans to kill your daughter with his own hand.
Clytemnestra:	Out of your mouth come the words of a crazed mind!
Old Servant:	I speak the truth!

Greek & Roman Plays for the Intermediate Grades © 1993 Fearon Teacher Aids

Clytemnestra:	Why? Why? What horror has entered his mind to commit such a deed?
Old Servant:	The prophet Calchas informed Agamemnon that the goddess Artemis will not allow the Greek fleet to sail unless Agamemnon sacrifices Iphigenia. You know all the mystery now!
Clytemnestra:	And the marriage was just a pretext to bring her here.
Old Servant:	Yes.
Clytemnestra:	Poor Iphigenia. I have escorted you to your death. I cannot hold back my tears.
Old Servant:	Weep, my lady, weep.
Clytemnestra:	Old servant, are you sure you speak the truth?
Old Servant:	I was on my way to you with a second message from Agamemnon telling you not to come.
Clytemnestra:	Why didn't you deliver the second message?
Old Servant:	Blame Menelaus! He is the cause of all our ruin, for he tore the letter from my hand.
Clytemnestra:	Do you hear this story, Achilles?
Achilles:	I hear the misery that has been inflicted upon you.
Clytemnestra:	You were used to trick my daughter to coming here.
Achilles:	I shall reproach Agamemnon for his actions.
Clytemnestra:	You are a demigod, Achilles, and I but a mortal. I cast myself at your knees to beg for your protection. True, the marriage plans were false! I brought my daughter to you in good faith. I implore you to raise your right hand in our defense. You are the child of a goddess, you are the only altar at which I can seek help!
Chorus:	Mothers possess a powerful spell when they fight to protect their children.
Achilles:	Your pride and anger lifts my soul. I shall make right these abominable wrongs. Your daughter, Iphigenia, will not die at the hands of her father. Be calm and comforted.

Greek & Roman Plays for the Intermediate Grades © 1993 Fearon Teacher Aids

Chorus:	Your words are worthy of you, Achilles.
Clytemnestra:	I sing your name in praise. Always will I praise you, Achilles. May the gods bless you for helping the unfortunate, such as I.
Achilles:	Listen to my plan. First you must speak to Agamemnon. Beseech him not to kill Iphigenia. If he refuses to listen to your plea, come to me.
Clytemnestra:	If I fail to change his mind, where can I find you?
Achilles:	Like a sentinel, I shall be near by.
Clytemnestra:	It shall be as you have spoken.
	(Exit Clytemnestra and Achilles.)
Chorus:	Poor Iphigenia, your head will wear a crown of sacrifice. Poor Iphigenia!
Chorus Leader:	Woe the times when men push righteousness behind them!
Chorus:	Poor Iphigenia!
	(Enter Clytemnestra.)
Clytemnestra:	Has Agamemnon arrived? Do you not hear the tears of my daughter? She moans and sobs, hearing of her father's plot.
Chorus:	Behold! Agamemnon arrives.
	(Enter Agamemnon.)
Agamemnon:	I am glad you are here. Send for Iphigenia to join me.
Clytemnestra:	Iphigenia, come! Your father wills you to come. Bring Orestes with you.
Chorus:	Iphigenia, come! Your father wills it so.
	(Enter Iphigenia carrying Orestes.)
Clytemnestra:	Behold, Agamemnon, she is here. She is obedient.
Agamemnon:	Why are you crying, Iphigenia? Why do you not look at me? Why do your eyes search the ground? Why is there terror in your face?

Greek & Roman Plays for the Intermediate Grades © 1993 Fearon Teacher Aids

Clytemnestra:	Agamemnon, my husband and King, answer this question with the courage of a man.
Agamemnon:	Speak.
Clytemnestra:	Do you intend to kill your child and mine?
Agamemnon:	What a vile question you ask.
Clytemnestra:	Answer my question!
Agamemnon:	Your question is not a reasonable one.
Clytemnestra:	Answer!
Agamemnon:	My secret has been betrayed.
Clytemnestra:	Yes, I know all. I know fully your intention. Your refusal to answer directly the question is your confession to this horrible deed.
Agamemnon:	Lying would only add greater shame to my misfortune.
Clytemnestra:	You would kill your daughter to win a war? Is your only thought to lead armies and win battles? Do not commit this sin. After you sacrifice a daughter, what prayers can you speak? Do you think your other children at home will greet you with smiles when you return from battle? Speak to me! Be wise, Agamemnon. Do not force me to become a woman of evil because of what you plan to do. Be wise and repent. Do not slaughter your daughter and mine!
Chorus:	Yield, Agamemnon, yield. Together save your child!
	(Iphigenia hands Orestes to a servant.)
Iphigenia:	Do not take away my life, father. The sweetness of life is too precious to me. Father, look into my eyes and see my heart. See, even little Orestes begs you to spare my life. I beseech you.
Chorus:	Be merciful, Agamemnon.
Agamemnon:	I love my children, but it is terrible for me to dare this thing and terrible not to dare it! It is the prophet

Greek & Roman Plays for the Intermediate Grades © 1983 Fearon Teacher Aids

Calchas who has decreed your death, lovely daughter, not I. The Greek army is maddened with desire to sail for Troy, and if I do not appease the goddess Artemis, the soldiers will kill us all. I do not dare change my mind. All Greece forces upon me this sacrifice of you. We are weak against this force. Oh daughter, Greece turns to you and to me for help.

(Agamemnon and servant carrying Orestes exit.)

Clytemnestra: Iphigenia, your father has betrayed you and now has fled.

Iphigenia: Oh mother, Artemis has chosen me for sacrifice, and I shall be slain by my father's hands.

Chorus: We pity you for your evil fate.

(Enter Achilles.)

Achilles: The whole army is shouting.

Clytemnestra: What are they shouting?

Achilles: It is about Iphigenia. They insist she be sacrificed to the goddess Artemis.

Clytemnestra: And did you not attempt to save her as you vowed?

Achilles: Yes, but I too am in danger.

Clytemnestra: What danger threatens you?

Achilles: They threaten to stone me to death. Every soldier has turned against me. Even my own men will not listen to reason.

Clytemnestra: Poor Iphigenia, all is lost now.

Achilles: The soldiers say I have become a slave to this false marriage.

Clytemnestra: The mob is a terrible, frightening thing.

Achilles: However, I will defend you both.

Clytemnestra: You, fight thousands of soldiers alone?

Greek & Roman Plays for the Intermediate Grades © 1993 Fearon Teacher Aids

Iphigenia in Aulis

Iphigenia: Mother, listen carefully to my words. Something has seized my heart and overwhelmed me. Mother, I want to die! I want to die for Greece gloriously! All Greece turns her eyes to me, and to me only. Through my sacrifice, the Greek fleet will sail, for Artemis will make the winds blow. Through my sacrifice, Greece will devastate Troy! Through me, the barbarians will no longer exist. As the savior of Greece, I will win honor, and my name will be blessed throughout the country. Mother, you gave birth to me not only for yourself, but for all Greece. Oh mother, if the goddess Artemis seeks my death, who am I to disagree? Who am I to oppose her divine will? It is right that I be sacrificed!

Chorus: Oh child, you play a noble role!

Achilles: Oh daughter of Agamemnon, I envy you! I envy you because Greece has chosen you and has ignored me. Your soul is noble, Iphigenia! If you change your mind, call my name, and I will rescue you.

(Exits.)

Iphigenia: Mother, do not weep for me. Do not make a coward of me.

Clytemnestra: What must I do but cry?

Iphigenia: After I am dead, do not mourn for me.

Clytemnestra: Is not losing a daughter reason for mourning?

Iphigenia: Mother, I am not lost, but saved! I say good-bye to all now, and my wish for Orestes, my little brother, is that he grow into a strong man. And mother, do not hate my father, your husband. Against his will he sends me to be sacrificed. It is the will of the gods.

Clytemnestra: He is unworthy of the title King! (Iphigenia starts toward the steps.) Iphigenia, daughter, do not leave me!

Iphigenia: Stop! I forbid you to have tears! (She climbs the steps. Clytemnestra exits.) Lift up your voices, people. Let us sing in honor of Artemis!

Chorus: Never will your glory fade away! Never! Never!

Iphigenia: Oh glorious day, to another world I soon go. Beloved day, farewell! (She slashes her throat and dies.)

Chorus: Look at the girl who walked to the altar of death!

Chorus Leader: All hail to the goddess Artemis!

Chorus: All hail to Artemis! Greece will be crowned with victory.

(Chorus slowly exits. Curtain slowly falls.)

Greek & Roman Plays for the Intermediate Grades © 1993 Fearon Teacher Aids

Iphigenia in Aulis

THE TROJAN WOMEN

By Euripides

INTRODUCTION

The chorus of women in *The Trojan Women* talk to us about the horrors of war. Their words, their actions, and their tears make it painfully clear that war is devastating, sorrowful, and tragic. After ten years of fighting, the City of Troy fell to the Greeks, and only the women survived. Euripides makes it very plain that often the innocent victims of war suffer the most. *The Trojan Women* is a protest against war uttered centuries ago by a sensitive playwright. The message is not unlike protests uttered now and in the past by many throughout the world.

Queen Hecuba's youngest daughter, Cassandra, has become a name associated with a pessimistic person who foresees doom and disaster, but who is never believed. In this play, she prophesies the misfortunes that will overwhelm the royal Greek family of Agamemnon. These misfortunes are dramatized by Aeschylus in his *Oresteian Trilogy*. Euripides was so fascinated with the destruction of Troy and the fates of the survivors that he approaches the subject again in *Hecuba*.

STAGING

It is most effective to have one platform large enough for only two characters at one time. As each main character presents his or her problem, he or she speaks directly to the audience while climbing the steps to the platform. The Greek chorus, here, the Trojan women, form a semi-circle around the platform as they answer the character who is speaking. If you have a spotlight, shine it on the speaker on the platform while the chorus makes subtle movements in the shadows.

COSTUMES

The women of Troy are disheveled and dressed in rags. If possible, cast the role of young Astyanax with a young child.

VOCABULARY

abominable
accentuate
accumulates
acquaintance
alas
allotment
ancient
barbarian
bemoaning
bore
brilliance
brine
choir
confronts
countenance
counterpart
culmination
decision
deliberately
descend
descendants
devise
dirge
disasters
doomed
drone
embark
endure
exists
exposed
feeble
fetch
foreign
frantic
frenzied
gallantly
ghastly
gleeful

glory
grief
grievous
hapless
haste
hauling
hearth
herald
heroic
humiliate
imprecations
inscription
intolerable
invoking
lair
lamentations
laurels
looms
maledictions
matricidal
merciless
misery
mistress
mortals
mourning
native
necessity
nobility
nuptials
oblivion
ordinance
ornament
particularize
perish
piteous
plundered
ply
prosperity

prostrate
provoke
radiance
rejoice
resurrected
sacred
scoundrel
serene
shed
shuddering
sober
solitary
staff
strain
survivor
swan song
swoon
tasks
tatters
toiled
tomb
tournament
towering
treacherous
usage
utter
veers
vengeance
virtues
wedlock
wits
woeful
woes
wretched
yearnings
yoke

CHARACTERS

Hecuba, old Queen of Troy
Cassandra, Hecuba's daughter
Andromache, Hecuba's daughter-in-law
Astyanax, Hecuba's grandson
Talthybius, herald of the Greeks
Chorus Leader, a Trojan woman
Chorus, Trojan women
Soldiers

THE TROJAN WOMEN

Hecuba: Up, up, poor soul, lift your head and your neck from the ground. Face life and admit that Troy no longer exists and that the royal family of Troy is doomed. Fortune veers, but be brave. I must sail with the stream and the wind of fate. Alas, I weep! And why should I not weep in my misery? My country is lost . . . my children . . . my husband. What a worry bed this earth is for my heavy, weary limbs. Oh, you Greek ships that crossed the purple brine and in the bay of Troy dropped anchor, soon you will carry me off to slavery. Yes, an old woman like me. Oh women of Troy, let us weep together. Troy is a city of smoking ruins, never to be resurrected again! I shall be like a mother hen, women of Troy, leading you in your song of sorrow. Oh how different my songs are now. Once I sang gleeful songs to the gods, and I was the one, as Queen of Troy, to stamp my foot as a signal for the dancers to begin.

(Enter the chorus leader.)

Chorus Leader: Hecuba! I heard your piteous lamentations ringing through the tents. Shuddering fear grips the hearts of the Trojan women who are bemoaning their slavery. Why do you wail such a bitter song? Has the time arrived for one of us?

Hecuba: My child, the crews of Greek rowers are stirring down the river.

Chorus Leader: Ah me! What does that mean? The time has come, I suppose, when the ships will carry me away from my native land.

Hecuba: I do not know, but I suspect the worst.

Chorus Leader: Woeful women of Troy, come and hear your doom. Come out of the tents. The Greeks are preparing to set sail for home.

Greek & Roman Plays for the Intermediate Grades © 1993 Fearon Teacher Aids

Hecuba: Oh please, do not bring frenzied Cassandra out here for the Greeks to insult. Please, do not add grief upon grief. Oh City of Troy, hapless Troy, this is your end. Hapless are they who have lost you, both the living and the dead.

(Enter the chorus.)

Chorus: Ah me! In fear and trembling we leave our tents to hear your words. Oh Queen, have the Greeks made their decision? Is it death for us, or are the Greek sailors already preparing to push off and ply their oars?

Hecuba: My children, I have been here since daybreak with my heart in a swoon of dread.

Chorus: Has some herald of the Greeks been here already?

Hecuba: The hour of allotment must be near.

Chorus: Oh Queen Hecuba, which one of the islands will they take us to? Unhappy us, to be sent so far from our City of Troy!

Hecuba: Alas! Whose wretched servant shall I be? Where, where on earth shall this old woman toil, useless as a drone, a feeble ghastly ornament? To be posted to watch at a door or to become a children's nurse? Poor me, I who in Troy was once paid the honors of a queen!

Chorus: Alas! How piteous are your lamentations!

Woman 1: No more shall I ply my flying shuttle in Trojan looms.

Woman 2: For the last time, I look upon the graves of my parents . . . for the very last time!

Chorus: Look, here comes a herald from the Greek army. What news does he bring? What news will he tell? What does it matter? We are already servants of the Greeks!

(Enter Talthybius.)

Talthybius: Hecuba, you know I made many trips to Troy as messenger for the Greek army. That makes me an acquaintance of yours of long standing. I am Talthybius, here to announce the latest news.

Greek & Roman Plays for the Intermediate Grades © 1993 Pearon Teacher Aids

The Trojan Women

Hecuba:	Here it comes, Trojan women. This is what I have long been dreading.
Talthybius:	The assignments have already been made, if that was your dread.
Hecuba:	Ah! Where do we go? To what city do they send us?
Talthybius:	You were each assigned individually to separate masters.
Hecuba:	Then who received whom? Is there good luck ahead for any of Troy's daughters?
Talthybius:	Yes, I can tell you, but you must particularize your questions one at a time.
Hecuba:	Then tell me, who received my daughter, poor Cassandra?
Talthybius:	King Agamemnon took her as a special prize.
Hecuba:	What? To be the servant of his wife, Clytemnestra? Ah me!
Talthybius:	No, she is to be his wife as well.
Hecuba:	Oh my poor daughter! And what of the daughter you lately took away from me? Where is she?
Talthybius:	You mean Polyxena? Of whom do you speak?
Hecuba:	Just her! To whom does the lot yoke her?
Talthybius:	She has been appointed to serve at the tomb of Achilles.
Hecuba:	Ah me! To serve at a tomb? My daughter? But what new usage or ordinance is this that the Greeks have?
Talthybius:	God bless your child. She rests well.
Hecuba:	What words are these? Tell me, does she see the sun?
Talthybius:	She is in the hands of fate. Her troubles are over.
Hecuba:	And what of Hector's wife, the unhappy Andromache? What luck had she?
Talthybius:	The son of Achilles took her also, as a special gift.

Greek & Roman Plays for the Intermediate Grades © 1993 Fearon Teacher Aids

Hecuba:	And whose servant am I, this ancient body who needs a staff in her hand to help her two legs walk?
Talthybius:	The King of Ithaca, Odysseus, received you for his slave.
Hecuba:	Ah me! An abominable, treacherous scoundrel I will have for a master, an enemy of justice, a lawless beast whose double tongue twists all things up and down and up, who turns every friendship to hate. Oh women of Troy, wail for me. I go to my doom. Ruin and misery are mine. The unluckiest lot has fallen to me!
Chorus Leader:	Oh Queen, you know your fate, but who is to be master of my life?
Talthybius:	Come women, you must fetch Cassandra out here at once. I will put her in my King's hands and then return for the others. Wait! I smell smoke! Are the Trojan women burning something? Are they starting fires within their tents? Their death may be very fine for them, but the Greeks won't like it, and I don't want to get myself into any trouble.
Hecuba:	It is no fire. It is not that. It is my child, frantic Cassandra. Here she comes hurrying out.
	(Enter Cassandra waving a smoking stick.)
Cassandra:	Look! Look! Look how I light up the sky. Yes, I am to marry one of royalty. Poor mother, your time is all taken up with mourning and lamentations for my dead father and our dear country. Therefore, I must now hold aloft the torch myself, for my own wedding. See its radiance, its brilliance! Lift high the high foot. On with the dance. Let it be as in the proudest days of my father's prosperity. The choir is sacred. Lead it, Phoebus, in thy temple among the laurels. Sing, mother, sing and dance, whirling in and out. Trip it with me, as you love me. Shout the marriage greeting to me, the bride. Wish her joy with songs and shouts.
Chorus Leader:	Hecuba, will you not seize your frantic daughter?
Hecuba:	Oh god Hephaestus, you carry the torches at the wedding of mortals, but it was cruel of you to fan this flame. How unlike the high hopes I had. Ah me! My

Greek & Roman Plays for the Intermediate Grades © 1993 Pearon Teacher Aids

The Trojan Women

child, my poor Cassandra, never, never, never did I think your nuptials would be held amidst the spears and lances of the Greeks. Give me the torch, Cassandra. In your frantic haste, you do not hold the torch straight. Our disasters have not made your mind sober. Women of Troy, take her torch. Let your tears answer her wedding songs.

Cassandra: Mother, crown my conquering head. Rejoice in the royal match I make. King Agamemnon will find me a most fatal bride! I shall kill him. I shall ruin his house. I shall take vengeance for my father and my brothers. But these things can wait. I shall not sing of the matricidal tournament my marriage will start, nor of the utter overthrow of the house of Agamemnon! It comes to this . . . . If a man is wise, he will shun war, but if war must come, it is a crown of honor for a city to perish in a good cause. In an evil cause there is infamy! Therefore, mother, you must not feel sorry for our country. This wedlock of mine is the means by which I shall destroy our worst enemies, mine and yours.

Talthybius: It is well that Apollo gave you crazy wits. Otherwise it would have cost you dear to be speeding my commanders from the land with such maledictions. Since you are not quite right in the mind, I'll let your words go down in the wind. Come with me to the ships, a fine bride for the King. (To Hecuba.) And you be ready when they come for you.

Cassandra: Yes, let me fly to my bridegroom's bed of death! Where is the King's ship? Where must I embark? There is no time to lose. Farewell, mother, do not weep. Oh dear country, oh my brothers under the earth, oh my father, you will not have long to wait for me. But I shall descend to the dead a conquering hero, having destroyed the house of Agamemnon, by whom our house was destroyed.

(Talthybius leads Cassandra out. Hecuba collapses.)

Chorus Leader: Nurses of old Hecuba, can't you see your mistress has fallen, prostrate and speechless? Take hold of her. Will you leave the old woman dying?

Greek & Roman Plays for the Intermediate Grades © 1993 Fearon Teacher Aids

Chorus: Lift her upright!

Hecuba: Leave me! Leave me, my daughters. Let me lie where I have fallen. I have full cause for falling, the things I have to endure, and have endured, and shall endure. Oh ye gods! It's poor helpers indeed I am now invoking, but still it's the fashion to call upon the gods when trouble overtakes us. This is my swan song. First, I will sing of my blessings and thus accentuate the pity of my woes. I was a queen. I married into a king's house, and there I bore my excellent children, of whose like no mother can boast, Trojan or Greek or barbarian. These children I saw fall in battle with the Greeks. And Priam, their father, his loss was not reported to me by others, for with my very own eyes I witnessed his death. I saw my city plundered, my daughters taken away from me, and no hope have I that I will ever see them again or they me! And finally, the crown of wretched misery, I go to Greece to an old age of slavery. They will put me to all the tasks that are intolerable to the aged. I shall be a door servant, me, the Queen of Troy. Or I shall have to bake bread and lay to rest on the hard ground my wrinkled back that once slept in palace beds. This poor body of mine will be dressed in rags and tatters, an insult to my former prosperity. Unhappy woman that I am! What a future confronts me. Oh Cassandra, my poor child. And Polyxena, poor girl, where, where are you? None of my daughters and sons are here to help their poor mother, so why then should you lift me up? What is there to hope for? Lead me to some lair where the stones will be my pillow. Let me fling myself on the ground there and waste out my cursed life in weeping.

Chorus: I sing a new strain, a strain of weeping.

(Enter Andromache and her young son Astyanax with soldiers on each side of them.)

Chorus Leader: Hecuba, look! Here comes Andromache, wife of your dead son, Hector, bound for a foreign land.

Chorus: Clutched to her skirt is her son, Astyanax. Hapless woman, where are they taking you?

Andromache: Our masters, the Greeks, are hauling me off.

Greek & Roman Plays for the Intermediate Grades © 1993 Fearon Teacher Aids

The Trojan Women

Hecuba:	Ah me.
Andromache:	Why do you lament? Lamentation is mine.
Hecuba:	Ah me.
Andromache:	Grief is mine.
Chorus:	Ah me.
Andromache:	Misery is mine.
Hecuba:	My child, wife of my son, gone is the glory, gone is Troy.
Chorus:	Gone, gone is Troy.
Hecuba:	The splendor, the fortune of the city, in smoke.
Andromache:	Oh come, my husband, I beseech you!
Hecuba:	You cry out for the one who is dead.
Andromache:	Come and save your wife!
Hecuba:	Oh cruel is the grief we bear.
Andromache:	Deep are our yearnings for the city that is gone.
Chorus:	Grief on grief accumulates!
Andromache:	Oh my husband, before the Temple of Pallas the yoke of slavery is placed upon Troy, and the end has come.
Chorus:	Oh our country, our poor country!
Andromache:	I weep at leaving you.
Chorus:	Now you see the bitter end.
Andromache:	To leave my own home where my baby was born.
Hecuba:	Oh my children, you have gone and left your mother in a deserted city. You have left me to the bitterness of dirges, lamentations, and fountains of tears. The dead shed no tears, for they have forgotten their grief.
Chorus:	What a sweet thing tears are to those burdened with pain.

Greek & Roman Plays for the Intermediate Grades © 1993 Fearon Teacher Aids

Andromache: Oh Hecuba, mother of Hector, of the hero whose spears destroyed so many of the enemy, do you see this sight?

Hecuba: I see the hand of the gods. Some men they raise from nothingness to towering heights, others they humiliate and destroy.

Andromache: Away we are led like stolen cattle, I and my son. Nobility enslaved!

Chorus: Strange are the ways of necessity.

Hecuba: Andromache, they have just now torn Cassandra away from me. She has been given to King Agamemnon.

Chorus: Sorrow outsorrows sorrow.

Andromache: Hecuba, I bring you more sorrow.

Chorus: Sorrow outsorrows sorrow!

Andromache: Your child, Polyxena, is dead! She was slain at the tomb of Achilles as an offering to the dead Greek soldiers.

Hecuba: So that is what Talthybius meant just now with his dark riddle?

Andromache: I saw her myself! I covered her with my robes and dropped my tears upon her.

Hecuba: Oh, my poor Polyxena. What a shameful death!

Andromache: She died as she died. In death, she was luckier than I who live!

Hecuba: Death and life are not the same, my child. Death is nothingness, but in life there is hope.

Andromache: It is better to die than to live in pain. The dead have no sorrows to hurt them. In Hector's house I toiled to master all the virtues of a good wife. I did not admit inside my doors gossip talk. My tongue was still and my countenance serene. This was the good reputation I had. And what is my reward from the gods? I am being delivered to the house of Achilles to marry his son. How can I be a wife in the house where my husband died? In you, my dear husband Hector, I had all the husband I

Greek & Roman Plays for the Intermediate Grades © 1993 Pearon Teacher Aids

wanted. You were wise, noble, wealthy, brave, and a truly great man. And now you are dead! I am being shipped captive to the yoke of slavery in Greece. I nurse no delusion, Hecuba, that things will ever be all right for me.

Chorus: Your misery is ours!

Hecuba: My dear Andromache, think no more of Hector's fate. Your tears will not bring him back from the dead. Respect your new husband, the son of Achilles, and bring up your son to be a mighty aid to Troy. Some day descendants of his may return and settle here, and Troy be again a city.

Chorus: Look Hecuba, Talthybius returns.

Hecuba: What brings him back? What new decisions?

(Enter Talthybius with soldiers.)

Talthybius: Andromache, wife of Hector, do not hate me. It is not my choice that I bring you the following command.

Andromache: What is it? I feel you are beginning a long song of sorrows.

Chorus: Sorrow outsorrows sorrow!

Talthybius: The Greeks have decided that the boy . . . . How can I speak the word?

Andromache: What? Is he not to have the same master as I?

Talthybius: No one will ever be his master.

Andromache: Are they leaving him here, sole survivor of Troy?

Talthybius: I don't know how to break the sorrowful news gently.

Chorus: Speak Talthybius! Speak your words of sorrow.

Talthybius: They are going to kill your child!

Andromache: Alas! My sorrows are too much.

Talthybius: The reasoning is that the son of a heroic father should not be allowed to grow up.

Chorus:	Sorrow outsorrows sorrow!
Talthybius:	They plan to hurl him from the battlements of Troy.
Chorus:	Sorrow outsorrows sorrow!
Talthybius:	Andromache, bear the agony of sorrow gallantly. Remember that you are powerless. Don't think that you are strong. There is no help for you anywhere. Your city is destroyed, your husband dead, yourself overpowered. The Greeks are able to contend with a solitary woman. Therefore do not invite a struggle. Don't do anything that will humiliate you and make things more objectionable. And another thing, I don't want you to mutter imprecations against the Greeks. If you say anything to provoke them, your son will not receive a decent burial. Say nothing Andromache. Make the best of the situation, and you yourself may find the Greeks kinder to you.
Andromache:	My dearest child, my special care, you are to leave your mother. Your father's gallantry has brought but death to you. Your father's virtues flowered unseasonably for you. Embrace your mother for the last time. Oh you Greeks, un-Greek are the tortures you devise. Why are you killing this innocent child? (Andromache hands Astyanax to Talthybius.) There! Take him, take him away. Is that what you want?
Chorus:	Andromache. Andromache. Your pain is deep!
Talthybius:	Come, child. Oh Greeks, pick another sort of herald for jobs like this, one who is merciless, one whose heart has more taste for brutality than mine.
	(Exit Talthybius with the child. Soldiers escort Andromache out.)
Hecuba:	Oh you Greeks, why do you fear this child? Were you afraid that someday he might raise fallen Troy? Then you are cowards after all. Our city is taken, yet you are afraid of a child, a little child. I do not admire a fear that has no basis in reason. I remember the days he would come to me and say, "Grandmother, I cut from my hair a great big curl for you." Ah me! What will be the verse inscribed on his tomb? Perhaps it will say,

Greek & Roman Plays for the Intermediate Grades © 1993 Fearon Teacher Aids

The Trojan Women

"Within this grave a little child is laid, slain by the Greeks because they were afraid," an inscription to make Greece blush!

Chorus: Hecuba, you touch our hearts.

Woman 3: Oh child, the earth will receive you.

Woman 4: What a bitter sorrow.

Chorus: Alas, what a bitter sorrow! Alas, poor Hecuba!

Chorus Leader: Look Talthybius returns again.

(Enter Talthybius and soldiers.)

Talthybius: I have two commands in one. You women, march to the awaiting ships when you hear the shrill note of the echoing trumpet, and you, old Hecuba, unhappiest of women, go with these soldiers whom Odysseus has sent to fetch you. The lot has made you his servant. He will take you away from Troy.

Hecuba: Ah wretched me! It has come at last, the culmination and crown of all my sorrows. I leave my country. Old legs, press on. Try hard. Oh Troy, that once held your head so high among barbarians, soon you will be robbed of your name and fame! Oh ye gods! Yet, why should I call upon the gods! In the past they did not hear when they were called.

Talthybius: Poor Hecuba! Your sorrows are driving you frantic. Soldiers, lead her away. Don't stand on ceremony. We must take Odysseus his prize and put her in his hands.

Hecuba: Oh Priam, King of Troy, my dead husband, do you see how they taunt us?

Chorus: He sees. Yes, he sees! But the city, the city, is a city no longer. Troy has fallen. Troy is dead!

Hecuba: Alas! Alas! Oh, alas!

Chorus: Our conquered country perishes. Its palaces are over-run by the fierce flames and the deadly spear!

Hecuba: Oh land that reared my children.

Chorus: Troy is dead!

Hecuba: My children, listen to the voice of your mother.

Chorus: Hecuba, you call on the dead with lamentations.

Hecuba: Yes, I call on them, as I lay my old limbs on the ground and knock on the earth with my two fists.

Chorus: Grievous is your cry!

Hecuba: We are driven off, we are hauled away to the halls where we must slave.

Chorus: Far from our fatherland.

Hecuba: Oh Priam, King of Troy, now my dead husband, unburied, unbefriended, I leave you.

Chorus: We walk soon to slavery.

Hecuba: Oh temples of the gods, oh city of my love.

Chorus: Soon, your name will be no more.

Hecuba: And the dust, like smoke, with wings outspread to heaven, will rob me of the sight of my home.

Chorus: The name of the land will pass into oblivion. Hapless Troy is finished!

(Trumpets sound.)

Hecuba: Ah! Oh trembling limbs, lead me on my path. On with you, poor limbs, to lifelong slavery!

(Hecuba exits escorted by soldiers. Talthybius follows.)

Chorus: Ah hapless city, hapless city, hapless city of Troy! Farewell! Farewell! Farewell!

(Chorus slowly exits. Curtain slowly closes.)

Greek & Roman Plays for the Intermediate Grades © 1993 Pearon Teacher Aids

The Trojan Women

ALCESTIS

By Euripides

INTRODUCTION

Alcestis is a play reminiscent of the Rod Serling scripts of TV's "Twilight Zone." It is a an, almost unbelievable tale about a loving wife, Queen Alcestis, who volunteers to die in the place of her husband, King Admetus. There is no other comparable situation in dramatic literature. The sacrifice of Alcestis and the role played by Hercules, the strong man of Greek mythology, will intrigue both your cast and your audience.

STAGING

One large platform, center stage, to indicate the palace will help your staging. The Greek chorus can be grouped around this platform. To the left can be a smaller, but higher, platform where Death makes speeches. To the right of the center platform can be another small platform where Apollo speaks.

COSTUMES

Death, of course, should appear in black. The god Apollo would look best in gold or bright yellow. The royal family, King Admetus and Queen Alcestis, should be robed in flowing white cloth with many folds. If possible, cast the roles of the two children with a boy and girl from a lower grade.

VOCABULARY

abused	deny	fate
affable	despair	feeble
belching	detestable	festival
bellowed	dignity	folly
bitterness	disposed	forfeit
brink	distinction	frowning
cancel	distress	generous
circumstances	doomed	gracious
concerned	emerged	grant
consenting	envy	grief
cowardice	fatal	grieve

hesitating	mockery	reproach
honor	mortal	sacrifice
hospitality	mourn	scoundrel
inhospitable	mourning	scowling
insolent	offerings	solemn
lament	opportunity	spite
lamentations	outwitted	steadfast
limp	perpetual	syllable
loathed	persuade	torment
lodging	prosper	tragedy
manifest	punctual	victor
melancholy	purified	wisdom
memorial	remedy	worthy

CHARACTERS

Apollo, Greek god
Death, Ruler of the Underworld
Admetus, the King
Alcestis, the Queen, Admetus' wife
First Child, Admetus and Alcestis' son
Second Child, Admetus and Alcestis' daughter
Pheres, Admetus' father
Hercules, Admetus' friend, a man of great strength
Chorus Leader
Chorus
Servants

ALCESTIS

Apollo: I, the god Apollo, have tricked Death in this house of Admetus! I, the god Apollo, have brought luck to this house. Finding my host Admetus worthy and god-fearing, I saved his life by tricking Death into consenting that Admetus should escape imminent death if he could find another to take his place. Admetus went to all of his friends, but they refused. He went to his father and mother, but they too said no. He found none but his wife, Alcestis, who dared to die for him, none but his wife who dared give up the sweet sunlight for him. See! Here comes Death himself. How punctual he is. He has come to take her. Alcestis, alone, is willing to take her husband's place in the arms of Death. (Enter Death, shrouded in black.) So, you have finally arrived, oh Death. You have remembered the fatal day.

Death: God Apollo, why are you still here? Are you not satisfied that you outwitted me to cancel the death of Admetus and have given me Alcestis instead? Is she not keeping her promise to forfeit her life?

Apollo: You need not fear . . . and yet, I might persuade you to . . .

Death: Never!

Apollo: Allow Alcestis to reach her old age.

Death: Never! My work is to take those due to die.

Apollo: So, you'll not grant my wish?

Death: Prince of Light, have you come to quarrel with me in this house again?

Apollo: Then you will not allow Alcestis to live longer?

Death: Never! You know what I am.

Greek & Roman Plays for the Intermediate Grades © 1993 Pearon Teacher Aids

Apollo:	Yes, I know . . . hated by men and women and loathed by the gods. (Exits.)
Death:	(To the audience.) Today this woman, Alcestis, must bend to my wish! (Death enters the house. Chorus enters.)
Chorus:	The house is silent. There is no one to tell us if we should mourn for our Alcestis. No servant stands at the door.
Chorus Leader:	Can anyone hear weeping? Any lamentations?
Chorus:	She is surely dead. Today she must go Underground. It must be so!
Chorus Leader:	The very thought is a wound to the soul.
Chorus:	It must be so. When goodness dies, all good people suffer, too. It must be so!
Chorus Leader:	I do not know what altar we could make sacrifices on to save her.
Chorus:	There is little hope. All sacrifices would be hopeless against evil. It must be so!
Chorus Leader:	Look! Here comes a servant to the door, weeping.
Chorus:	Tell us, is she alive or dead?
Servant:	She is alive and dead.
Chorus:	How can that be?
Servant:	Her soul stands on the brink.
Chorus:	Oh poor King Admetus! To lose such a wife.
Servant:	Noble she is indeed, but Admetus will not see the truth until he has lost her.
Chorus:	Can nothing be done to save her?
Servant:	Time will not wait. The fatal day is here.

Greek & Roman Plays for the Intermediate Grades © 1993 Fearon Teacher Aids

Chorus: No one under the great sun is the equal of Alcestis.

Servant: What greater sacrifice than to take the place of death for someone else? There is no higher excellence.

Chorus Leader: There must be great distress within the heart of Admetus.

Servant: He is weeping. I will go in and say you are here. (Exits into the house.)

Admetus: (From within.)
Oh gods, is there no escape from this evil?

Chorus: Oh Zeus, can we find no remedy?

Admetus: (From within.)
Is there no help?

Chorus: Pray to the gods. They have great power!

Chorus Leader: Look! Queen Alcestis is coming. King Admetus is with her.

(Enter Alcestis supported by Admetus and her two children holding on to her robes.)

Chorus: Oh lament, my land and city. Weep, weep to see her go!

Alcestis: Oh sun and white clouds, soon you will vanish.

Admetus: How have we harmed the gods? Why should you die? (Alcestis stumbles and nearly falls.) Do not give in. The gods are powerful and may be merciful.

Alcestis: I hear someone calling, "Why are you hesitating? Why do you delay? Come!" Do you not hear the voice, oh husband? He is angry with me!

Admetus: You break my heart when you talk like this.

Alcestis: I feel a hand touching me. Don't you see? Death is frowning at me. (Admetus holds her back.) Why are you holding me back? Let me go! I must take this strange journey.

Greek & Roman Plays for the Intermediate Grades © 1993 Fearon Teacher Aids

Alcestis

Admetus:	We who love you are heartbroken.
Alcestis:	I have no strength to stand. I must lie down for I am too near to Death! Oh children, be happy in the sweet sunlight.
Admetus:	To hear you say farewell is torture worse than death. Don't leave me and your children. Rise and live! How can I go on living when you are dead?
Alcestis:	Admetus, you know I must die! Before I go, listen to my wishes. Love the children as I do.
Chorus:	You need not be afraid, Alcestis. Admetus is a good man. He will respect your wishes.
Admetus:	You are my only Queen. I shall carry my grief for you not for one year, but as long as I live. My hatred shall be toward my mother and father and my friends, for only you were willing to give up your tender life for my life.
Chorus:	Your grief is our grief.
Alcestis:	You shall be mother and father to them now.
Admetus:	I take them from you, but what shall I do without you?
Alcestis:	Time will soften pain.
Admetus:	Take me with you!
Alcestis:	It is enough that I die.
Admetus:	Oh Death, so detestable to steal a wife!
Alcestis:	My eyes are heavy . . . . It is now very dark.
Admetus:	Don't leave us!
Alcestis:	I am now nothing. (She dies.)
Admetus:	Alcestis! Alcestis!
Chorus:	Alcestis is dead! She has gone!
First Child:	What shall we do? My mother is gone into the darkness.

Second Child: Her eyes are shut. Her hands are limp. She has left us to a lonely life.

Chorus: Admetus, you must bear this tragedy. You are not the first to lose a wife. Death comes to all!

Admetus: I know! Let every citizen dress in black, and for a year I forbid the sound of music in the city. She is worthy of all honor, for she alone has taken my place in death.

(Servants carry Alcestis into the house followed by Admetus and the children.)

Chorus: Oh Alcestis, our love goes with you. Let Death remember no braver woman ever crossed with him to the silent shore. Would we could save you from the blackest of waters.

(Enter Hercules.)

Hercules: My good friends, is Admetus at home?

Chorus: What brings you to our fair city?

Hercules: An errand to capture four wild horses.

Chorus Leader: You will have a fight on your hands.

Hercules: I have never run away from a struggle.

(Enter Admetus.)

Admetus: Welcome to my house, Hercules.

Hercules: You are covered with a black cloth. Are you in mourning?

Admetus: I have a burial to perform today.

Hercules: Is it one of your children?

Admetus: No, my children are within.

Hercules: Your parents?

Admetus: No, they are both well.

Greek & Roman Plays for the Intermediate Grades © 1993 Pearon Teacher Aids

Hercules: Surely not your wife Alcestis?

Admetus: She is dead, and she is not. It tortures me.

Hercules: Is this a riddle of some sort?

Admetus: Do you not know her fate?

Hercules: I know she promised to die in your place.

Admetus: Then how can I say she really lives?

Hercules: Don't grieve now! Wait till the time comes.

Admetus: (Not willing to tell Hercules that Alcestis is already dead.) Whoever is doomed to death is already dead.

Hercules: Most men see a difference between being alive and being dead.

Admetus: I find it difficult to make the distinction.

Hercules: Come now. Who is this dead friend you are mourning? Is it one of your family?

Admetus: No, but there were ties between us.

Hercules: How did she happen to die in your house?

Admetus: She came to live here when her father died.

Hercules: I wish I had found you in happier circumstances. (He turns to leave.)

Admetus: Where are you going?

Hercules: I must find lodging with some other friend.

Admetus: I will not hear of it. If you do not use my house as a lodging, I will be deeply hurt.

Chorus: A guest is a heavy burden in a house that mourns.

Admetus: The dead are dead. Come, use my house. I will not allow you to use another's house. Come.

Greek & Roman Plays for the Intermediate Grades © 1993 Fearon Teacher Aids

(Hercules enters the house.)

Chorus: Admetus, are you insane to entertain a guest with such mourning upon your house? What are you thinking of?

Admetus: To turn him away would not have solved my problem, and I would have had one friend less. My sorrow would be no less. To label my house as inhospitable would have burdened me with one more calamity.

Chorus: How could you keep from telling him your sorrow?

Admetus: If he had known the truth, he would not have entered. I am aware that what I have done will be misunderstood, but my house has yet to learn to shut the door in the face of a guest.

(Admetus enters his home.)

Chorus: It is a gracious house, friendly to strangers and a home to friends.

Chorus Leader: Weeping, his eyes wet, weeping the new dead, he still throws his doors wide for a stranger.

Chorus: Yet, in such folly, if the heart be true, lies full wisdom, too. He who fears the gods will prosper well.

(Enter Admetus and servants carrying the body of Alcestis.)

Admetus: My friends, we are ready for the funeral.

Chorus Leader: But look! Your old feeble father comes by foot. His servants are carrying gifts for offerings to the dead.

(Enter old Pheres and his servants.)

Pheres: My son, I have come to carry some of your grief. No one can deny that Alcestis was a noble wife. She has shed a new dignity upon all living women by her noble sacrifice. Take my gifts, oh son, so that she may go in peace to the world of gray shadows.

Alcestis

Greek & Roman Plays for the Intermediate Grades © 1993 Fearon Teacher Aids

Admetus: Father, you are not one of my friends, and I did not invite you to this funeral. My dead wife does not accept your gifts. You, who are old and feeble, did not come to my aid when I faced danger. You let her die! You were so afraid to die, and with so little life left in you. I refuse to be known as your son. I am dead so far as you are concerned!

Chorus: Say no more Admetus! There is enough sorrow in your heart.

Pheres: Insolent boy! To whom do you think you are speaking, a slave? You enjoy life, and don't you think I enjoy it? There is no law of the Greeks that says a father should die for his son. You talk of my cowardice! What about your bravery? What a weak hero you are—a man who allows his wife to die in his place!

Chorus: You have both abused each other enough. Say no more!

Admetus: Dying is different for an old man. I am still young.

Pheres: A man has but one life to live—his own!

Admetus: Her tomb will be a memorial to your cowardice.

Pheres: I killed her, did I? You say I killed her?

Admetus: Do not turn to me when you need help.

Pheres: Take a dozen wives, and let them all die for you.

Admetus: Leave my house. Let me bury Alcestis. Go! Be gone!

Pheres: I go. You, being the one who allowed her death, should know the best way to bury her!

(Exits with his servants.)

Admetus: (Yelling after him.)
Go back to your wife, also known as my mother. I renounce you both! Neither of you shall enter my house again. Never! Servants, let us continue with the burial of noble Alcestis.

Greek & Roman Plays for the Intermediate Grades © 1993 Fearon Teacher Aids

Chorus: Farewell, Alcestis! Farewell! May Death be gentle to you.

(Admetus, servants, and chorus carry Alcestis out to the burial ground. Enter a servant from the house.)

Servant: A worse guest I have never seen! He saw that our King was in mourning, but still stayed. He ate while singing silly songs. He put myrtle leaves on his head and acted the clown. He bellowed and never considered our King once! He kept me so busy serving him, I did not have the opportunity to reach out and bid a proper farewell to our Queen, the mother of us all. How often Alcestis saved us from punishment when Admetus was angry. This guest, how I hate him, bursting into this house with all its trouble.

(Enter Hercules, crowned with myrtle, holding a large goblet.)

Hercules: Servant, come here! Why so solemn? You should not be scowling before a guest. You should be affable. Away with all this melancholy.

Servant: I am not disposed to merrymaking.

Hercules: She was a stranger who died, wasn't she?

Servant: My master carries hospitality too far.

Hercules: Is there some real trouble he has kept from me?

Servant: He has lost his wife, Alcestis!

Hercules: What? The Queen is dead, and he entertained me in spite of that?

Servant: He was too honorable to turn you from his house.

Hercules: Poor King, to lose Alcestis!

Servant: We all feel that our life has ended, too.

Hercules: Where is he burying her?

Servant: Down the straight road. (Exits into the house weeping.)

Greek & Roman Plays for the Intermediate Grades © 1993 Fearon Teacher Aids

Hercules: For the sake of Admetus, I must bring Alcestis back from the dead. I will wrestle with Death himself. I will bring Alcestis back into the sunlight. Admetus must never say that his hospitality was wasted upon a scoundrel.

(Exit Hercules. Enter Admetus and chorus.)

Admetus: Oh gods, the way home is hateful to me. Oh house full of sorrow, how can I cross your door? All language is too poor to express my sorrow. I shall never feel warm again in the full sunlight. If only I were dead!

Chorus: You must enter your sad home. Within your walls weep out your bitterness. Prepare yourself never again to see the face of Alcestis!

Admetus: You touch me where the wound is deep. I envy those who have not married, for the loss of a good companion is too much to bear.

Chorus: Drink your full cup of pain, for you cannot wrestle with Fate.

Admetus: You should have let me leap into her deep grave and die with her. Death would have gained two souls instead of one. Friends, what have I to live for?

Chorus: Fate holds you in an unyielding grip. Your weeping will not raise Alcestis. The noblest of all women will stay dead!

Chorus Leader: My King, look! Hercules is returning.

(Enter Hercules followed by a veiled woman.)

Hercules: When I came to your house you were in trouble, and you did not share your trouble with a friend. But I will not add my reproach to your suffering. See this woman? Take care of her until I return, for I still must capture four wild horses. A time will come when you will thank me for her.

Greek & Roman Plays for the Intermediate Grades © 1993 Fearon Teacher Aids

Admetus: When I hid my wife's unhappy fate from you, I did not mean to wrong you. If you had gone to another house, I should have been hurt twice over. As for this woman, Hercules, take her to some other house for it is Alcestis I must remember always. Yet . . . she stands like Alcestis . . . . Why must you torment me, Hercules? As I look at her, I seem to be with Alcestis! What unspeakable misery this is for me. I taste the full bitterness of my loss.

Chorus: A mortal must accept what the gods give!

Hercules: Try to be brave. There is no future in perpetual mourning.

Admetus: There is no future for me in anything.

Hercules: Time will cancel your pain.

Admetus: Yes, if time is Death himself!

Hercules: Perhaps a new wife will . . .

Admetus: Never! Not another syllable.

Hercules: Will you never take another wife?

Admetus: I shall never be called a bridegroom again. Heaven strike me dead if I remarry.

Hercules: I see your love for your dead Alcestis is steadfast.

Admetus: I swear this by Zeus! This woman must go elsewhere.

Hercules: I beg of you to let her enter your house.

Admetus: Your begging is hateful to me.

Hercules: In time you will thank me. Take her into the house.

Admetus: I will not touch her! Servant, show her in.

Hercules: I will not turn her over to servants.

Admetus: I will not touch her . . . . There is the house.

Greek & Roman Plays for the Intermediate Grades © 1993 Pearon Teacher Aids

Hercules: Your own right hand!

Admetus: You force your friendship too far!

Hercules: Your hand! Your own right hand, Admetus!

Admetus: (Looks away as he offers his hand to the woman.) Here it is.

Hercules: Hold her hand tightly. Now, look at her Admetus! Look!

(Alcestis slowly removes the veil.)

Admetus: Is this joy or some mockery sent by the gods? Is this a cruel trick?

Hercules: This lady before you is truly Alcestis. Speak to her!

Admetus: Alcestis, I thought you were lost forever!

Hercules: May the gods not envy your happiness too much.

Admetus: Oh friend, may the gods keep you in their warmth and guard you forever. You alone, Hercules, have saved me and my house from despair. But how did you save her?

Hercules: I fought with Death himself and emerged the victor!

Admetus: Why is she silent? Will she not speak again?

Hercules: You will not hear her voice for three days until she is purified. Take her in, Admetus, my good friend. Now I must leave you to complete my errand.

Admetus: Stay, Hercules, stay. Join in our feast of thanksgiving.

Hercules: I shall return later to the house that displayed such generous hospitality. (Exits.)

Admetus: May every happiness go with you. And now, citizens, I command you to celebrate with song, dance, and festival. Our life begins again! I am the happiest of all mortal men! (He escorts Alcestis into the house.)

Chorus: The gods manifest themselves in many forms. Heaven
works in the dark with riddles and confusion. What
could not be has become! It is the way of the gods! That
is what you have seen today.

(Chorus exits slowly. Curtain falls on an empty stage.)

Greek & Roman Plays for the Intermediate Grades © 1993 Fearon Teacher Aids

HECUBA

By Euripides

INTRODUCTION

After the violence and victory of war have subsided, the
forces of greed, revenge, and power raise their ugly heads.
Euripides' tragedy *Hecuba* depicts the aftermath of war.
The Trojans were thoroughly defeated by the Greeks after
ten years of fighting, and their city and army were utterly
destroyed. Hecuba, the Queen of Troy, survived, only to
face more sorrows. Her daughter was sacrificed at the tomb
of Achilles, the dead Greek hero who killed Hector, the
leader of the Trojan soldiers and Hecuba's eldest son. Her
youngest son was sent to Thrace for his own safety, but
there is intrigue and mystery about his well-being and the
treasure that was sent with him. Somehow Hecuba man-
aged to retain her sanity and scheme revenge. A number of
the characters in this play, as in other Greek dramas, also
play prominent roles in Homer's *Iliad* and *Odyssey*. It is
interesting to compare this version of Troy's defeat with
Euripides' other play on this same subject, *The Trojan
Women*.

STAGING

It is not necessary to use a platform in this play, but it does
help to have the defeated Trojans assume kneeling or
fallen postures indicating defeat, while the Greek warriors
stand erect. The climax can be spellbinding as the Trojan
women descend upon Polymestor, King of Thrace. Be sure
he is completely surrounded and out of sight as he receives
his punishment.

COSTUMES

The captive Trojan women dress in rags, while the victorious Greek conquerors wear full-length robes of a solid
color. The soldiers' costumes come only to the knees. When
the spirit of Polydorus appears, it is always effective to
have one light shining on him, while the rest of the stage is
in darkness.

VOCABULARY

anguish
apparition
aside
atrocity
attendants
behalf
brief
callous
cease
chaos
commit
concerns
contemptuous
cunning
decision
decree
dedicate
deed

delicate
dignity
disaster
displayed
entrusted
greed
heralds
hesitate
implore
impression
incident
invoke
merciful
misconstrued
mislead
mourn
nobility
opposition

ordeal
plea
predict
priceless
ramble
rejoice
renounce
reprieve
revenge
revive
sheer
shorn
skeptical
sympathize
verdict
victim

CHARACTERS

Agamemnon, King and commander-in-chief of the
   Greek army
Odysseus, Greek Army Officer
Talthybius, a Greek herald
Polymestor, King of Thrace
Hecuba, Queen of Troy
Spirit of Polydorus, Hecuba's dead son
Polyxena, Hecuba's daughter
Servant
Chorus Leader
Chorus
Attendants
Soldiers

HECUBA

Spirit: I am the spirit of Polydorus, the son of Hecuba and Priam, King of Troy. My father, afraid that Troy would fall to the Greek army, sent me away so I would be safe from harm. With me, he sent a large sum of gold so that I would always be provided for. My father entrusted me to his friend Polymestor, King of Thrace, but as soon as Troy fell to Greece, Polymestor unmasked himself and showed his greed. Polymestor, the so-called friend of my father, killed me and stole my gold. My soul searches for Hecuba, my mother. Today, poor mother, not only will you find my body cast up on shore, but you will see the end of life for your daughter and my sister, Polyxena. I go now, for I see my mother approaching and still trembling from her dream about me. (Enter Hecuba stumbling to the ground.) Poor mother, poor old fallen Queen! Poor mother, left in bitter slavery, shorn of your pride and dignity.

(Spirit exits.)

Hecuba: I am too weak to stand, too weak. Women of Troy help me! Oh light of Zeus, what dreams you send to me. I saw an apparition of honor, my son, Polydorus, had died and now Polyxena, my daughter, will die as well! My heart shivers with fear of the dreams I dream. Oh gods, beat back my horrible dreams. Save my children!

(Enter the chorus.)

Chorus: In haste we come to you, Hecuba.

Chorus Leader: We bring you news that will pain your heart.

Chorus: We do not have the power to lighten your heart.

Chorus Leader: The Greek decree has been announced. Your daughter, Polyxena, is to be sacrificed. Agamemnon, commander-in-chief of the Greek army, spoke in your behalf.

Chorus: But Odysseus voted no!

Chorus Leader:	Odysseus is coming here to take Polyxena from your arms.
Chorus:	Hecuba, rise and go to Agamemnon. Plead your case with Agamemnon. He will listen. Fall at his knees!
Chorus Leader:	Invoke the gods.
Chorus:	Rise, Hecuba, rise!
Hecuba:	I am childless, homeless, my husband murdered, and my city burned. What can I do? What can I say?
Chorus:	Rise, Hecuba!
Hecuba:	Oh women of Troy, you are heralds of evil. The news you bring crushes me. (Enter Polyxena.) Your mother brings you wretched news, daughter Polyxena.
Polyxena:	I am not afraid, mother. Speak the truth.
Hecuba:	The Greeks have decreed your death!
Polyxena:	Oh my poor mother, how much you have suffered in one lifetime. It is you I pity. It is for you I cry, not for myself. There is so much suffering about us that I call it happiness to die.
Chorus:	Look Hecuba. Odysseus comes!
	(Enter Odysseus attended by soldiers.)
Odysseus:	Hecuba, the Greeks have decreed that your daughter, Polyxena, is to die in memory of Achilles, our fallen hero. Accept this decision without opposition, for nothing you say or do will change our minds.
Hecuba:	Oh gods, why do I live? Is there no end to my suffering? Why does mighty Zeus keep me alive? Odysseus, I realize I am now only a servant, but may I present you with one brief question?
Odysseus:	One brief question, yes.
Hecuba:	Think back, Odysseus, think back. Remember once how you fell at my knees and begged for your life. I was a Queen then and showed you mercy. Remember?
Odysseus:	Yes, I remember the incident.

Greek & Roman Plays for the Intermediate Grades © 1993 Fearon Teacher Aids

Hecuba: I let you have your life. I set you free. Remember?

Odysseus: You are the reason I am alive today.

Hecuba: And now I am at your feet. I beg for mercy back! Let Polyxena, my daughter, live. She is my comfort, the staff I lean on in my old age. She is all I have now. I was Queen once upon a time, but now I am nothing. Be merciful, Odysseus. Show pity. Convince the Greeks that what they do is wrong!

Chorus: Listen to a mother's heartbroken cry. Surely, no man could be so callous.

Odysseus: Hecuba, in your sorrow you twist the facts. I am not your enemy, and also remember that I owe you your life, not your daughter's. Achilles, our fallen warrior, deserves the greatest honors, and Polyxena has been chosen to be sacrificed in his memory. I have given my word to this.

Hecuba: I see I talk to the empty air. Polyxena, you implore him. Fall on your knees and beg for your life.

Polyxena: No, I shall not beg for life! I shall not call on Zeus for help. Once I was daughter of a King, but now I am a lowly servant. With my eyes still free, I renounce the light of day and dedicate myself to death. Take me, Odysseus, and lead me where you will, for I see nothing worth living for. And you, mother, help me to die nobly. I prefer to die than to live in such a manner.

Chorus: Polyxena is truly of noble birth. There is greatness in her words.

Hecuba: Yes, I am proud of you, my daughter, but there is still anguish within my heart. Odysseus, take me instead. Kill me, Odysseus, but save her. I am old, she is still young.

Odysseus: The spirit of Achilles demands Polyxena, not you, old woman.

Hecuba: Kill us both then.

Odysseus: One victim is enough.

Greek & Roman Plays for the Intermediate Grades © 1993 Fearon Teacher Aids

Hecuba

Hecuba:	Like ivy to an oak, I shall stick to her!
Odysseus:	Control yourself, old woman.
Hecuba:	Never will I allow her to die.
Odysseus:	Strong words, old woman. I had the impression that I was master here and you but a servant.
Polyxena:	Be gentle with my mother, Odysseus. Mother, do not struggle with those who are stronger than you. Mother, give me your hand as we kiss each other for the last time. Now I look upon the light of the sun for the last time. Farewell, mother! What message shall I give to my father and brothers?
Hecuba:	Tell them that I am the queen of sorrow!
Polyxena:	Lead me out, Odysseus, before I break my mother's heart even more.
	(Odysseus shrouds Polyxena in black and leads her out.)
Hecuba:	Polyxena, Polyxena, no! Oh gods, look upon me and weep.
Chorus:	Oh winds of the ocean, where are you blowing us? Our city is wasted in ashes and smoke, wasted in a wilderness of war. We live as servants, soon forced to foreign lands.
Chorus Leader:	Behold. Here comes Talthybius.
	(Enter Talthybius.)
Talthybius:	Women of Troy, where can I find Hecuba, your Queen?
Chorus:	There, buried in tears, she lies in the dust.
Talthybius:	This cannot be! Hecuba, Queen of Troy? Hecuba, her proud head fouled in the dust? Rise, Hecuba! Lift your head to the light of the sky.
Hecuba:	Why do you disturb my sorrow? Who are you?
Talthybius:	I am called Talthybius, the herald of the Greeks. I bring you a message from King Agamemnon.

Greek & Roman Plays for the Intermediate Grades © 1993 Fearon Teacher Aids

Hecuba:	The only news I wish to hear is that the Greeks have decreed my death. No other news interests me.
Talthybius:	My message is that Polyxena is now dead.
Hecuba:	My poor Polyxena!
Talthybius:	I cried when your daughter died, and I cry again as I tell you the full story. As the son of Achilles prayed to his father's spirit and prepared Polyxena to die, she displayed such bravery and nobility that the Greek army began to chant, "Free her, Free her!" But, Polyxena said, "No! Here is my throat. Do not hesitate to slit it." Torn between pity and duty, he hesitated, but then with his sword of gold he did it! The soldiers were silent and then slowly covered her body with leaves with much respect. You are blessed, Hecuba, to have had a daughter of such nobility.
Chorus:	Disaster falls from the heavens!
Talthybius:	And now you know all, Hecuba.
Hecuba:	Nothing is left. Gone, everything is gone! (Exit Talthybius.) Oh daughter, I cannot forget your death. I cannot stop crying! I ramble in despair! (Hecuba exits.)
Chorus:	Worse than grief surrounds us. War and the ruin of our houses! Mothers mourn for their sons and daughters!
	(Enter a servant.)
Servant:	Where is Hecuba? Where is the Queen?
Chorus:	What new sorrow do you cast in her path? Will her anguish never cease?
	(Enter servants carrying the covered body of Polydorus.)
Servant:	I cannot speak gently about this grief.
Chorus:	Here comes Hecuba now.
	(Enter Hecuba.)
Servant:	Oh my Queen, more sorrow for your eyes and heart.

Greek & Roman Plays for the Intermediate Grades © 1993 Pearon Teacher Aids

Hecuba

Hecuba:	Why have you brought my daughter's body here? I thought the Greek soldiers would give her decent burial.
Chorus:	Poor Hecuba, she thinks it is the body of her daughter.
Servant:	This is the body of your son, Polydorus.
Hecuba:	I am going mad! Oh merciful gods, let me die! I wail in my madness!
Chorus:	What suffering we hear.
Hecuba:	How were you killed, my son? What evil hand took your life?
Servant:	I found his body washed up by the waves.
Hecuba:	Drowned? Drowned or murdered?
Chorus:	Was this your dream, Hecuba? Who murdered him?
Hecuba:	Who but the King of Thrace, Polymestor, our friend. To him we sent Polydorus to be safe from harm. Oh horror! Horror!
Chorus:	Was he killed for his gold? Murdered by a friend?
Hecuba:	What does the word friendship mean now?
Chorus:	How heavily the anger of the gods falls upon you, Hecuba, most miserable of women!
Chorus Leader:	Look, Agamemnon comes!
	(Enter Agamemnon.)
Agamemnon:	What is this corpse?
Hecuba:	(To the audience.) Shall I beg for mercy or keep my tongue still?
Agamemnon:	Who is this man?
Hecuba:	(To the audience.) Suppose he is contemptuous of me and casts me aside as a servant?
Agamemnon:	If you do not speak, I cannot help you, Hecuba.

Hecuba: (To the audience.)
Perhaps he will understand my wish?

Agamemnon: Very well, apparently you have nothing to say to me, and thus I leave.

Hecuba: (To the audience.)
Why do I hesitate? He is my only hope, win or lose. (She falls to Agamemnon's knees.) I implore you, Agamemnon, to help this old woman who falls at your feet.

Agamemnon: You know you have your freedom.

Hecuba: Freedom I care not for. I seek revenge! For revenge, I will stay a servant forever.

Agamemnon: What revenge, Hecuba? Revenge on whom?

Hecuba: Revenge on Polymestor, King of Thrace, who murdered my son for his gold.

Agamemnon: Poor Hecuba, your suffering has no end.

Hecuba: Honor my request, oh noble Agamemnon.

Agamemnon: My position now has become a delicate one. Put yourself in my position. The King of Thrace is well liked by my soldiers, and your son was our enemy. I would like to help you, but first I must keep my army happy. And who would help you?

Hecuba: (Pointing to the chorus.)
These women.

Agamemnon: How foolishly you speak. These women have no strength.

Hecuba: Cunning makes us strong, and there is power in numbers. Open your heart to my plea.

Agamemnon: I am skeptical.

Hecuba: What is your answer, mighty Agamemnon? (Agamemnon nods yes.) Servant, deliver the following message to Polymestor, the King of Thrace. Tell him that Hecuba, once Queen of Troy, has important business that concerns him. Now, run! (Servant runs out.)

Greek & Roman Plays for the Intermediate Grades © 1993 Fearon Teacher Aids

Hecuba

One more favor, Agamemnon. Defer the funeral pyre of my daughter that her brother may burn with her.

Agamemnon: Let good and evil receive their just rewards. (Agamemnon exits. Servants carry out the body of Polydorus.)

Chorus: Poor City of Troy, now among the fallen cities. Your glory men and women will speak no more. Let the winds blow your dust far away.

Chorus Leader: Look, Hecuba, the King of Thrace arrives.

(Enter Polymestor with servants. Hecuba looks away.)

Polymestor: Poor Hecuba, my dear friend. What sadness overcomes you in your ruined Troy? The gods have made a chaos of your life, tossing you about, a puppet of tragedy. And with all my sorrow for you, your loss still remains. (Hecuba continues to look away.) Are you angry with me, Hecuba, for not coming to you sooner? I was on the point of coming, when your servant delivered your message.

Hecuba: I haven fallen so low that I am embarrassed to face you, Polymestor.

Polymestor: I sympathize with you, Hecuba. I understand. Of what help can I be to you?

Hecuba: I wish to speak with you privately. Send your attendants away.

Polymestor: Servants, be gone. Hecuba is my friend. (His attendants leave.) Now, Hecuba, how can I help you?

Hecuba: First, how is my son, Polydorus, who was sent to you for protection?

Polymestor: Be at peace in this matter. He is well and safe from harm.

Hecuba: You have proven to be a kind friend. Does he still remember me, his mother?

Polymestor: He speaks of you often. In fact, he wanted to come and visit you in secret.

Hecuba: Is the gold he had with him still safe?

Greek & Roman Plays for the Intermediate Grades © 1993 Fearon Teacher Aids

Polymestor: Very safe. It is locked in my palace and very well guarded.

Hecuba: I trust you will continue to guard it well. Do not let it tempt you.

Polymestor: Put your mind at rest, Hecuba. Have no fears about the gold.

Hecuba: Now, the reason for sending for you.

Polymestor: Yes?

Hecuba: Since you are a man of honor, I think you should have the following information.

Polymestor: Yes?

Hecuba: Within my rags, I was able to smuggle away some priceless jewels. Would you keep them for me?

Polymestor: Yes!

Hecuba: Come close so none will see their brightness.

(Polymestor comes very close to Hecuba and the chorus surrounds him, hiding him from sight. Polymestor screams.)

Polymestor: Help! Murder!

(The chorus of women gouge out his eyes. Polymestor screams in agony. The chorus returns to its place.)

Chorus: Now your debt falls due! The gleam of gold mislead you.

(Polymestor stumbles about.)

Polymestor: Where shall I run? Oh gods, heal my bleeding eyes!!

Chorus: You suffer now as you made others suffer.

Hecuba: Never again will you see the light of day. I have my revenge!

Polymestor: Soldiers, servants, help me! Kill these women of Troy. You murderous hags. Help! Oh gods, where can I run?

Chorus: You suffer now as you made others suffer!

Greek & Roman Plays for the Intermediate Grades © 1993 Pearon Teacher Aids

(Enter Agamemnon.)

Agamemnon: The sound of a scream brought me here.

Polymestor: It is the voice of Agamemnon. Help me!

Agamemnon: Oh, awful sight! Who did this to you Polymestor? Who hated you so much as to do this?

Polymestor: She, Hecuba, and the other women. They have destroyed me!

Agamemnon: Hecuba, is this atrocity your doing? What is the meaning of this?

Polymestor: Is she here? Tell me where, and I will rip her limb from limb.

Agamemnon: No more of this inhuman savagery. I shall listen to both sides and then judge.

Polymestor: Listen well, Agamemnon. Polydorus, her young son, was sent to me for safekeeping, and I admit I did away with him. I took his life because I was afraid that someday he might revive the strength of Troy and attack Greece. I did my deed for Greece and for you, Agamemnon, and this is my reward!

Hecuba: He claims he killed my son Polydorus for you and Greece. I call him a liar! The truth is he killed my son for his gold. It was his sheer greed and nothing more!

Chorus: Your cause is just, Hecuba.

Agamemnon: To sit as judge in such a case is not a pleasure for me. I have no choice but to pass a verdict. Polymestor, I find you guilty of murder as charged. You in your plea have misconstrued the facts.

Hecuba: I rejoice in my revenge!

Polymestor: Enjoy it now, for the sweetness of revenge that you enjoy will soon vanish. I predict that you will be changed to a dog with blazing eyes and drowned at sea.

Hecuba: What do I care how I die. Revenge is mine!

Polymestor: And you, Agamemnon, you shall be killed by a woman called your wife.

Agamemnon:	Clytemnestra, my wife, would never commit such an act.
Polymestor:	She shall lift the ax, and your blood will spill to the floor. A blood bath awaits you at home, oh mighty Agamemnon!
Agamemnon:	Servants, drag him away. Gag his mouth!
Polymestor:	My words are out, and I have touched you with them. The god Dionysus has told me all.
Agamemnon:	Cast him on a desert island so none can hear him. (Attendants drag Polymestor out.) May the gods grant that this ordeal is at an end! And may all be well in my home.
	(Agamemnon and Hecuba exit.)
Chorus:	We are servants of life. There is no reprieve for us. We, the Women of Troy, find life harsh.
	(Chorus slowly exits and curtain closes on an empty stage.)

Greek & Roman Plays for the Intermediate Grades © 1993 Fearon Teacher Aids

Hecuba

PROMETHEUS BOUND

By Aeschylus

INTRODUCTION

The world of the ancient Greek gods truly comes alive in *Prometheus Bound*, the story of a god who defied the ruler of the gods and gave the gift of fire—and hence art, science, and civilization—to human beings. Zeus was so angered by this disobedience and the god's refusal to repent, that he dictated that Prometheus be punished for all eternity. Aeschylus has succeeded admirably in depicting the power and will of Zeus.

STAGING

The stage should be completely bare, except for a huge rock in the center. It can be made of chicken wire covered with papier-mâché or piles of wooden blocks covered with heavy wrapping paper to create an irregular form. An illusion of lightning and thunder is vital. Flick lights on and off rapidly to simulate lightning, and shake a large piece of flexible metal off stage to resemble the rumble of thunder. Use full lighting at the beginning, and as the play progresses, dim the lights gradually until, at the end, there is only one light shining on Prometheus and the rock to which he is bound.

COSTUMES

Prometheus should wear a simple tunic, but the characters representing gods can be richly clothed in flowing robes.

VOCABULARY

affection	bonds	craves
aggressive	boulder	defy
agony	bound	desolation
ailment	calamity	destruction
anguish	calculation	detested
appease	celestial	dethrone
arrogant	comradeship	discard
ascended	concern	discuss
astray	counsel	disposition
bitter	crafts	efforts

entangled
fate
feeble
fetters
folly
fondness
forethought
forth
fury
gadfly
gaze
goad
harshness
humble
immortals
insolent
intention
intolerable
kin

lacking
loitering
lunatic
mandated
mortal
oblivion
obstinate
perishing
pity
plight
predicament
privileges
rage
rebel
remote
respecting
respite
responsive
reveal

scorch
scurry
sensible
slight
subject
swarming
swirl
tedious
underlings
uttering
vain
whence
witless
wrath
wretched
wronged
yoked

CHARACTERS

Prometheus, a Greek god in disfavor
Hephaestus, Greek god of fire
Strength
Violence
Oceanus, Greek god of the ocean
Io, a priestess
Hermes, herald of Zeus
Chorus Leader
Chorus, daughters of the ocean

PROMETHEUS BOUND

Strength: We have come to the very end of the world . . . the most remote region of the earth. This is desolation itself! Clamp this rebel, Prometheus, to the rock. Remember that this act has been mandated by Zeus himself. Remember, Hephaestus, that this rebel stole fire from you and gave it to human beings.

(Strength and Violence bind Prometheus to the rock.)

Hephaestus: Your work is done, Strength and Violence, and yet I do not have the heart to lay hands on a fellow god. And yet I must, for it is so ordered by Zeus. To disobey Zeus would be insane. Poor Prometheus, you will never see a human form again. The hot sun will scorch your skin, and the night air will cover you with frost. No one yet born will set you free. Many groans and cries shall come from you, and all in vain, for mighty Zeus is difficult to appease.

Strength: Do not waste your time in pity. You should hate this fellow god who stole fire from you to give to the mortals.

Hephaestus: The ties of comradeship and kin are strong.

Strength: That is true, but dare you defy Zeus?

Hephaestus: Oh Strength, you have always been so aggressive and lacking in pity.

Strength: Don't waste your time on Prometheus, for it will gain him nothing. Cast him round with fetters quickly lest Zeus see you loitering. Clamp them on his wrists and peg him to the crag. Now his feet.

Hephaestus: There, the job is done. Poor Prometheus, how I weep for your suffering!

Strength: Are you weeping for someone whom Zeus frowns upon? Be careful, Hephaestus, for mighty Zeus may frown on you for showing so much concern about Prometheus.

(Exit Hephaestus.)

Greek & Roman Plays for the Intermediate Grades © 1993 Pearon Teacher Aids

Violence: Now do you feel so superior, Prometheus? How are your mortal friends going to free you from these bonds?

Strength: The gods named you incorrectly when they named you Forethought.

(Exit Strength and Violence.)

Prometheus: Because I love humankind, I suffer! You see me, a wretched god, bound to a boulder, laughed at by the winds, hated by the gods. I must bear my fate as best I can. Hear me, oh celestial space. Hear me, oh deep oceans. Hear me, mother earth. Hear my groans of anguish! Something comes. Everything that moves frightens me. It is coming closer, closer, closer to me!

(Enter the chorus.)

Chorus: Be not afraid, for we come in fondness. We come to this rock to be your friends.

Prometheus: Daughters of the ocean, gaze upon me! See what a cruel grip I am in.

Chorus: We look, Prometheus, and fear spreads through our eyes. We fear for your withering body.

Prometheus: Oh, if only Zeus in his anger had cast me deep into the earth, hidden from the eyes of my enemies that laugh in the wind at me.

Chorus: You feel the anger of Zeus.

Prometheus: There will come a day when mighty Zeus will need me. He will need me to show him the plot that will dethrone him of his power. But not until he frees me from my chains will I speak my secret.

Chorus: Oh Prometheus, you are too free with your tongue. You are too bold! Mighty Zeus is hard of heart. He has a disposition that none can change.

Prometheus: The day will come when his harshness will soften, and he will rush to my side with affection.

Chorus: Reveal it all to us. Tell us the tale that caused you to be bound to this rock.

Prometheus: When mighty Zeus ascended to the throne of the gods, he gave to each god several privileges, but to humans he gave nothing. His intention was to blot out this breed called human beings. Only I dared to defy mighty Zeus and save them from oblivion. That is why I am bound to this rock.

Chorus: Our hearts are pained!

Prometheus: Yes, I am a thing of pity to look upon.

Chorus: Is there more to your tale?

Prometheus: I gave the people fire! And from this fire they will learn a thousand arts.

Chorus: Then this is why Zeus punishes you?

Prometheus: Yes, and gives me no respite.

Chorus: Is there any limit to this plan of yours?

Prometheus: Only Zeus can decide the limit of my suffering.

Chorus: What hope is there for you, Prometheus? Do you not see the error of your ways? It is not a pleasure for us to say that you have erred.

Prometheus: It is easy to give advice when you are on the outside of calamity. I knew that by helping humans I would bring troubles upon myself. I knew!

(Enter Oceanus.)

Oceanus: I arrive after a tedious journey. I heard your words of anger, and if you continue with such angry words, soon Zeus will hear them and your present condition will be like child's play. Prometheus, discard this angry mood. You must become humble if Zeus is to forgive you. I will try to free you, but remember a vain tongue is subject to correction.

Prometheus: You cannot overcome the power of Zeus. He is not easily overcome. Do not become entangled with my problem, or perhaps you, too, will feel the wrath of Zeus.

Oceanus: You are better at advising others than yourself. I am sure that Zeus will grant me the favor of releasing you.

Greek & Roman Plays for the Intermediate Grades © 1993 Fearon Teacher Aids

Prometheus Bound

Prometheus: Your trouble will serve no purpose. Keep away from me, for I am unlucky.

Oceanus: Do you see some danger for me because I want to help you?

Prometheus: Your efforts will be useless. Your actions will only make Zeus your enemy.

Oceanus: Your words advise me to leave.

Prometheus: Leave. Get out! Leave now!

Oceanus: Your words fall on very responsive ears. I take my leave. (Exits.)

Chorus: We weep, Prometheus, for your perishing fortune. Our eyes are like fountains. Zeus is shaking his arrogant spear in your face.

Chorus Leader: The sufferings you are bearing are beyond all measure.

Chorus: Your pain is as endless as the booming waves as they hit the shore.

Chorus Leader: The dark thunder on earth echoes your pain.

Chorus: The swollen streams swirl in your agony.

Prometheus: My heart is eaten away when I see how I have been insulted. I found human beings to be witless, and I made them master of their minds. They lived like swarming ants in holes in the ground, and all their actions lacked intelligent calculation. It was I who gave them numbers, sounds of letters, crafts, yoked beasts, carriages, and ships. Yes, it was I who gave them all these discoveries, but now I cannot discover a way for myself to escape.

Chorus: You are astray and bewildered. You are too confused to cure your own ailment.

Prometheus: All the arts that mortals possess have come from me, Prometheus, and yet I cannot solve my own sad predicament.

Chorus Leader: You had no fear of Zeus by respecting humans too much.

Chorus: How thankless were all your benefits to mortals.

(Enter Io.)

Greek & Roman Plays for the Intermediate Grades © 1993 Pearon Teacher Aids

Io: What land is this? Where am I? Who is this tied to a rock unprotected from wind and storm? What have you done to suffer such a death? Where has my miserable wandering brought me? Help! The gadfly stings me again! Oh, oh, oh! It stings me again! Why am I driven to madness by the stings of the gadfly? Alas, I can find no escape to my problems.

Prometheus: Are you not Io, the one who looked at Zeus too often? Are you not Io who caused Hera, the wife of Zeus, to become jealous?

Io: Who are you? Who are you? Who are you who knows so much of me? Yes, I am the victim of Hera's jealousy and am constantly goaded by her gadflies. I am constantly moving, tortured, and hungry. Tell me, if you know, what will cure me of these stings? Tell this unlucky maid the secret.

Prometheus: You see before you the one who gave mortals the gift of fire.

Io: Why are you bound to this rock?

Prometheus: The wrath of Zeus!

Chorus: Tell us your story.

Io: My dreams were all of Zeus . . . night after night. Hera, his wife, could not abide my dreams and punishes me with these horns you see upon my head and my constant moving as the gadfly stings me.

Chorus: Such intolerable sufferings. Alas, alas, for your fate. We shudder when we look upon your misfortune.

Io: Alas, alas for me!

Prometheus: What will you do when you hear of the evils that are to come?

Chorus: Is there more to come?

Prometheus: A wintry sea of agony and ruin.

Io: Why don't I throw myself from a high mountain top and end my troubles? It would be better to die once than to suffer endlessly.

Greek & Roman Plays for the Intermediate Grades © 1993 Fearon Teacher Aids

Prometheus:	For me there is no limit of suffering till Zeus is dethroned.
Io:	Will that ever happen, Prometheus?
Prometheus:	It will come! I promise!
Io:	Alas, alas, the gadfly strikes again. The gadfly's sting goads me on. (She dashes off the stage in pain.)
Chorus:	Her wanderings are bitter because of Hera's jealousy.
Chorus Leader:	This is a fight that none can fight, for the anger of Zeus is too powerful.
Prometheus:	Yet, this Zeus shall fall someday. He sits confidently upon his throne, but his crashing fall will come.
Chorus:	You seem to wish for his destruction.
Prometheus:	He will suffer more than I do now.
Chorus Leader:	Speak not so loudly.
Chorus:	Have you no fear of uttering such words, Prometheus?
Prometheus:	Am I not destined to wither away and die? Why should I fear?
Chorus:	But he might make your pain even worse.
Prometheus:	Then let him do so.
Chorus Leader:	Look, here comes Hermes, the herald of Zeus.
Chorus:	He comes with news.
	(Enter Hermes.)
Hermes:	You, Prometheus, who sinned against immortals, you, the thief of fire, I speak to you. You, who boast that mighty Zeus will fall from his throne, speak. And do not speak in riddles, but set forth the truth, for Zeus is near the end of his patience with you.
Prometheus:	You'll find nothing from me, so scurry back from whence you came.
Hermes:	You are obstinate and insolent, and that is what has brought you to your present plight.

Prometheus:	I prefer my painful plight to your position as a messenger boy.
Hermes:	I am the trusted messenger of Zeus.
Prometheus:	I do not discuss important matters with underlings, such as you.
Hermes:	It seems you still have not learned the art of common sense. So you won't tell Zeus what he craves to know?
Prometheus:	You waste your time. You might as well be speaking to the waves for an answer. I will not kneel to my detested enemy!
Hermes:	Like a young unbroken colt you speak. You fight the reins, but you are too feeble to win. Consider what punishments will flash upon you if you do bow to the wishes of Zeus. Tell him what he wants to know! Listen to my wise counsel.
Chorus:	The words of Hermes are most sensible. Listen to his counsel, Prometheus.
Prometheus:	Let the air burst with thunder, let hurricanes upheave the trees, let the waves roar in savage fury, but I am a god who Zeus cannot kill!
Hermes:	Your words remind me of a lunatic. (To the chorus.) Daughters of Oceanus, quickly leave this place, for soon the roar of thunder will be intolerable to your ears.
Chorus:	We are not cowards. We will stay with Prometheus. We do not desert our friends.
Hermes:	Then do not blame Zeus for what happens to you, for you have been warned. A calamity will strike, and you will be trapped. Your own folly will trap you in this net of destruction. (Exits.)
Prometheus:	The earth rocks and dust begins to dance! The four winds battle and sea and sky rage. All this Zeus sends to me to make me afraid. (Wild lightning and thunder commence. The chorus scatters in all directions, leaving Prometheus alone.) Oh earth, sky, and moon, you see how I am wronged!

(The storm rages as the curtain slowly closes.)

Greek & Roman Plays for the Intermediate Grades © 1993 Fearon Teacher Aids

Prometheus Bound

THE ORESTEIAN TRILOGY

By Aeschylus

INTRODUCTION

A trilogy is a group of three plays that can be presented separately or at the same performance. They are sequential in action and in time, and some of the same characters appear in all three dramas. In Aeschylus' *Oresteia*, the only Greek trilogy to have survived, the dramatist repeatedly points out that human beings must eventually be punished in some harsh manner for their sins and crimes.

In *Agamemnon*, the first play of the trilogy, the seed of the tragedy that overwhelms the ancient Greek royal family is revealed. Ten years before the play opens, King Agamemnon was preparing to lead the Greeks in their long war with Troy, when the goddess Artemis refused to send winds to permit the fleet to sail until he sacrificed his daughter, Iphigenia. The army forced him to agree to his daughter's death, an act for which his wife, Clytemnestra, never forgave him. This episode is related in *Iphigenia in Aulis* by Euripides. King Agamemnon was not an evil person, but he was trapped by the will of the gods. After his victory over Troy, depicted by Euripides in *Hecuba* and *The Trojan Women*, Agamemnon was destroyed by his revengeful wife and treacherous cousin.

The Libation Bearers, the second part of the trilogy, continues the family tragedy. Ten years have elapsed, and the main characters are now Electra and Orestes, Agamemnon's eldest daughter and only son. This is a drama of revenge, with much the same theme and characters as in Sophocles' *Electra*.

In *The Furies*, the third part of the trilogy, Orestes is an old man hounded by evil spirits who constantly condemn him for taking the life of his mother. He admits his guilt, but says he was driven to avenge his father's death. The goddess Athena forgives him because he has suffered enough remorse and unhappiness over his deed.

STAGING

Staging *Agamemnon* is extremely simple. One fairly large platform with steps leading up to it and steps behind it can designate the entrance to the palace. The main characters, such as Queen Clytemnestra, should speak from the platform.

For *The Furies*, two platforms can be added to the stage, one to the right of the center platform for Athena to stand on and one to the left for the god Apollo. The Furies can be all over the stage, usually rolling on the floor and huddled together.

COSTUMES

All of the characters in the first two plays of the trilogy can wear normal Greek dress—floor-length robes of a solid color—with the exception of Electra, who should be dressed in rags. The Furies who appear at the end of *The Libation Bearers* are underground spirits and extremely ugly. Any weird and unusual costumes will suffice. No clothing can be too extreme for depicting the Furies.

In *The Furies*, Athena and Apollo, of course, should be resplendent in appearance, while the Furies should be ugly. Make sure that Orestes looks quite old. Wearing a white wig or beard and carrying a staff to help him walk will age him.

AGAMEMNON VOCABULARY

achieved	dealt	heed
alleluia	defiance	heir
approve	defiling	hence
assured	demean	herald
astonish	deny	ignorant
awaiting	desserts	ills
baffled	dirge	incredible
banish	dissonant	insistent
banishment	entangled	just
beacon	extreme	keen
befallen	faltering	knell
bidding	fancies	loyalty
blissful	fate	mortal
boast	fiery	mourn
brow	foretold	omen
censure	frenzied	plunder
condemned	grief	pronouncements
content	grovel	prophecy
contrived	harbored	prostrate
cruelty	hearth	reproach

revere	scheme	unashamedly
revolt	secure	unravel
rightful	slavery	vengeance
royal	spoils	vigils
rumors	supreme	void
sacked	task	wisdom
sacrifice	tranquillity	yield
scent	treachery	yoke

AGAMEMNON CHARACTERS

Agamemnon, King of Greece
Clytemnestra, Agamemnon's wife, the Queen
Aegisthus, Agamemnon's cousin
Cassandra, Princess of Troy, now a servant
Chorus Leader
Chorus, Greek citizens
Herald
Servants
Soldiers

AGAMEMNON

Chorus: Queen Clytemnestra, we come obedient to your bidding.

Chorus Leader: Since our King, Agamemnon, is away at war and his throne empty, we pay homage to his wife, our Queen!

Chorus: Have you received some message? Is it good news? Pray speak. We long to hear!

Clytemnestra: I bring good news as certain as the dawn that springs from the night.

Chorus: Share your news, oh mighty Queen.

Clytemnestra: We, the Greeks, have captured Troy!

Chorus: Incredible! We can't believe it!

Clytemnestra: Troy is ours! Is that not plain enough for you?

Chorus: Happiness fills our eyes with tears!

Chorus Leader: What proof? What evidence have you?

Chorus: Perhaps it was a dream?

Clytemnestra: A dream! I do not deal with the fancies of my sleep. I am not an ignorant woman!

Chorus: Speak! When was Troy captured?

Clytemnestra: This very night.

Chorus: What messenger could fly so fast from Troy to here?

Clytemnestra: The god of fire! Beacon lit beacon in relays of flame to bring me the news.

Chorus: We offer thanks to heaven! Tell us the good news again.

Greek & Roman Plays for the Intermediate Grades © 1993 Fearon Teacher Aids

Clytemnestra:	Today the Greeks hold Troy! The women of Troy are prostrate over dead husbands and brothers; aged grandfathers mourn the deaths of their sons and grand-sons. The people of Troy are now our servants! Our soldiers have earned a well-deserved rest, a blissful sleep without the care of standing guard. After a night and day of plunder, all that remains for them is a safe journey home. May the gods grant them a safe trip.
Chorus:	We prepare ourselves again to praise the gods!
	(Clytemnestra enters the palace.)
Chorus Leader:	Oh Zeus, supreme of heavenly powers!
Chorus:	Great Zeus, we revere thee!
Chorus Leader:	Look! A herald approaches our shores with brow covered with olive leaves.
Chorus:	Now may the proof be good.
	(Enter the herald.)
Herald:	After ten years, this dawn has brought me home. Yes, today I am home. Oh hear my prayer of thanks, Greek gods!
Chorus:	Herald of the Greek army, welcome home! We bid you joy.
Herald:	For ten years, I prayed for this moment! Come death, for now I am content!
Chorus:	Love for your fatherland has worn you out.
Herald:	My cloak is wet with tears of joy. Having taken Troy, the glory of Greece is sung in every temple.
Chorus Leader:	This news belongs by right first to Clytemnestra, our Queen.
	(Enter Clytemnestra from the palace.)

Greek & Roman Plays for the Intermediate Grades © 1993 Fearon Teacher Aids

The Oresteian Trilogy

Clytemnestra: Long before this, I shouted at the joyful news when the first fiery midnight message told me that Troy was sacked and shattered! Now citizens, do you believe that Troy is ours? Was it a woman's weak dream I had? Soon King Agamemnon will tell me all about it. What greater joy for a wife than to hear her husband is returning home from war, safe and sound? Tell my husband to come with all speed and he will find a wife as loyal as he left her, a wife who was the watchdog of his house. (Clytemnestra exits into the palace. Herald exits.)

Chorus: Come then, my King, destroyer of Troy. We hail you and give you honor!

Chorus Leader: We thought you wrong, oh King, when you first attempted this war. We thought you were sailing far off the course of wisdom.

Chorus: We thought you wrong when you offered your daughter in sacrifice.

Chorus Leader: You have come home victorious!

Chorus: From our open hearts we wish you well!

(Enter Agamemnon followed by Cassandra.)

Agamemnon: My first act on returning to my royal hearth is to thank the gods who led me hence and led me home again. May victory never leave my side!

(Enter Clytemnestra from the palace.)

Clytemnestra: Citizens of this city, I unashamedly announce my loyalty and love for my husband who has returned after ten long years. To sit at home for so many years is extreme cruelty for a wife, but now all this has passed. The rumors of his being wounded and dead were more painful, however. If all the rumors of his wounds were true, his body would be like a fish net. These rumors of your death, oh mighty King, convinced me to send your young son, Orestes, away to another city safe from

The Oresteian Trilogy

revolt within this city. He is safe, have no fear. The late night vigils awaiting your return to safety have worn out my eyes. Even in my dreams I would start up, imagining all the ills that had befallen you. But now, all my grief is ended. Servants, spread the royal cloth for King Agamemnon to step upon.

Agamemnon: Guardian of my home, call him fortunate whose life will end harbored in tranquillity.

Clytemnestra: Now you have come to your dear home. Your return is like a spring warmth after a bitter winter.

Agamemnon: I will enter the house with an easy mind. Servants, take in this girl called Cassandra. She is part of the spoils of victory. Treat her with kindness. The man who is the gentle master, the gods look upon complacently. No one likes to bear the yoke of servanthood.

(He enters the palace.)

Clytemnestra: Alleluia! Zeus! Zeus! Fulfill my dreams! Ripen my prayers, and your part, oh mighty Zeus, is to make the ripe fruit fall! (She enters the palace.)

Chorus: What is this insistent fear that sets a steady beat within our hearts?

Chorus Leader: What is this evil omen that haunts us?

Chorus: What is this sore dream that we cannot spit out?

Chorus Leader: My heart is outrunning my tongue to unravel this scheme!

Chorus: We hear a dissonant dirge . . . a dissonant dirge!

(Enter Clytemnestra from the palace.)

Clytemnestra: You there . . . you called Cassandra. Come within. It has been your fortune to have the gods place you in this house to share our holy water. I want to speak to you, Cassandra!

Chorus: It is you she has addressed.

Greek & Roman Plays for the Intermediate Grades © 1993 Fearon Teacher Aids

The Oresteian Trilogy

Chorus Leader:	Obey her. Clytemnestra waits!
Chorus:	You are a captive in the toils of destiny. You must obey.
Chorus Leader:	You must obey, Cassandra!
Chorus:	Cassandra, do you choose defiance?
Clytemnestra:	I had hoped to persuade her.
Chorus:	Clytemnestra speaks the best for you. Obey!
Chorus Leader:	She bears herself like a wild beast.
Clytemnestra:	She is mad. She hears only her frenzied thoughts! I'll speak no more thoughts to demean myself. (She enters palace.)
Chorus:	Unhappy girl, yield to your fate and wear the yoke of servanthood.
Cassandra:	Apollo! Apollo! Alas!
Chorus:	Why call upon Apollo? He is not the god of mourning.
Cassandra:	Oh horror! Horror! Apollo!
Chorus:	Again she calls upon him.
Cassandra:	All this way you have led me just to destroy me again!
Chorus Leader:	She speaks of her own sufferings.
Cassandra:	What is this fearful house to which you have led me?
Chorus:	This is the house of Agamemnon, our beloved King. It is not a false house.
Cassandra:	What is she planning? What is she plotting? She who hunts is called wife and queen!
Chorus Leader:	This strange girl seems like a hound with a keen scent.
Chorus:	She is picking up a trail that leads to murder!
Cassandra:	Soon, very soon, it will fall. Oh horrible treachery. I call it treachery!

Greek & Roman Plays for the Intermediate Grades © 1993 Fearon Teacher Aids

Chorus: We are baffled by her pronouncements.

Cassandra: I fear and fear again. Not alone will he suffer, for I see myself entangled in his death net! Oh cruel Apollo! Why have you led me here? Why must I share the death he must die?

Chorus: This strange girl is insane.

Cassandra: Quick! Be on your guard! The bull, keep him away from the cow! Too late. Oooohhh! She strikes! He falls . . . murdered!

Chorus: Are her words void of meaning or do we fail to understand her message?

Cassandra: Someone is plotting vengeance! A lion? Yes, but a cowardly lion! Female murders male. Yet she posed so glad at his return . . . . Listen to her shout of triumph! If you distrust my words, what does it matter, for soon that which will come will come. Soon your eyes will see, and you will cry out in pity, "She spoke the truth!"

Chorus Leader: If you speak the truth, why do you stay? Why do you not run?

Cassandra: There is no escape. There is no cure. What the gods have decreed will come to pass.

Chorus: Arrows of prophecy, I cannot guess your target.

Chorus Leader: Let us pray to the gods.

Cassandra: While you are praying, others prepare to kill.

Chorus: Alas, I pity you for the death you have foretold.

Cassandra: My only prayer is that the blow be mortal and my eyes closed in sleep without a struggle.

Chorus Leader: What man could boast he was born secure who heard this tale?

Cassandra: I go. I go into the land of the defeated, the end of Agamemnon and of me. (She starts toward the palace, but suddenly turns away.)

Greek & Roman Plays for the Intermediate Grades © 1993 Pearon Teacher Aids

The Oresteian Trilogy

Chorus:	What is it?
Chorus Leader:	What do you see?
Chorus:	What terror has turned you back?
Cassandra:	In this palace, I sense that death is certain. The palace reeks with fumes of murder.
Chorus:	Poor soul!
	(Cassandra enters the palace. There is long silence as the chorus remains frozen still.)
Agamemnon:	(From within the palace.) Help! Help! She murders me!
Chorus:	Listen to the cry . . . the stroke of death!
Agamemnon:	She strikes again! Help!
Chorus:	Let us act! No time for faltering now.
Chorus Leader:	No words of ours can raise the dead to life.
Chorus:	We are wasting time.
Chorus Leader:	We must know the facts for sure and then be angry.
	(Agamemnon and Cassandra come stumbling out of the palace and fall at the feet of the chorus. Clytemnestra appears at the door.)
Clytemnestra:	I stand where I struck, above my victims. I will not deny that I contrived it. My task has been achieved. I struck him twice, and the third stroke was his death knell.
Chorus:	Your words astonish us!
Chorus Leader:	You boast about the murder of your husband, our King!
Clytemnestra:	Approve or censure as you will.
Chorus:	What poison did you eat or drink that drove you to such an action?

Greek & Roman Plays for the Intermediate Grades © 1993 Fearon Teacher Aids

Chorus Leader:	The people will banish you from the city.
Clytemnestra:	This man you called King and I called husband took my child, Iphigenia, and sacrificed her to appease the gods. He sacrificed his own daughter. He is the one you should have banished from the city. And now to bring home this strange girl named Cassandra and perhaps take her as his new wife? They both received their just desserts.
Chorus:	Oh evil spirit falling upon this house.
Chorus Leader:	Then you dare say you are not guilty of this double murder?
Clytemnestra:	When he sacrificed my dear Iphigenia, was he not the one who began the horror that runs through this house? My tears in rivers ran. He paid with death for this act, dealt by the sword of his own beginning.
Chorus:	We are at a loss for thought. Where, where lies right?
Clytemnestra:	This is not for you to decide. Do not mourn, for Iphigenia, his daughter, will greet him with kisses in the land below.
Chorus:	Reproach answers reproach.
	(Enter Aegisthus with soldiers.)
Aegisthus:	Oh blessed day, when justice speaks! This man lying here warms my heart! I was condemned to banishment by Agamemnon's father, but I am the rightful heir to the throne, and now it is mine! I planned this killing!
Chorus:	Justice will curse you Aegisthus!
Chorus Leader:	Your head will not escape the curses of the people, mixed with stones.
Aegisthus:	Be careful, lest you stumble and be hurt.
Chorus:	You weakling! Agamemnon went to war while you stayed at home.

Greek & Roman Plays for the Intermediate Grades © 1993 Fearon Teacher Aids

The Oresteian Trilogy

Chorus Leader:	You are now King, you who plotted Agamemnon's death, but did not dare to do the deed yourself.
Aegisthus:	The trick was to have it be another's work. And now I rule in Agamemnon's place and will marry Clytemnestra. Whoever is disobedient will wear a most heavy yoke.
Chorus:	What of Orestes, the son of Agamemnon?
Chorus Leader:	Perhaps fortune may have him return and prove the final victor?
Clytemnestra:	Go home, citizens! Go home and yield to fate before you suffer.
Chorus Leader:	We will not grovel at your feet!
Aegisthus:	Some later day I'll settle scores with you.
Chorus:	Grow fat defiling justice.
Chorus Leader:	Perhaps Orestes will return.
Chorus:	Yes, perhaps Orestes will return!
Aegisthus:	You will pay a severe price for your words.
Chorus:	Be not too self-assured, Aegisthus.
Clytemnestra:	Pay no heed to their foolish sounds. You and I are rulers of this house. You and I are now strong and shall order all things well. (She and Aegisthus enter the palace.)
Chorus:	(Turning to audience.) Perhaps Orestes, Agamemnon's son, will return in triumph. Perhaps!
	(Chorus slowly exits, leaving the stage bare.)

THE LIBATION BEARERS VOCABULARY

advise
agony
ally
anthems
anvil
arranges
bearer
bellowed
bitter
challenges
climax
coalesce
comfort
concern
condemns
conscience
debased
declare
deed
defy
dereliction
despise
destiny
detested
devotion
distracted
divulge
embrace
entangled
exile
fancied
fate
fetch
foreign

forges
fortune
fulfilled
fury
gall
gossip
grapple
grief
handmaidens
haunts
haven
hospitality
imaginary
informed
inmost
instruct
invoke
justice
justified
kenneled
libations
lock
loyal
misery
mournful
obvious
offerings
orphaned
pollution
portends
proportions
ranks
reared
redeem

render
resounding
rite
ritual
rumor
sanctify
scarlet
scroll
sear
sights
solemn
sorrow
soul
spirits
stroke
succumbed
summon
suppliant
sway
texture
tomb
tread
tyranny
unmourned
upright
urn
utter
vagabonds
vengeance
viper
visible
weary

The Oresteian Trilogy

THE LIBATION BEARERS CHARACTERS

Orestes, son of Agamemnon and Clytemnestra
Electra, Orestes' sister
Clytemnestra, Orestes' mother
Aegisthus, Orestes' stepfather
Cilissa, Orestes' old nurse
Pylades, Orestes' companion
Servant
Chorus Leader
Chorus
Furies

THE LIBATION BEARERS

(Orestes and Pylades standing at Agamemnon's tomb.)

Orestes: Oh god Hermes, I invoke you to be my champion. Receive my prayers. Fight in my cause! I return as an exile to my native land to pray at my father's tomb. I beg your forgiveness, father, that I was not here to break my grief upon your murder nor to stretch my hand when they took your murdered corpse away. I place a lock of my hair on your tomb to honor you, father.

Chorus: (With Electra, enter the palace carrying urns as they walk toward the tomb.)
Who is coming? What does it mean? Surely that is Electra, my beloved sister, wrapped in deepest sorrow. Yes, she walks in bitter sorrow. They bring urns to pour on my father's tomb. Oh Zeus, grant me vengeance for my father's murder. Be gracious to me. Be my ally! Come Pylades, let us hide in the shadows to overhear this suppliant rite. (They hide in the background.)

Chorus: We come with mournful, solemn tread, with offerings for the dead. Straight from the house we come with our libations. Terror bellowed through the house the night you were murdered, Agamemnon! What can wash off the blood once spilled? Oh tomb, soaked in sorrow!

Chorus Leader: Poor house in dereliction.

Chorus: How can our libations sanctify the ground where blood lies spilt? Behind our veils we weep. Covered in black cloth we suffer!

Electra: Come, you handmaidens. What shall I say as I pour the urns of grief? Advise me. Shall I say I bring these libations from a loving wife, my mother? Shall I say she pours her love on Agamemnon's tomb? I have no heart for such words! Oh friends, stay with me, for we carry a common hatred. Advise me.

Greek & Roman Plays for the Intermediate Grades © 1993 Pearon Teacher Aids

The Oresteian Trilogy

Chorus Leader:	By your father's sacred tomb, I will speak the inmost thoughts of my heart.
Electra:	Speak from your devotion to my dead father.
Chorus:	Utter a solemn prayer for those who were loyal to your father.
Electra:	Whom do you mean?
Chorus:	Yourself and all those who despise your mother, Clytemnestra, and your stepfather, Aegisthus . . . murderers of your beloved father!
Electra:	Who else should be added to our ranks?
Chorus:	Think of Orestes, your brother, even though he is far from home.
Electra:	You advise me well.
Chorus:	After that, add the names of the murderers.
Electra:	What words are these? Why do you instruct me so?
Chorus:	Pray that someone may come to give them their just rewards.

(Electra goes to the tomb and as she pours, she begins her prayer.)

Electra:	Oh god, Hermes, carry down my prayers to the land of the dark where the spirits guard my father's soul. As I pour my libations, I call upon you, father, to pity me and my poor brother, Orestes. We are vagabonds whose mother betrayed us. I am like a slave, and Orestes is in exile. Answer my prayer, oh father! Let some good chance bring Orestes home. Let those who killed you taste wickedness for wickedness! These are my prayers, poured out with these libations. Let earth, justice, and all the gods come to our aid.
Chorus:	Oh misery, misery! Oh, for a person who is strong with a spear to unloosen this house.
Chorus Leader:	Oh, for a person of strength!

Greek & Roman Plays for the Intermediate Grades © 1993 Fearon Teacher Aids

Chorus: Oh, for someone to redeem this house.

Electra: But listen! Here is news!

Chorus: Speak, Electra, speak.

Electra: Here is a lock of hair cut off and placed upon the tomb as a gift.

Chorus: Whose hair? Instruct us, please.

Electra: Look! Same color, same form, same texture! Like mine!

Chorus: Can this be a secret gift from Orestes?

Electra: It is nobody's hair, but his!

Chorus: Poor Electra! Poor Orestes! Never to embrace as brother and sister again.

Electra: Could this lock of hair speak some loving message to end the torn suffering of my heart? If only my brother could join my sad ritual and bring honor to our father's tomb. Oh gods, what storms you toss in our journey of life. Handmaidens, look! These footprints. Two sets of footprints. Look! One set of prints has the same measurements as mine, same form, same proportions! My heart throbs painfully.

(Orestes and Pylades step forward.)

Orestes: Tell the gods that your prayers have been answered!

Electra: What have the gods fulfilled for me?

Orestes: He for whom you prayed stands before your eyes.

Electra: And how do you know for whom I prayed?

Orestes: Orestes, him I know. You longed for him.

Electra: How exactly have my prayers been answered?

Orestes: Do you see me and still not know me? See this scarf, your own hands' work. The dogs of the house knew me, but Electra does not know her own brother?

Greek & Roman Plays for the Intermediate Grades © 1993 Fearon Teacher Aids

The Oresteian Trilogy

(Electra casts herself at his feet.)

Electra: Oh dearest treasure of my father's house! Dear, dear face. You are four joys in one to me! Faithful brother, you have returned to your sister. Sweet seed of hope!

Orestes: Oh Zeus, mighty Zeus! Direct us! Look upon two orphaned children of an eagle father! A father who died entangled in the coils of an evil viper called wife and mother. Electra and Orestes stand within your sight. Guide us!

Chorus: Children, silence! Some gossip tongues might divulge your secret meeting.

Orestes: Apollo will not forsake us now! The oracle spoke to me and said, "Blaze like a bull upon those who murdered Agamemnon." Shall I not trust the oracle?

Chorus: Oh spirit of right, let these things be done!

Orestes: Father, my sad father, guide us in action. Help me to return your house to its moment of glory.

Electra: Listen, my father! Two of your children stand before you weeping, casting sorrowful anthems on your tomb. Show us how to outsmart ruin.

Chorus: Help them, oh gods!

Electra: Oh Zeus! Mighty Zeus! Bring down your fist with a blow! Bring back justice.

Chorus: Murder screams for the spirit of justice!

Orestes: Oh Zeus, where shall we turn?

Electra: Merciless mother, you who had the gall to bury him unmourned.

Chorus: Yes, shout this outrage out.

Electra: My mother and stepfather debased me! They kenneled me like a vicious dog. My tears fell in secret.

Chorus: Sink this tale deep into your hearts, oh gods. This is the way things are!

Orestes: Be with those you love, my father.

Electra: And I, with all my tears, echo my brother.

Orestes: Father, be with us against those we hate.

Chorus: Right against right!

Electra: Oh gods, be just in what you bring to pass!

Chorus: Too long has destiny been delayed. It comes. It comes to those who prayed!

Orestes: Oh father, who succumbed to death in a most unkingly way, grant my prayer and over your house give me sway.

Electra: And I, too, father, need from you a grace . . . to murder Clytemnestra and Aegisthus and then escape.

Orestes: Great earth, set my father free above to see the fight.

Electra: Great gods, grant us success.

Orestes: Remember how they robbed you of your life.

Electra: Remember how they tangled you in their net.

Orestes: Will you not waken, father, to these challenges?

Electra: Will you not raise upright your beloved head?

Chorus: You must strike and prove your destiny!

Orestes: So be it! But I do not understand the libations upon this tomb from my mother. What was her motive?

Chorus Leader: It was a dream she had that filled her with guilt.

Chorus: A dream that she gave birth to a snake.

Chorus Leader: She woke screaming from her sleep.

Orestes: Then I shall turn snake to kill her! This is what the dream portends.

Greek & Roman Plays for the Intermediate Grades © 1993 Pearon Teacher Aids

The Oresteian Trilogy

Chorus: So be it.

Orestes: My plan is simple. Electra must go inside the palace to keep our plans undiscovered. I, with Pylades, my companion, will disguise ourselves as travelers and ask to see Aegisthus. Once I enter and face my stepfather, I'll flash my sword through his heart and lay him dead. Now you, Electra, keep a good lookout within and see that all our plans coalesce. All others, keep a silent tongue.

(Orestes and Pylades exit to disguise themselves. Electra enters the palace.)

Chorus: The anvil of justice is firm. Destiny forges and hammers her steel already.

Chorus Leader: The gods produce a son to the house at last to pay the murderers for their pollution.

Chorus: The gods produce soon a moment of terror.

Chorus Leader: Near the heart the pointed sword waits.

Chorus: Life must fall for life.

Chorus Leader: None can break the holy laws of heaven and hope to find the deed forgiven.

Chorus: Now the wheel has turned with time, blood in blood for ancient crime!

(Orestes and Pylades return disguised as travelers. Orestes pounds on the door.)

Orestes: Servants . . . servants! Hear you not this pounding upon this door? Is anyone at home? Does Aegisthus find the word hospitality foreign to him? (Servant opens the door.) Go and tell the masters of this house a weary traveler comes with news for them. Be quick about it. The night shadows become obvious, and it is the time when travelers must find a haven for the night.

(Clytemnestra appears at the door.)

Greek & Roman Plays for the Intermediate Grades © 1993 Pearon Teacher Aids

Clytemnestra: Strangers, you have only to declare your needs and this house is yours. You shall be given the rest you deserve. Look after them, servant, in a manner worthy of a house like ours.

Orestes: Madam, we are weary travelers with a very special message for the parents of Orestes. Tell them he is dead. Please don't forget to tell them. They should decide whether he should be brought home or buried in the land where he settled. This is the message, I tell you. I do not know to whom I speak, but his father should be informed.

Clytemnestra: Oh misery! Oh curse that haunts this unhappy house. Nothing escapes your watch. Poor Orestes! Death has recorded his name on his scroll.

Orestes: I only wish I could have introduced happier news to such a gentle house.

Clytemnestra: Someone had to bring the news, but now it is time to bring you some comfort after your long travel. Servant, conduct these gentlemen into our house and grant them every wish. See that they are comfortable. Meanwhile, we will get in touch with the master of this house to share this grief.

(Exit all, except the chorus.)

Chorus: Oh gods, you must listen and help Orestes. Now the time is ready to break. The sword will show its edge!

(Enter Cilissa.)

Chorus Leader: See! Orestes' old nurse in tears.

Chorus: Where do you go, Cilissa?

Cilissa: I summon Aegisthus as commanded by Clytemnestra. She puts a sad face on before her servants to hide the smile inside her eyes. Her sad look is false! Aegisthus will also be pleased to hear the message of the strangers. But never have I had to bear a hurt like this. My darling, baby Orestes, is dead. I was his nurse when he was very young. He wore me out, bless his little heart. I was so skilled in handling him that his father put him

Greek & Roman Plays for the Intermediate Grades © 1993 Pearon Teacher Aids

in my charge almost from the day he was born. Oh my poor Orestes. I am so unhappy. And now, I'm on my way to fetch the man who was his family's ruin. Yes, Aegisthus will be glad enough to hear of Orestes' death.

Chorus Leader: What is your message for Aegisthus?

Cilissa: My message is that he is to come with his bodyguards.

Chorus Leader: Say no such thing to our detested master. Put on a cheerful face and tell him Clytemnestra wants him to come at once . . . and alone.

Cilissa: What does all this mean?

Chorus: Go! Do as you are ordered! The gods will see to matters that concern the gods.

(Cilissa hurries out.)

Chorus: Oh Zeus, father of the gods, grant now that the fortune of this house be planted firm.

Chorus Leader: Zeus, bring a reign of goodness.

Chorus: Grant that this house may raise its eyes from the dust and welcome Orestes as its master.

(Enter Aegisthus.)

Aegisthus: I have been asked to come. There is a rumor that Orestes is dead. Is this true or just gossip? Give me an answer!

Chorus: Go inside and find out. No news is sure at second hand. (Aegisthus enters the palace.) Zeus! Zeus! How shall we begin our hopeful prayer?

Chorus Leader: Keep a bold heart, Orestes!

Chorus: Finish your fearful deed, Orestes. It is fate, and none condemns you.

Chorus Leader: The gods are on your side.

Chorus: May right by victory be justified!

Greek & Roman Plays for the Intermediate Grades © 1993 Fearon Teacher Aids

(The cry of Aegisthus is heard from within.)

Chorus Leader: Whose voice was it?

Chorus: Who has won?

Chorus Leader: Who rules the palace now?

(Servant enters from the palace.)

Servant: Help! Help! Aegisthus is dead. Aegisthus is no more. Help! Can't you hear me? Are you all deaf or fast asleep? Clytemnestra beware! Your neck is on the razor's edge . . . beware!

(Clytemnestra enters from the side.)

Clytemnestra: What is this sound I hear resounding through the house? Speak!

Servant: The dead come to life to kill the living!

Clytemnestra: The dead come to life? Ah, I know what you mean. Fetch me a weapon. The long, bitter story reaches its climax.

(Enter Orestes and Pylades from the palace.)

Orestes: Yes, it is you I seek! You, whom I call mother. Your second husband is dead!

Clytemnestra: Aegisthus dead? No!

Orestes: In the same grave with him you'll lie.

Clytemnestra: Wait! You are my son, my blood, and flesh. Orestes, remember that I am your mother!

Orestes: Pylades, what shall I do? Her words sear my brain. Should I weaken and not finish the deed. Advise me quickly.

Pylades: What of the words of the oracle? What of all your solemn oaths to the gods?

Orestes: Yes, Pylades, you advise me well.

Greek & Roman Plays for the Intermediate Grades © 1993 Fearon Teacher Aids

Clytemnestra:	I reared you up from babyhood. Let me grow old with you!
Orestes:	You ask me to share a home with you who murdered my father?
Clytemnestra:	Fate, my son, fate is half to blame for that.
Orestes:	Then fate arranges for your dying now!
Clytemnestra:	Orestes, does a parent's curse mean nothing to you?
Orestes:	You gave me birth, then flung me out to misery.
Clytemnestra:	Your heart, it seems, is set on taking another's life.
Orestes:	You are the one, not I, who does the killing.
Clytemnestra:	Beware, Orestes, of a mother's curse. It will hound you!
Orestes:	A father's curse will hound me if I let this go!
Clytemnestra:	So, you are the snake in my dream?
Orestes:	Yes! Your nightmare saw things straight. You killed a man you never should, now suffer what you never would!

(Orestes forces his mother into the palace followed by Pylades.)

Chorus:	Be brave, Orestes, in your part. Seal your ears to her cries of "My son! My son!"
Chorus Leader:	Perform the scarlet stroke, Orestes!
Chorus:	Erase the criminal and the crime!

(The cry of Clytemnestra is heard. Enter Orestes carrying Clytemnestra's blood-stained cape.)

Orestes:	The double-headed tyranny of our land has reached its end. My father's enemies, once so full of pride, speak no more. Was she guilty or not guilty? This whole business tortures me!

Greek & Roman Plays for the Intermediate Grades © 1993 Fearon Teacher Aids

The Oresteian Trilogy

Chorus: No man can hope to spend life untouched by pain.

Orestes: But I am blind to where this pain will end. I ask you, friends, was I justified in killing my mother?

Chorus: You must not load your lips with such doubt.

(The Furies enter from the back of the stage.)

Orestes: Look, everyone, look! Like shadows of conscience, they search for me. I cannot stay here!

Chorus Leader: What fancied sights torment you? We see no shadows.

Chorus: What have you to fear?

Orestes: They are not imaginary. I see them! I see them! Clear as day! They come toward me.

Chorus Leader: Your mind is distracted.

Orestes: Oh Apollo, help me! Help me!

Chorus: Grip yourself and do not be afraid. You have won!

Orestes: You do not see them, yet I see them. I must escape!

(With a cry of agony, Orestes rushes out, followed by the Furies.)

Chorus Leader: Good fortune go with you.

Chorus: May the gods watch over you and bring you peace. (Turns to audience.) Where is the end? Oh, when shall it finish? When shall it sate, this fury-bound hate?

(Chorus slowly exits, leaving the stage empty.)

Greek & Roman Plays for the Intermediate Grades © 1993 Fearon Teacher Aids

The Oresteian Trilogy

THE FURIES VOCABULARY

abhorred
abide
accursed
accusers
acquittal
advised
advocate
amazed
ancient
answerable
avail
awareness
blight
boast
branded
brooding
cast
cause
cavern
concentrate
conscience
consent
cunning
debt
deceit
deed
deny
devotion
dignity
discerned
disgraced
dwell

elude
emotions
entreat
escort
exile
foes
foiled
fugitive
guardian
guilt
hound
implore
influenced
integrity
invoke
judged
jurors
justice
kin
lenient
libations
malice
mocks
mortals
murmur
mutter
neglected
ordain
outcasts
persecute
plague
plea

plead
pledged
prey
protector
province
pursue
quench
rage
reconciled
relieve
respite
retribution
ripe
ritual
sacred
sanctuary
scent
scorn
sear
session
snare
steadfast
tended
torment
tribunal
unspeakable
urn
vapors
verdict
wrath

THE FURIES CHARACTERS

Apollo, Greek god of healing, prophecy, music, and poetry
Hermes, Greek god of travelers and messenger of Zeus
Orestes, son of Agamemnon and Clytemnestra
Athena, Greek goddess of wisdom, war, and peace
Spirit of Clytemnestra, dead wife of Agamemnon
12 Furies, daughters of the night
Chorus, citizens of Athens

THE FURIES

Apollo: I am your constant guardian, Orestes, and I will not fail you. It was I who first encouraged you to take your mother's life, and it is I who will deliver you from your present painful state. Look upon these ancient, ageless ones asleep upon the floor. They were born out of evil, and evil is the dark where they dwell. They are abhorred by the gods and mortals. They plan to hound you on land and sea, but keep your courage firm and constant. Pray to the goddess Athena as planned. Implore her help.

Orestes: Your promised help will be my strength, oh Apollo. Knowledge of justice and right is your power.

Apollo: Orestes, remember. Let your steadfast heart not be betrayed by any fear. Look upon this temple as a sanctuary. Hermes, be his guardian and prepare him for his introduction to Athena.

(Exit Apollo, Hermes, and Orestes. Enter the spirit of Clytemnestra.)

Spirit: Listen to me in your sleep, oh Furies. I, Clytemnestra, call to you. Awake! Of what use are you asleep? Often have I poured libations in your honor and offered prayers in your name, gifts, banquets, and now you forget. Like a fawn, Orestes has left the temple and escaped. He mocks you! Listen, you powers of darkness, and hear my plea. I entreat you to punish Orestes for his deed of murder! (The Furies mutter in their sleep.) Awake! I, Clytemnestra, call upon you to awake! You murmur and mutter in your sleep while your prey has vanished! (Again, the Furies mutter in their sleep.) Do you not hear me? Orestes has escaped! Orestes, my son, who killed me has escaped! Will you not wake? (Furies continue to mutter.) Still asleep? Wake and stand up. Do your work. Evil is your province, so do it! (Furies continue to murmur.) Your rage is being wasted in sleep.

Furies: (In their sleep.)
After him! Catch him! Catch him! Catch him!

Spirit: Only in your dreams you hunt your prey. How can you forget my pain? Awake, and torment his wicked heart. Storm at him and bite his conscience. Storm at him with hot lashes of your tongues. Destroy his hope of respite. Oh Furies, hunt him to the death!

(Furies awake. Spirit of Clytemnestra exits.)

Furies: Wake! Wake! Wake each other. All awake! We must shake off our heavy sleep. Someone was warning us. (They notice that Orestes has gone.)

Fury 1: We have been foiled!

Furies: What has happened?

Fury 1: Orestes has escaped. Our prey has vanished. Our snare is empty!

Furies: While we slept, our right stole away.

Fury 2: Out of my dreams I thought I heard a warning of this.

Furies: Who has ever mocked us? This is too painful to bear!

Fury 3: Orestes is accursed. He shall find no sanctuary to relieve his guilt!

Furies: Fate's curse is branded on his forehead!

(Enter Apollo.)

Apollo: I command you to leave this sacred temple at once! What place have you within these walls? Take your foul odor from this place. The gods abhor you!

Furies: Now it is our turn to speak!

Fury 4: It was you who encouraged Orestes to kill his mother. You are answerable for this crime, too.

Apollo: I encouraged him to avenge his father's death.

Greek & Roman Plays for the Intermediate Grades © 1993 Fearon Teacher Aids

Fury 5:	Orestes uses you as his protector.
Apollo:	It was I who suggested he come to this temple for sanctuary.
Furies:	Yes, and we are here as his escort.
Apollo:	You do outrage by your presence here.
Furies:	It is our duty to be here.
Apollo:	What duty?
Furies:	We hound. He kills his mother!
Apollo:	And what of a wife who kills her husband? What of that?
Fury 6:	That is not the same, for husband and wife are not of kin.
Apollo:	To persecute Orestes this way is most unjust. You concentrate upon his crime, but are most lenient with the crime of his mother, Clytemnestra. I shall take this case to goddess Athena herself.
Furies:	We will never let Orestes go. We will trace him by his mother's blood. We will hound him!
Apollo:	And I, Apollo, will stand by him. I command you to leave the Temple of Athena!
	(Furies slowly exit, muttering curses at Apollo. Apollo exits. Orestes enters.)
Orestes:	Oh goddess, Athena. I kneel in your temple. Supported by Apollo, I come. I know I am a fugitive and that my conscience is stained with blood, but even so, I implore you to receive me. I have traveled over land and sea seeking peace of mind, but to no avail. Oh Athena, at your temple I stand to be judged. Hear me and be merciful, I beg you.
	(The Furies, having picked up the trail of Orestes, have sneaked back into the temple.)

Greek & Roman Plays for the Intermediate Grades © 1993 Fearon Teacher Aids

Furies:	As hounds, we track Orestes. His scent is strong.
Fury 7:	Guard every door, lest he attempt to escape again.
Furies:	No hope can rescue him now. For your guilt we want your life.
Fury 8:	Your flesh will wither in payment for your crime. Down to the world of death you shall go!
Furies:	You shall not elude our watchful eye.
Orestes:	I invoke you, goddess Athena, for aid. Come and save my soul!
Furies:	Our judgment is just and true. Neither Athena nor Apollo can save you from the darkness of our power.
Fury 9:	We claim our price of blood.
Furies:	Oh brooding night, hear us! We come for punishment.
Fury 10:	We are ripe for ritual!
Furies:	We sing a song full of terror. Oh brooding night, hear us. We come for punishment.
Fury 11:	Our part is to torment.
Furies:	Oh brooding night, hear us. We come for punishment!
Fury 12:	We pour deep darkness on his mind.
Furies:	Oh brooding night, hear us. We come for punishment!

(Athena enters the temple.)

Athena:	From distant vapors, I heard my name invoked. I am amazed by this strange company in my temple. Who are you who crawl upon the ground?
Furies:	We are the daughters of night. We live deep under the earth.
Athena:	Why are you here?
Furies:	To drive out a murderer!

Greek & Roman Plays for the Intermediate Grades © 1993 Pearon Teacher Aids

The Oresteian Trilogy

Athena:	So, you pursue this man?
Furies:	Yes! Orestes has murdered his mother.
Athena:	Was there not some stronger power that influenced him to perform such a deed?
Furies:	Who truly has the power to influence a son to kill his mother?
Athena:	You grant to me the final decision in this case?
Furies:	Since you are daughter of Zeus, we do. We trust your wisdom.
Athena:	(To Orestes.) It is your turn to speak.
Orestes:	Oh goddess Athena, I will speak the truth. You knew my father, Agamemnon, well, for together you won victory over the city of Troy. Upon returning home, my father met a disgraceful death at the hands of my mother. With her black-hearted heart, she trapped him in her snare of cunning and deceit. After years of exile I returned home, and in just retribution for my father, I killed my mother. The god Apollo whispered many thoughts in my ear. He told me that if I neglected to revenge my father's murder, many tortures would sear my soul. Oh Athena, it is for you to judge whether I was right or wrong in my actions. Goddess Athena, I will abide by your decision, whether it be life or death for me.
Athena:	My temple will grant you sanctuary until your case has been decided. But this is too grave a situation for one person to judge. I'll choose the wisest citizens of my beloved city of Athens. They will judge you with integrity and truth.
	(Athena leaves the temple.)
Furies:	Oh sword of justice, fall upon Orestes. Today he must begin to pay his debt to justice.
Fury 1:	Today our watchful rage will sleep until a verdict has been reached.

Furies: Oh sword of justice, fall upon Orestes. Today he must begin to pay his debt to justice.

Fury 2: Our anger will not hurt his guilty soul until a verdict has been reached.

Furies: Oh sword of justice, fall upon Orestes. Today he must begin to pay his debt to justice.

Fury 3: Soon Orestes will perish unwept and unknown.

Furies: Oh sword of justice, fall upon Orestes. Today he must begin to pay his debt to justice.

(Athena returns with a jury of twelve citizens. Apollo also enters.)

Athena: Let the trumpets of the city announce that the trial of Orestes is about to begin. Let all who hear recognize that his court is in session. I ordain that justice now and always be well discerned.

Furies: Wait! Wait! What right does Apollo have to meddle in this tribunal?

Apollo: Orestes has my protection. Since I encouraged him to avenge his father's murder, I am here as his advocate. Oh goddess Athena, with your heavenly wisdom, begin this case.

Athena: The trial begins. The case is open. Furies, you are the accusers, speak! Make a full statement of the charge.

Fury 4: First, do you admit killing your mother?

Furies: Answer our question! Did you?

Orestes: I cannot deny it. Yes, I did.

Furies: Good. Good. We win the first point.

Orestes: It is too soon to boast. I am not defeated as yet.

Fury 5: How did you kill her?

Furies: Answer our question. How did you kill her?

Greek & Roman Plays for the Intermediate Grades © 1993 Fearon Teacher Aids

Orestes: With a sword.

Furies: Good. Good. We win the second point.

Orestes: It is too soon to boast. I am not defeated yet.

Fury 6: Who persuaded you to commit such a deed?

Furies: Answer our question. Who advised you to commit such a deed?

Orestes: The god Apollo! I trust him. My dead father, Agamemnon, will also send me help.

Fury 7: Yes, trust the dead now. Your right hand struck your mother dead.

Orestes: She was guilty!

Furies: Tell the court, if you can.

Orestes: She killed her husband, my father.

Fury 8: But you still live and are not punished.

Orestes: Why did she live and go unpunished?

Fury 9: Agamemnon, her husband, was not of her own blood.

Orestes: Oh Apollo, help me. I do admit killing Clytemnestra, my mother, but give evidence to show that my cause was right. Plead my cause.

Apollo: Listen, you outcasts of heaven!

Furies: You dare plead for his acquittal?

Apollo: Mark the truth of what I say. Clytemnestra was not the true mother of Orestes. From the very moment of his birth, Orestes was handed to a nurse who tended to his growth. She fed him, changed him, and loved him. The nurse was his mother, for she watched every step he attempted. Her heart was happy when he was happy and sad when he was sad. Yes, the nurse was his honest mother. I have said all I have to say and await to hear the decision of the jurors.

Athena: Citizens of Athens, you have heard the facts and emotions of both sides. As you now prepare to cast your vote, guard well the truth. Each of you has a white stone and black stone in your hand. If you decide that Orestes is innocent, cast the white stone in the urn, and if you decide that Orestes is guilty, cast the black stone in the urn. Be faithful to your consciences so that people may sleep in peace.

Furies: Do not scorn us, or we will deal with you harshly.

Apollo: Let your consciences listen to almighty Zeus!

Furies: If we fail to win this case, we will infest the land with an unspeakable plague!

Apollo: You will not win. The gods will win for Orestes!

Orestes: Oh Apollo, my life is held only by a slender thread.

Furies: Oh deep darkness, smile in our favor.

Orestes: This is a moment of life and hope or despair and death for me!

Furies: To us, it is a moment of great honor or disgrace!

Athena: As Athena, goddess of the city of Athens and daughter of mighty Zeus, I order the voting to begin. (Each citizen, one at a time, places a white or black stone in the urn. Athena slowly counts the votes, and it is a tie—six white and six black.) The vote is a tie, and to break the tie, I, Athena will cast my stone. With much thought and an awareness of right and wrong, I cast a white stone into the urn. Orestes is acquitted. Orestes is free!

Orestes: Oh goddess Athena, my constant devotion for bringing me from exile to a safe passage home. Zeus has remembered the memory of my father, Agamemnon, and through his daughter, Athena, has delivered me to safety. Farewell citizens of Athens! May death come to all foes of your city, but always success and victory to you.

Greek & Roman Plays for the Intermediate Grades © 1993 Fearon Teacher Aids

(Exit Orestes and Apollo.)

Furies: Vengeance! Vengeance!

Fury 10: Vengeance shall fester until our hearts pour over the land.

Furies: Anger for our insult!

Fury 11: A blight shall stamp itself upon plant and child.

Furies: Poison for our pain!

Fury 12: We are intent to get revenge. The face of the earth will be covered with infectious sores.

Furies: We seek revenge!

Athena: Let me entreat you to soften your threats. It was an even vote, which brought you no disgrace. Quench your anger. Do no harm to our land. In return, I, Athena, promise you a bright home here in this land . . . a holy cavern where you will receive homage from all the citizens of Athens.

Furies: Vengeance shall fester in our hearts. Soon Athens will be in despair and cry in pain!

Athena: No one has dishonored you. Calm your swelling wrath. I promise you a home here in Athens that will give you honor and dignity. Share with me a home in our lovely city of Athens.

Furies: We have been disgraced and stand in shame!

Athena: I beg you not cast upon our fields a sickness. Let there not be war within our city. Again, I offer you a home within our beloved city of Athens.

Furies: We have been disgraced and stand in shame!

Athena: I do not weary of offering you friendly words. Live with us in peace. Do not turn with malice upon our people.

Fury 1: What place do you offer us, divine Athena?

Greek & Roman Plays for the Intermediate Grades © 1993 Fearon Teacher Aids

Athena: A place where you will be accepted by all, a place free from all regret.

Furies: You promise us all this?

Athena: My word is pledged forever.

Furies: Our anger melts away.

Athena: You are among friends in Athens.

Furies: We consent to share the home of Athena. No harm will come to the fields of Athens and the people will live in joy.

Athena: We wish you joy in return. Now we will guide you to your new home.

Chorus: Pass onward to your new home, daughters of ancient night.

(Slowly the citizens lead the Furies off stage.)

Athena: Oh great, all seeing Zeus, guard our city! Thus god and fate are reconciled. Let every voice sing with joy!

(Curtain slowly closes as Athena stands with arms uplifted.)

Greek & Roman Plays for the Intermediate Grades © 1993 Fearon Teacher Aids

The Oresteian Trilogy

THE HAUNTED HOUSE

By Plautus

INTRODUCTION

This Roman comedy is obviously about a haunted house, but it is also about a little white lie that grows and grows until it becomes one gigantic lie that is completely out of hand. A good subtitle for this play might be, "When the Cat's Away, the Mouse Will Play." The dialogue in Roman comedies is simple and direct, and if the cast delivers it clearly, the audience will respond with loud laughter.

STAGING

Two houses should be represented on the stage. This is easily done by having two separate doors, one stage left and one stage right. Any suggestion of a door will be sufficient. The most important element in presenting a successful Roman comedy is neither the scenery nor the costumes, but maintaining the fast pace of the dialogue and having the characters enter and exit promptly from the two houses.

COSTUMES

The elderly Romans can wear floor-length togas, while younger characters can wear shorter robes. The servants wear tunics to their knees.

VOCABULARY

abomination	domicile	influence
accustomed	drachmas	involved
achieved	dusk	javelin
anxious	encourage	jig
benefit	excelled	knell
beseech	exterminate	meddling
budge	extravagance	misery
bumpkin	fetch	obnoxious
ceremony	fodder	relieved
cinders	garlic	scoundrel
convenient	host	scullion
deposit	impious	tuppence
discussion	imprisonment	vermin
disgraceful	inconvenient	yoke

CHARACTERS

Theopropides, the father
Philolaches, Theopropides' son
Tranio, Theopropides' servant
Grumio, Theopropides' servant
Callidamates, Philolaches' friend
Phaniscus, Callidamates' servant
Pinacium, Callidamates' servant
Simo, next door neighbor
Misargyrides, moneylender
Two friends of Philolaches
Four Servants

THE HAUNTED HOUSE

Grumio: Tranio! Tranio! Come out of that house. Come out, you smelly scullion! I know you're hiding in there. If you ever come back on the farm, I'll give you what you deserve. You in there, you're ruining your master's house. Come out here, I say!

(Tranio comes out of Theopropides' house.)

Tranio: Well, well, well, if it isn't Mr. Pig! You forget that you are in the city, not the country to which you are accustomed. There is no need to yell so. Please go back to your farm where you belong. Get away from this door! Are you waiting for this? (He begins to strike Grumio.)

Grumio: Why are you hitting me?

Tranio: For being alive and annoying me.

Grumio: Oh, how I wish our master would come home. And when he does, he will see how you're eating him out of house and home . . . and wasting all his money.

Tranio: That's a lie!

Grumio: I know you think me a country bumpkin, while you look upon yourself as a witty city chap. When the master discovers what a sneaky servant you have been, you'll soon be sent to the country in irons. Go ahead and waste your master's goods and encourage his son to do the same, your time will come. Go ahead . . . be merry while you can. Go ahead . . . drink and eat all day and night. Was that what the master told you to do while he was away? Is this being a good servant? His son was considered to be the best behaved young man in town. But now, under your influence, he's an entirely different person.

Tranio: I don't see what business it is of yours what I do. Don't you have some cattle or pigs to look after back on the farm? If I like eating and drinking and staying up late, that's my affair, so there!

Greek & Roman Plays for the Intermediate Grades © 1993 Pearon Teacher Aids

Grumio: (To the audience.)
He certainly is sure of himself, ain't he?

Tranio: Boy, do you stink! What is it I smell? Pig, goat, or garlic?

Grumio: We can't all stink of perfumes like you.

Tranio: Jealous, jealous, jealous! That's what you are, my dear Grumio. Jealous, jealous, jealous! I'm doing well, and you're not.

Grumio: When the master comes home, you will be hustled through the streets under a yoke.

Tranio: Oh, be quiet or I'll exterminate you right on this spot!

Grumio: Do you have any fodder for me to take back to the cattle?

Tranio: You bore me. Bore me! Bore me!

Grumio: OK! Eat, drink, and be merry. Fill your bellies, you and the master's son, but when the master comes . . .

Tranio: Be quiet! Go back to the farm where you belong. I'll have the fodder sent over to the farm tomorrow some-time. Now I'm busy. I have to go marketing for some fish for supper . . . . Well, why are you standing there, bird brain?

Grumio: They'll be calling you worse things before long. You'll see!

Tranio: "Before long" they can do what they like, provided things can stay as they are for the present.

Grumio: Those sound like famous last words to me. This I know, that things happen quicker than you expect them.

Tranio: Go away! Go away! Remove yourself! Go back to the farm. I can't waste anymore time on you. (Exits.)

Grumio: (To the audience.)
He doesn't give a tuppence for my warnings. Oh gods, please have the master come home soon before the house and farm go to complete ruin. It's been three years now since the master went away. Three years is a long time, as you well know. In a few months, all will

Greek & Roman Plays for the Intermediate Grades © 1993 Fearon Teacher Aids

be ruined—the farm, the house—and the master's money will all be spent. Oh well, I tried to stop that smart-alecky city servant! It's been nice chatting with you, but I had better go back to the farm, for I'm a hard-working country servant.

(Grumio exits. Enter Philolaches from the house in his pajamas, still half asleep.)

Philolaches: (To the audience.)
So, I overslept! . . . Yes, once I was a model child and the best in my class. I excelled at throwing the discus and javelin, fencing, and numbers. And now I'm out of shape! The house is falling apart, too. The beams are rotten through and through. I'm afraid the whole house will soon collapse, but nothing can be done about it for I'm in debt! I guess I spent too much of my father's money. I guess I'll go in and take a wee bit of a nap.

(Philolaches enters his house. Enter Callidamates, acting silly.)

Callidamates: (To the audience, staggering.)
I'm his best, best friend! Let's sing to him to wake him up . . . help me sing. (Singing.)

> For he's a jolly good fellow.
> For he's a jolly good fellow.
> For he's a jolly good fellow.
> That nobody can deny!
> That nobody can deny!
> That nobody can deny!
> For he's a jolly good fellow,
> That nobody can deny!
> Say, I feel a bit dizzy! Say, is anybody home?

(Enter Philolaches.)

Philolaches: Hello, my good friend.

Callidamates: Philolaches! Greetings to the best pal on earth. (He staggers into the arms of Philolaches.)

Philolaches: You had better sit down.

Callidamates: I think I'll just go to sleep.

Greek & Roman Plays for the Intermediate Grades © 1993 Fearon Teacher Aids

The Haunted House

(Enter Tranio, very upset.)

Tranio: (To the audience.)
It's all over, my friends. The master is returning from his travels. He's back! Jupiter and all the gods have turned against me! Does anybody in the audience want to take my place? I have a feeling I'm going to have a dozen spears stuck in my hide.

Philolaches: Wake up my dizzy friend, Tranio is back.
Now we shall get something to eat.

Tranio: Philolaches!

Philolaches: What's the matter?

Tranio: We are dead! Dead! Dead!

Philolaches: We are?

Tranio: Your father is back!

Philolaches: No! No! No!

Tranio: Yes! Yes! Yes!

Philolaches: Oh no!

Tranio: We are finished!

Philolaches: Who saw him?

Tranio: My two eyeballs saw him, that's who saw him!

Philolaches: You actually saw him?

Tranio: Of course I did.

Philolaches: Well, it's the end of me! Oh Tranio, what shall I do?

Tranio: Wake him up!

Philolaches: Wake up, Callidamates. My father is back! Wake up!

Callidamates: Long live the father of Philolaches!

Philolaches: He'll live all right. I'm the one who is dying.

Callidamates: Let's have a little party!

Greek & Roman Plays for the Intermediate Grades © 1993 Fearon Teacher Aids

Tranio:	Get up and be quiet!
Philolaches:	What am I going to do, Tranio? Soon my father will be here, and he'll find me in pajamas entertaining a drunken pal, the house in bad shape, and most of his money gone. Poor me!
Tranio:	He's asleep again! Wake him up and let's drag him out of here.
Philolaches:	Wake up, Callidamates. My father is coming!
Callidamates:	Where is he? I'll kill him, and then he will go away!
Tranio:	Be quiet, you silly fool. You'll have us all killed. Let's drag him into the house. (With much effort, they drag Callidamates into the house.)
Philolaches:	All is lost.
Tranio:	Never say die, Philolaches. I think I have an idea. Suppose I can fix it so that when your father arrives, he never enters the house? Suppose I manage to persuade him to run in the other direction?
Philolaches:	Impossible!
Tranio:	Listen! Go inside the house and keep your silly friend quiet. Lock all the doors. Warn all the servants to be absolutely still, as if there wasn't a living soul in the house.
Philolaches:	Right.
Tranio:	And nobody, absolutely nobody, must answer the door when your father knocks.
Philolaches:	Tranio, I commit all my life and hope into your hands. (He enters the house.)
Tranio:	(To the audience.) Now, let him come upon the scene. I'll put on a good show for the old man. I'll hide here in the corner. (Enter Theopropides.)

Greek & Roman Plays for the Intermediate Grades © 1993 Fearon Teacher Aids

The Haunted House

Theopropides:	Thank you, Neptune, for bringing me home safe and dry! Never again will I set foot upon your water. I never want to set eyes upon you again. (To the audience.) Well, I'm back after three long, long years in Egypt. I'm sure my son will be very glad to see me after all this time.
Tranio:	(To the audience.) I'd be glad to see someone bringing news of his death.
	(Theopropides attempts to open the door of his house.)
Theopropides:	Why is the door locked? It is daytime. (He begins to knock.) Is anybody home? Open this door, I say!
Tranio:	Who can that be outside our house?
Theopropides:	Tranio! My loyal servant, Tranio!
Tranio:	Master! Oh gentle master, you are at last safe at home with people who love you.
Theopropides:	Tell me, what's going on here?
Tranio:	What, sir?
Theopropides:	There's no one at home to answer my knocking. Not a living soul. I have bruised my knuckles pounding on this stupid door.
Tranio:	You haven't touched the house, have you? Tell me it's not so!
Theopropides:	Of course I touched it. How could I help but touch it, if I knocked on the locked door? Why shouldn't I touch it?
Tranio:	Alas, alas all is lost! (Starts crying.)
Theopropides:	What ails you?
Tranio:	You have done something most horrible!
Theopropides:	I think you must have a fever or something. Are you ill?
Tranio:	What a terrible, impious thing you have done.
Theopropides:	Tranio, calm yourself and tell me what I have done.

Greek & Roman Plays for the Intermediate Grades © 1993 Fearon Teacher Aids

Tranio:	Oh master, quickly come away from that house. (He drags Theopropides away.) Avoid this house. Avoid it! Avoid it! Fly, sir, fly! I implore you to fly from this house! Are you sure you touched the door?
Theopropides:	(To the audience.) Poor Tranio is off his rocker.
Tranio:	Alas, alas! You have caused the death of . . .
Theopropides:	Whose death? Speak!
Tranio:	You have caused the death of all your house!
Theopropides:	May the gods and goddesses cause your death for talking this way!
	(Two of Philolaches' friends enter and start to knock on the door.)
Tranio:	Quickly! Keep those people away from the door.
Theopropides:	You two, keep away from the house!
Tranio:	Quickly! Cast yourselves upon the ground.
	(Everyone falls face first to the ground.)
Theopropides:	Tranio, for the love of the gods, please explain what all this is about.
Tranio:	I shall. Listen! Seven months ago we all left the house, and no living soul has set foot inside since.
Theopropides:	Why?
Tranio:	Everyone get up and look around to see if we are being overheard.
	(Everyone searches about.)
Theopropides:	Yes, we are quite alone.
Tranio:	Look again, just to be sure.
	(Everyone searches about again.)
Theopropides:	I tell you, there is no one about. We are the only people here.

Greek & Roman Plays for the Intermediate Grades © 1993 Fearon Teacher Aids

The Haunted House

Tranio:	Oh master, a horrible, horrible crime has been committed!
Theopropides:	What horrible, horrible crime?
Tranio:	A horrible crime! An old and ancient horrible, horrible crime!
Theopropides:	What crime? What crime? Out with it!
Tranio:	Listen, and I shall speak.
Theopropides:	Yes? Yes?
Tranio:	A host murdered his guest in this very house. He was the very man who sold you this house many years ago.
Theopropides:	Murdered his guest?
Tranio:	Yes! Murdered and robbed his guest, and then buried the body in this very house!
Theopropides:	How did you ever discover this terrible occurrence?
Tranio:	Listen, and I shall speak. One evening after your son and all the servants had retired to bed, your son let out a terrible yell!
Theopropides:	My son did?
Tranio:	Please don't interrupt. Just listen. Your son yelled! The dead guest had appeared to him in his sleep!
Theopropides:	Really?
Tranio:	Don't interrupt. Listen!
Theopropides:	All right. All right! I shall be still. Not another word from me.
Tranio:	The dead man said to your son, "My host slew me and buried me in this house without benefit of a burial ceremony. You must leave this house, for it is a house of abomination. This house is a domicile of sin!" That is what the ghost said to your son.
	(A noise comes from the house.)
Theopropides:	Hark, what was that noise from the house?

Greek & Roman Plays for the Intermediate Grades © 1993 Fearon Teacher Aids

Tranio:	Yes, what was it?
Theopropides:	I think someone is at the door!
Tranio:	The ghost walks!
Theopropides:	Oh merciful gods! The dead are coming to drag me to Hades! My blood is frozen!
Tranio:	(To the audience.) Those fools inside the house are going to ruin everything. If I'm found out, may the gods be merciful!
Theopropides:	What are you muttering about, Tranio?
Tranio:	Oh, sir, come away from that door, I beseech you! Fly away, sir, fly away before it's too late!
Theopropides:	To where shall I fly? Say, why don't you have to fly away, too?
Tranio:	I have made my peace with the dead, so I have nothing to fear.
Callidamates:	(From within.) Hey, Tranio!
Tranio:	(Speaking into the keyhole.) Why do you call my name, oh ghost? It was not I who knocked on the door. It was not I who disturbed your peace.
Theopropides:	Tranio, what is happening?
Tranio:	Oh, I'm so relieved! It was you calling my name. For a moment, I thought it was the ghost of the man crying out to me because you had knocked on the door. Oh, Theopropides, master, do as I tell you and leave.
Theopropides:	Do what?
Tranio:	Cover your head, don't look back, and fly away!
Theopropides:	But aren't you going to fly with me?
Tranio:	I told you before that I have made my peace with the dead.
Theopropides:	I know, I know, but why are you so frightened then?

Greek & Roman Plays for the Intermediate Grades © 1993 Pearon Teacher Aids

Tranio: Oh master, please don't worry about me. You go away as safely as you can.

Theopropides: Oh Hercules, come to my assistance.

(Theopropides and the two visitors hurry off.)

Tranio: (To the audience.)
A pretty clever scheme, eh? (He unlocks the front door with his key and enters. Enter Misargyrides.)

Misargyrides: (To the audience.)
This has been a bad year for me, Misargyrides, the moneylender. In fact, it has been a lousy year! From dawn to dusk I haven't been able to lend a penny to a single soul in the forum and, of course, I don't make any money on the interest.

(Tranio comes from the house most cheerful, until he sees Misargyrides.)

Tranio: (To the audience.)
Oh my word, what now? This will finish me forever! That looks like Misargyrides, the moneylender, who lent money to my master's son, Philolaches. And of course the money was spent foolishly. Everything will be lost if my master discovers about the loan . . . I'll speak to the moneylender anyway, just to . . . . Oh No! Here comes my master! Oh noooo! Why is he returning so soon? I really am in a mess! He mustn't find out. I must cause more confusion to confuse everyone. My dear audience, it's no fun to have a guilty conscience such as mine. (Enter Theopropides.) Where have you been, master?

Theopropides: I've just met the man who sold me the house.

Tranio: I hope you didn't tell him all I told you about the guest.

Theopropides: I certainly did. Every detail!

Tranio: (To the audience.)
Oh no! My beautiful scheme is blown to bits!

Theopropides: What are you muttering about?

Tranio:	Did you really and truly tell him?
Theopropides:	Everything.
Tranio:	Does he admit to what he did to the guest?
Theopropides:	No! He denies it all.
Tranio:	Denies it? The liar! The scoundrel! I think you should bring charges against him.
Misargyrides:	(To the audience.) That looks like Tranio, the servant of Philolaches. They owe me money, and I can't get a penny of interest from them. (He starts toward Tranio. Tranio, seeing this, tiptoes toward him to stop him from coming too close.)
Theopropides:	Where are you tiptoeing to?
Tranio:	Uh . . . no where. (To the audience.) I surely was born under an unlucky star. I can't have the master discover that we borrowed money. I'm full of misery. Fire on both sides! I'll speak to him.
Misargyrides:	(To the audience.) It's a good sign that Tranio is coming toward me. Perhaps he has the money he owes me.
Tranio:	A very good day to you, Misargyrides.
Misargyrides:	Never mind wishing me a good day, what about the money you and Philolaches owe me?
Tranio:	Oh be quiet. That's all you talk about.
Misargyrides:	(To the audience.) Sounds like he doesn't have a cent for me again.
Tranio:	It just so happens that you couldn't have come at a better time, you old tightwad!
Misargyrides:	Am I or am I not going to get the money you owe me?
Tranio:	You needn't yell, for I know you have a lovely voice. (To the audience.) I have a splendid plan that will solve my problem. Watch how clever I am, my friends. I have

Greek & Roman Plays for the Intermediate Grades © 1993 Fearon Teacher Aids

decided to involve my master in this discussion, and all will be well. You'll see! I will start a loud argument, so my master will overhear everything. Don't worry . . . you'll soon see how clever I am.

Misargyrides:	My money, please.
Tranio:	(Yelling.) Why don't you be a good little boy and go home.
Misargyrides:	Go home?
Tranio:	Come back in about an hour.
Misargyrides:	Why should I run back and forth like an idiot? I'll wait here for an hour.
Tranio:	You are an obnoxious beast!
Misargyrides:	The money! The money!
Tranio:	Money, money, money! It seems that's the only word in your vocabulary.
Misargyrides:	Not an inch will I budge until I get my money.
Tranio:	Shout as much as you like. You are the most obnoxious vermin I ever saw.
Misargyrides:	That sort of language doesn't frighten me in the least.
Theopropides:	(Approaching.) This is a rather hot argument you two are having. Tranio, what is this money he keeps screaming about?
Tranio:	Silly moneylender, this is the father of Philolaches, and I'm sure he will give you the money his son borrowed from you.
Misargyrides:	And I'll take it!
Theopropides:	Tranio, pray tell, what is this all about? Why does my son owe him money?
Tranio:	Oh master, cast the money in his dirty old face.
Misargyrides:	(To the audience.) A bag of money hurled in my face would please me. I'll take it anyway I can get it.

Greek & Roman Plays for the Intermediate Grades © 1993 Fearon Teacher Aids

Theopropides:	What money are you speaking of?
Tranio:	Your son owns him a little debt.
Theopropides:	How much is little?
Tranio:	Well, about . . . uh . . . uh . . . four thousands drachmas.
Theopropides:	Has my son really borrowed that much money?
Tranio:	Oh master, say you'll give it to him, and let's get rid of this nuisance.
Theopropides:	And what has become of the four thousand drachmas my son borrowed?
Tranio:	Oh, it's there all right.
Theopropides:	Well, if it's there you can pay it.
Tranio:	Well, it's not exactly there. You see, your son purchased a house with it.
Theopropides:	Why, that's splendid! I'm delighted that Philolaches is going into business. A very smart lad I have. What sort of house is it?
Tranio:	Words fail me!
Theopropides:	What do you mean, words fail you?
Tranio:	It's a beautiful house. Oh master, do pay him, or I shall faint from looking at his stingy face.
Theopropides:	Very well. I'll pay you tomorrow moneylender.
Misargyrides:	Tomorrow will be fine. I'll go then and return tomorrow. (Exits.)
Tranio:	(Yelling after him.) And may the curses of all the gods follow you! (To the audience.) That moneylender nearly ruined it all for me.
Theopropides:	Stop muttering, Tranio, and tell me where this beautiful house is that my son has purchased.

Greek & Roman Plays for the Intermediate Grades © 1993 Fearon Teacher Aids

The Haunted House

Tranio:	(To the audience.) Now I'm truly sunk!
Theopropides:	Answer my question.
Tranio:	Excuse me, sir, I'm simply trying to remember the location of the house.
Theopropides:	Why is it so difficult to remember?
Tranio:	(To the audience.) If you're going to lie, you might as well make it a big one.
Theopropides:	Well? Have you remembered yet?
Tranio:	Yes! Yes! It has come to me. My memory has returned at last. The house your son purchased is the house right next to your own house. This one!
Theopropides:	Are you joking?
Tranio:	(To the audience.) It won't be much of a joke, if he doesn't pay the money or the moneylenders.
Theopropides:	Well, let's take a look inside. Knock on the door, Tranio.
Tranio:	(To the audience.) Ye gods! What am I going to do now? This is the utter end! My lies have trapped me again. We can't enter that house.
Theopropides:	Hurry, Tranio, and knock on the door. Ask them to show us about. I am most anxious to look over the house my son has purchased.
Tranio:	But sir, we just can't barge in like that. The ladies of the house might have objections.
Theopropides:	Perhaps you're right. You find out if this is a convenient time for us to visit. I'll wait down the street while you arrange things. (He walks to the far end of the stage.)

Tranio: (To the audience.)
He is constantly upsetting my plans. (Simo, the owner of the house, comes out.) Well, here comes old Simo, himself. A bit of luck at last. I'll stand to one side and plan my next move.

Simo: (To the audience.)
That was the best meal my wife ever cooked for me. I feel comfortably full. It truly was delicious. I think I'll walk into town before I take my afternoon nap.

Tranio: (To the audience.)
I'll fix it so that old Simo helps me out of the trap I'm in. Watch! (To Simo.) May the gods cast their blessings upon you, Simo.

Simo: Why thank you, Tranio. What are you doing out here?

Tranio: Why I'm talking to the nicest man in town . . . you.

Simo: Thank you, Tranio, but I can't say I'm talking to the nicest servant in town. Tell me, what's been going on in your master's house since he has been away?

Tranio: What do you mean?

Simo: Come now! You know what I'm talking about. All those parties, drinking, card playing, and spending your master's money so foolishly.

Tranio: I can't deny anything you say, but have mercy, for before you, you see a servant who is about to die. My master is back!

Simo: Well, I guess that means imprisonment for you.

Tranio: Please don't give me away.

Simo: I'll not say a word.

Tranio: Would you do me one more favor?

Simo: Anything to help a drowning man.

Tranio: Would you let my master look over your house?

Simo: That's a silly thing for him to do. My house is not for sale.

Greek & Roman Plays for the Intermediate Grades © 1993 Pearon Teacher Aids

The Haunted House

Tranio:	I realize that, but my master is planning to enlarge his own house and wants to follow some of your plans, since your house is so beautiful.
Simo:	Why, certainly. He has my permission to copy any of my ideas that he likes.
Tranio:	(To the audience.) The gods are with me! Don't you think I'm clever? Thank you. (To Simo.) I'll call my master now. Theopropides, sir!
Theopropides:	Is it all arranged?
Simo:	I understand you would like to look over my house?
Theopropides:	Yes, if it's not too inconvenient for you.
Simo:	By all means go in and take a good look around. Go anywhere in the house, just as if it belonged to you.
Theopropides:	As if?
Tranio:	(Whispering to Theopropides.) See how sickly he looks. Don't upset him more by reminding him you have purchased his house. It will only make him more ill.
Theopropides:	I understand what you mean.
Tranio:	You got a real bargain, so don't give the impression that you got the better deal. Don't say a word about having bought the house.
Theopropides:	Very sensible of you, Tranio, very sensible indeed.
Simo:	Please enter the house.
Theopropides:	Thank you. I will. Come, Tranio.
	(They all enter Simo's house. Enter Phaniscus, a slave of Callidamates.)
Phaniscus:	(To the audience.) I'm here to bring my master home. He is visiting Philolaches and probably has been drinking a great deal. I'm the only one of his slaves who is any good. I take good care of my master, Callidamates, and that's why he's good to me.

(Enter Pinacium, another slave of Callidamates.)

Pinacium: Hey, Phaniscus, why didn't you wait for me?

Phaniscus: Go away and leave me alone.

Pinacium: Don't be so sure of yourself, just because you're the master's favorite.

Phaniscus: You know something? Looking at you makes my eyes sore.

Pinacium: Very funny.

Phaniscus: I'm not going to get in an argument with you. My job is to bring Callidamates home safely.

Pinacium: You'd do anything to remain his favorite.

Phaniscus: I don't have to listen to you.

Pinacium: And I don't want any more of your lip, either.

(Phaniscus knocks on the door.)

Phaniscus: Is my master Callidamates here? Open the door some-body. I'm sure Callidamates told me he was going to visit his best friend, Philolaches.

(Theopropides and Tranio emerge from the house next door.)

Tranio: Well, master, what do you think of the house your son bought?

Theopropides: I'm most pleased. We certainly got a wonderful bargain.

Tranio: I deserve some credit, for I persuaded Philolaches to borrow the money to buy the house.

Theopropides: Good work, Tranio. But now go and find my son and tell him I have returned.

Tranio: Very good, sir. (To the audience.) I'll go in by the back door and join my fellow jokers. I'll tell them how well I handled everything. Perhaps a little reward . . . well, don't you think I deserve it? I certainly do!

(Tranio enters the "Haunted House" by the back door.)

Greek & Roman Plays for the Intermediate Grades © 1993 Fearon Teacher Aids

The Haunted House

Phaniscus:	This is very strange! Not a sound is coming from within the house.
Theopropides:	(To the audience.) What are those two doing at my house? Why are they both looking through the keyhole?
Phaniscus:	I shall knock again. Open the door! I have come to fetch my master, Callidamates!
Theopropides:	Just a moment! Why are you trying to break into my house?
Pinacium:	What's it to you, old man?
Theopropides:	I beg your pardon. How dare you speak to me in such a fashion!
Pinacium:	Why are you meddling in other peoples' business?
Theopropides:	Obviously you have come to the wrong house.
Phaniscus:	Our master is in this house drinking.
Pinacium:	And we have come to fetch him home.
Theopropides:	You don't seem to understand. Nobody lives in this house any more.
Phaniscus:	Doesn't young Philolaches live here?
Theopropides:	He used to live here, but he moved away sometime ago.
Pinacium:	Well, he lived here yesterday.
Theopropides:	You are most mistaken. No one has lived in this house for the last six months.
Pinacium:	You must be dreaming.
Phaniscus:	He certainly does live here. I know that for the last week there has been a party going on in this house.
Theopropides:	Tell me, who has been giving these parties?
Pinacium:	Philolaches.
Theopropides:	Which Philolaches are you speaking of?
Phaniscus:	I think his father's name is Theopropides.

Greek & Roman Plays for the Intermediate Grades © 1993 Fearon Teacher Aids

Theopropides:	(To the audience.) If he is speaking the truth, this will be the death of me. I must ask him some more questions. (To Phaniscus.) You say that this Philolaches has been entertaining his friends in this house and that one of his wild friends is your master, Callidamates?
Pinacium:	Yes!
Phaniscus:	Ever since his father went on a long journey he has been partying almost every night.
Pinacium:	That's the truth.
Theopropides:	And then he bought the house next door?
Pinacium:	Wrong!
Theopropides:	But he gave the owner a deposit of four thousand drachmas.
Pinacium:	Wrong again!
Phaniscus:	Are you a friend of the man's father?
Theopropides:	You have just sounded the death knell of his poor old father.
Pinacium:	He certainly has been living in great luxury and extravagance. The money that Philolaches spends is unbelievable.
Theopropides:	He has brought his poor father to his grave!
Phaniscus:	Doesn't anyone hear me knocking on this door?
Pinacium:	Let's go. Nobody is home. (Phaniscus and Pinacium exit.)
Theopropides:	(To the audience.) Oh! Oh! Oh! This is the end of me. All these things I have heard have burned my heart into hot red cinders. (Simo enters.) Ah! Here comes the man from whom my son purchased the house. Simo, I understand my son gave you four thousand drachmas?
Simo:	Your son hasn't ever given me a penny.

Greek & Roman Plays for the Intermediate Grades © 1993 Fearon Teacher Aids

The Haunted House

Theopropides:	Then it was Tranio, his servant, who gave you the four thousand drachmas?
Simo:	No. Perhaps you have had a dream about all this?
Theopropides:	Didn't my son give you some money when he bought your house?
Simo:	Are you saying your son bought my house? All I can say is that your son bought nothing from me. He didn't even borrow a cup of sugar from me.
Theopropides:	O ye gods, I'm dying!
Simo:	This sounds like some of Tranio's mischief!
Theopropides:	Tranio has fooled me in a most disgraceful manner. Help me!
Simo:	Certainly. What can I do?
Theopropides:	Lend me some of your servants.
Simo:	Enter my house and pick whom you like. (They both enter Simo's house. Enter Tranio.)
Tranio:	(To the audience.) Well, I got everyone out of the house the back way, so that problem is settled.
Theopropides:	(Theopropides enters with four servants.) Ugh . . . yeow . . . it looks like the jig is up! I'm trembling all over. You, Tranio, are to be punished! Grab him! Pin him to the ground! (The servants pounce on Tranio.)
Tranio:	How about if I say I'm sorry?
Theopropides:	As I live, I'll see you dead first!
Tranio:	Oh sir, one lie led to another. I couldn't help it.
Theopropides:	And the punishment I'm going to give you I can't help either. Someone in the audience hand me a chair. Thank you. Now, servants, place this tricky little Tranio across my knees so I can talk to him with my hand! (Servants place Tranio over Theopropides' lap.) Audience, how many whacks shall I give him? Five? Ten? Twenty?

Greek & Roman Plays for the Intermediate Grades © 1993 Fearon Teacher Aids

The Haunted House

(As Theopropides spanks him, Tranio cries out in pain.)

There, now you are pardoned!

(Tranio jumps off the stage and runs up the aisle crying as he holds his rear end.)

Audience, now our little comedy has come to an end. Here's a final warning for you . . . one little lie leads to another, and another, and another! And now, clap your hands to show we are friends.

(Curtain closes.)

The Haunted House

THE MENAECHMI TWINS

By Plautus

INTRODUCTION

The fact that William Shakespeare adopted the plot of this Roman comedy for his successful play, *A Comedy of Errors*, and that is was later the basis of the Broadway musical, *Boys From Syracuse*, is proof enough that this rollicking comedy of confusion and fun has appealed to audiences for hundreds of years.

The Menaechmi Twins is about a pair of identical twin brothers who were separated when they were very young, and from the opening curtain, one joke after another spills forth, rivaling some of the situation comedies on television. As written by the Roman playwright, Plautus, the audience will sense what will ensue before the characters of the play realize what is going to happen to them, and this causes much audience laughter in anticipation of the humorous situations that arise. There is only one difficulty presenting this comedy, and that is that the cast must always stay in character no matter how funny the situation or how much the audience laughs. In other words, the cast must always keep a straight face!

STAGING

Only two doors are needed to represent the two houses on stage. Any type of opening can represent a door. Reality is not essential.

COSTUMES

People of high birth wear floor-length robes, while servants wear pieces of cloth that come only to their knees.

VOCABULARY

abiding
absolute
accusations
armlets
auctioneer
brute
chariot
clinic
concerned
crate
curse
debts
decency
declare
delirious
dinghy
dowry
emancipation
embroidered
entitled

fiery
fulfill
furthermore
garland
gills
goldsmith
hallucinations
hysteria
indication
lecture
mentioned
mistress
monotonous
obligation
opinion
patron
perjurer
personified
pestering
prescription

proverbial
psychosis
purlieus
rabid
requested
scaly
scheme
severity
sheer
skirmish
souvenir
spry
staff
statement
swindlers
thievery
threatening
whiff
whisk
yarns

CHARACTERS

Menaechmus I, a young man living in Epidamnus
Mrs. Menaechmus, his wife
Senex, Menaechmus' father-in-law
Peniculus, companion of Menaechmus I
Lady E, Menaechmus' neighbor
Cylindrus, Lady E's cook
Menaechmus II, Menaechmus I's twin brother
    from Syracuse
Messenio, Menaechmus II's servant
Decio, servant of Mrs. Menaechmus
Doctor
Servant girl
Servants

THE MENAECHMI TWINS

Peniculus: Hello, dear audience. Hello. Hello. Hello! My name is Peniculus, but some who know me better call me Whisk Broom, because when I come to dinner, I sweep the table clean. Some people have called me a sponger, because I like free meals. Oh well, I suppose I am a sponger of sorts. I'm a friend of Menaechmus, and he lives behind that door you see on stage. The other door belongs to Lady E. If you keep your eyes open, you'll see a great deal of action coming and going from those two doors.

(Menaechmus I enters from his door, shaking his fist at his house.)

Menaechmus I: You're a pretty poor wife, you are! And you're mean and bad tempered! If you weren't all these things, you'd show some sympathy for your husband's likes and dislikes. And furthermore, if you do anything like that to me again, I'll throw you out. I'll get a divorce. You can go home to your father. Every time I want to go out, you hang onto me, you call me back, you keep asking me questions, "Where am I going?" "What am I going to do?" "What's my business?" "What will I bring home? "What have I been doing while I was away?" Wife? I married no wife! I married a custom's inspector, for I have to declare everything, past, present, and future! The trouble with you is that I've spoiled you. There isn't a thing that you want that you don't have—fancy dresses and shining jewelry. Now, keep your nose out of my business. And I won't be home for dinner tonight . . . so there!

Peniculus: (To the audience.)
He's putting on quite a show, bawling out his wife, but I'm the one he's really punishing. If he has dinner out tonight, he'll be hurting me, for there goes my free meal.

Menaechmus I: (To the audience.)
Hurrah! That was telling her off, wasn't it? (Pulls a dress from under his tunic.) Not more than a minute

Greek & Roman Plays for the Intermediate Grades © 1993 Fearon Teacher Aids

	ago, I stole this dress from my wife, and I'm going to give it to Lady E who lives next door. A neat trick, eh?
Peniculus:	Are you going to share that souvenir with me?
Menaechmus I:	Who is it?
Peniculus:	It's me.
Menaechmus I:	(Turns around.) Oh, am I glad to see you! What good luck. How are you? (They shake hands.)
Peniculus:	How are you?
Menaechmus I:	(Still shaking hands.) What's on your mind?
Peniculus:	Nothing, but I've got my hand on the best friend a man ever had.
Menaechmus I:	My wife doesn't know where our party is going to be, and we have the whole day to burn.
Peniculus:	We'd better be going, for the day's half gone already.
Menaechmus I:	Ssshhhh! I think she's listening at the door. Come over here! (He walks on tiptoe far away from the door, with finger on lips.)
Peniculus:	All right. (Imitates him.)
Menaechmus I:	Now we're safe, away from the lion's den.
Peniculus:	Well, you surely would make a good chariot racer.
Menaechmus I:	What do you mean?
Peniculus:	You keep looking over your shoulder to see if your wife is catching up with you.
Menaechmus I:	Say, what do you think?
Peniculus:	What do I think? I think whatever you think. If it's "yes" with you, it's "yes" with me, and if it's "no" with you, it's "no" with me.
Menaechmus I:	How are you with smells?
Peniculus:	Smells?

Menaechmus I:	If you smell something, can you tell what it is?
Peniculus:	None better!
Menaechmus I:	All right. Take a whiff of this dress and tell me what it smells like.
Peniculus:	(Sniffing.) Thievery!
Menaechmus I:	Smell again.
Peniculus:	Dinner!
Menaechmus I:	Blessings on you. You guessed correctly both times. I stole this dress from my wife, and now I'm going to take it next door to Lady E. When she sees this dress, she will quickly prepare the most delicious dinner for you, for me, and for herself.
Peniculus:	Great! Shall I knock on Lady E's door now?
Menaechmus I:	Knock gently.
Peniculus:	What are you afraid of? The doors aren't made of glass. (Lady E opens the door, and Peniculus knocks her on the head.)
Menaechmus I:	Stop, stop you fool! See, she's there.
Lady E:	Why, Menaechmus, hello!
Peniculus:	What about me?
Lady E:	To me, you just don't count.
Peniculus:	(To the audience.) Don't count, eh? Well, even the fellows who don't count still eat.
Lady E:	Menaechmus, what's that you're holding?
Menaechmus I:	Your gain and my wife's loss.
Lady E:	(Fingering the dress.) Oh, Menaechmus, you are my favorite neighbor.
Peniculus:	(To the audience.) All sweet talk, so long as she sees something to grab.

Greek & Roman Plays for the Intermediate Grades © 1993 Pearon Teacher Aids

The Menaechmi Twins

Menaechmus I:	(Holding dress out to Lady E on bended knee.) Great was the danger when I stole this on this very morn!
Peniculus:	(To the audience.) He was scared to death!
Menaechmus I:	Take it, it's yours. Four golden coins I paid for it when I bought it for my wife a year ago.
Peniculus:	(To the audience.) Four golden coins cast down the drain.
Menaechmus I:	(Standing up.) You know what I'd like you to do?
Lady E:	(Stroking the dress.) For such a nice neighborly gift, I'll do whatever you want.
Menaechmus I:	Well then, have a dinner prepared for the three of us at your house.
Peniculus:	And buy something fancy from downtown. Buy some split pigs' heads or something like that. When those appear on the table in their gravy, they give me the appetite of a hawk!
Menaechmus I:	As soon as you can.
Lady E:	Why, of course.
Menaechmus I:	We'll just step downtown and then be right back.
Lady E:	Enjoy yourselves. Come whenever you like. The dinner will be awaiting you.
Menaechmus I:	Come, Peniculus.
Peniculus:	You bet I'll come. I'll keep an eye on you. I'll be right at your heels. I wouldn't lose you today for all the wealth of the gods in heaven. The thought of that dinner makes my head spin.

(Menaechmus I and Peniculus exit.)

| Lady E: | Cylindrus! Cylindrus, come out immediately! |

(Cylindrus appears from Lady E's house.)

Cylindrus: Yes, mistress.

Lady E: Get a basket and go along now and buy some food. Here's some money, six coins. See that you buy just enough for three, neither too little nor too much.

Cylindrus: Who'll be here for dinner?

Lady E: Menaechmus, myself, and Peniculus.

Cylindrus: Oh no! That's ten you've mentioned! Peniculus easily takes the place of eight.

Lady E: Well, I've told you who's coming, you decide.

Cylindrus: The dinner is practically ready, mistress.

Lady E: Hurry back.

Cylindrus: I'll return quickly. (Cylindrus exits and Lady E enters her house. Enter Menaechmus II, followed by Messenio, who is carrying a small sea chest.)

Menaechmus II: Sailors know no greater pleasure, in my opinion, Messenio, than when from the water, they catch their first sight of land in the distance.

Messenio: (Grumbling.)
The pleasure's greater, to be perfectly frank, if when you get there, you see that the land is your own. Now I ask you, master, why have we come to this place called Epidamnus? Are we going to run in on all the islands, like the tide?

Menaechmus II: We're looking for my brother, my twin brother.

Messenio: Yes, but are we never going to come to the end of looking for him? It's six years since we started spending our time this way. We've been to Spain, Marseilles, all over the Adriatic Sea, up and down the whole Italian coast, anywhere you can go by sea. If you were looking for the proverbial needle in the haystack, you'd have found it by now, if there were any needle. We are looking for a dead man among the living, for we would have found him long ago, if he were still alive.

Greek & Roman Plays for the Intermediate Grades © 1993 Pearon Teacher Aids

The Menaechmi Twins

Menaechmus II:	That's exactly what I'm looking for, someone who can tell me for sure that he knows my brother is dead. Once I've found that out, I won't spend another minute looking for him. But until I do, as long as I live, I'll never stop looking. My brother means a great deal to me.
Messenio:	Let's go home, or are we going to write a book entitled "Around the World with Menaechmus"?
Menaechmus II:	Do what you're told! You must take it and like it. Don't fuss at me so much. We're going to do this my way, not yours.
Messenio:	(To the audience.) Well, he certainly put me in my place, short and to the point. A long lecture couldn't have told me more, but even so, I can't help but say more things to my master. (To Menaechmus.) Excuse me, master, but when I take a look at our purse, we are traveling very, very light. I think that if you don't go home when you run out of money, you'll be sorry. You know how these people here are! In Epidamnus, the people like their fun. Besides, a lot of swindlers live in this town.
Menaechmus II:	Just give me the purse.
Messenio:	What do you want with it?
Menaechmus:	I'll protect us against your doing anything you shouldn't do.
Messenio:	Take it and keep it. I don't care what you do. (Cylindrus returns from market with a basket of food.)
Cylindrus:	(To the audience.) I've done a good job of buying and bought just what I wanted. I'll put a good dinner on the table tonight. But look, there's Menaechmus! Here's where I catch it from my mistress. The company is already at the door, and I haven't even returned back from the market. I'll go up and speak to them. Hello, Menaechmus.
Menaechmus II:	(Surprised.) How do you do! But . . . I don't think we have met.

Greek & Roman Plays for the Intermediate Grades © 1993 Fearon Teacher Aids

Cylindrus:	You don't think we have met? Don't you know who I am, Menaechmus?
Menaechmus II:	No, I really don't.
Cylindrus:	Where's the rest of the company?
Menaechmus II:	What company are you talking about?
Cylindrus:	Why, that sponger friend of yours.
Menaechmus II:	Sponger friend of mine? (To Messenio.) The fellow is crazy!
Messenio:	(Whispering to Menaechmus.) Didn't I tell you there were a lot of swindlers here?
Menaechmus II:	What sponger are you looking for, my friend?
Cylindrus:	Peniculus. His nickname is Whisk Broom.
Messenio:	I have a whisk broom in my sea chest.
Cylindrus:	Menaechmus, you're a little too early for dinner. I'm just returning from marketing.
Menaechmus II:	I know for sure that you're not right in the head making a perfect nuisance of yourself to a complete stranger.
Cylindrus:	I'm Cylindrus. Don't you know me?
Menaechmus II:	Cylindrus or Dolyndrus, go away. I don't know you, and I don't even want to know you!
Cylindrus:	But your name is Menaechmus?
Menaechmus II:	As far as I know. You talk sensibly enough when you call me by my name, but where did you ever meet me?
Cylindrus:	Where did I ever meet you? Why, the lady who lives here is Lady E. I'm her servant.
Menaechmus II:	Now you listen carefully, old servant. I don't know who your mistress is, and I don't know who you are.
Cylindrus:	You don't know who I am? Many the time I've served you food and wine in this house.

Greek & Roman Plays for the Intermediate Grades © 1993 Fearon Teacher Aids

The Menaechmi Twins

Messenio:	(To the audience.) Does anyone have anything I could use to dent this fellow's head? His story is becoming monotonous.
Menaechmus II:	You served food and wine to me? Why, I've never been to this town before today. I have never seen this place until now!
Cylindrus:	You say this is your first hour in the City of Epidamnus?
Menaechmus II:	I most certainly do!
Cylindrus:	(Pointing to the house of Menaechmus I.) Don't you live in that house?
Menaechmus II:	No! No! No!
Messenio:	(To the audience.) There seems to be an echo in this room.
Cylindrus:	(To the audience.) This man is crazy!
Menaechmus II:	A curse upon this house.
Cylindrus	(To the audience.) Why, he's putting a curse on his own house. (To Menaechmus.) I don't think you're feeling quite well, putting a curse on your own home.
Menaechmus II:	(To the audience.) Good grief, what a windbag. (To Cylindrus.) I can't stand the sight of you!
Cylindrus:	(To the audience.) He often jokes with me like this. He's the funniest fellow when his wife is not around. (To Menaechmus.) I beg your pardon.
Menaechmus II:	What do you want?
Cylindrus:	See all the food I have in my market basket. Have I purchased enough for the three of you, or should I get some more? (Menaechmus II threatens to strike him.) I mean, for you, the sponger, and the lady.
Menaechmus II:	What lady, what sponger are you speaking of?

Messenio:	What the devil is the matter with you? Why are you pestering him?
Cylindrus:	What business is it of yours? I don't know you. I'm speaking to this man, whom I know.
Messenio:	By heaven, you are out of your head.
Cylindrus:	Well, I'll go prepare dinner. It won't take me long. Don't go too far away from the house. Nothing else you want, is there?
Menaechmus II:	Yes . . . for you to leave the country!
Cylindrus:	(Growls under his breath.) Be better if you'd leave yourself. (Stops as he realizes Menaechmus has heard him.) I mean, go in and take your place while I put this food on the fire. I'll go in and tell Lady E you're waiting out here, so that she can ask you to come in. (Exits into Lady E's house.)
Menaechmus II:	Thank the gods he has gone! Well, Messenio, that was no lie you told me about this place. I'm finding that out.
Messenio:	Just you watch! I think it's an evil woman who lives there, judging from what her crazy servant said.
Menaechmus II:	But I wonder how he knew my name?
Messenio:	Oh, there's nothing so remarkable or mysterious about that. Servants often go to the wharves if a foreign ship comes in. They attempt to find out where the fellows come from and what their names are. When they meet the sailors, they stick to them like glue until they steal all of their money. I think we had really better watch out.
Menaechmus II:	Yes, that is good advice.
Messenio:	Be careful, master.
Menaechmus II:	Quiet! The door is opening. Let's see who is coming out.
	(Lady E enters from her house.)
Lady E:	Menaechmus, why are you waiting out here? My door is always open to you. My house is more yours than your own is. Everything is almost ready and is just what you requested. Please go in and take your place at the table.

Greek & Roman Plays for the Intermediate Grades © 1993 Fearon Teacher Aids

The Menaechmi Twins

Menaechmus II:	Who is this woman talking to?
Lady E:	Why, I'm talking to you.
Menaechmus II:	Have we ever had any dealings before? Do we have any now?
Lady E:	Menaechmus, how you talk!
Menaechmus II:	Messenio, this woman is crazy. I'm a complete stranger, and yet she talks to me like an old friend.
Messenio:	Didn't I tell you that's what always happens here? These are just the little leaves falling, but stay here three days, and the tree will fall on our heads. This place is nothing but a trap for your money! Let me talk to her. (To Lady E.) I beg your pardon. May I have a word with you?
Lady E:	What is it?
Messenio:	Where did you meet this gentleman?
Lady E:	Where? Why, right here in the city of Epidamnus.
Messenio:	Right in Epidamnus? But my dear lady, he has never set foot in this city before today!
Lady E:	Ha-ha-ha! Aren't you the funny one! Menaechmus, please go into the house. You'll be more comfortable within.
Menaechmus II:	Good heavens, the woman calls me by my right name. I can't help wondering what this is all about.
Messenio:	She has a whiff of that purse you have there.
Menaechmus II:	Yes, that's it. Thanks for the warning, Messenio. Here, you take it.
Lady E:	Let's go in and have dinner.
Menaechmus II:	Very kind of you, but no thanks.
Lady E:	Then why did you tell me to prepare dinner for you awhile back?
Menaechmus II:	Who, me? I told you to?
Lady E:	Yes, of course you did. You told me to prepare dinner for you and your friend, the sponger.

Greek & Roman Plays for the Intermediate Grades © 1993 Fearon Teacher Aids

Menaechmus II:	What sponger? (To the audience.) This woman is out of her mind, for sure!
Lady E:	Peniculus, you know, the one they call Whisk Broom.
Menaechmus II:	Who is the Whisk Broom you keep talking about?
Lady E:	The fellow who came with you when you brought me the dress you stole from your wife.
Menaechmus II:	What? I gave you a dress that I stole from my wife? Are you crazy? (To the audience.) This woman is asleep on her feet, like a horse.
Lady E:	Why are you making fun of me?
Menaechmus II:	Now what is it I say I didn't do, that I did?
Lady E:	That you gave me your wife's dress a short time ago.
Menaechmus II:	I still say I didn't! I haven't ever had a wife and I haven't one now! And since the day I was born, I've never been inside this town. I had breakfast on the ship, then I came out here and ran into you.
Lady E:	Really, Menaechmus! What nonsense you speak. What ship are you talking about? What is this all about?
Menaechmus II:	A very plain, old, wooden crate of a ship.
Lady E:	Now please, stop joking and come inside for dinner.
Menaechmus II:	Really, my dear lady, you are looking for somebody else, not me.
Lady E:	Menaechmus, really! Your father's name was Moschus.
Menaechmus II:	Everything you say is right enough.
Messenio:	(Whispering to Menaechmus.) She certainly knows all the answers about you.
Menaechmus II:	(Whispering to Messenio.) I don't think I can go on refusing her invitation.
Messenio:	Don't you do it! You're a goner if you step inside that door!
Menaechmus II:	Oh, be quiet. Everything is going to be all right. (To Lady E.) When I kept saying "no" to you, I had a reason

Greek & Roman Plays for the Intermediate Grades © 1993 Fearon Teacher Aids

for it. I was afraid of this fellow, afraid he'd tell my wife about the dress and the dinner. Shall we go in now, if you're ready?

Lady E: Are you going to wait for the sponger?

Menaechmus II: Of course I'm not going to wait for him. I don't give two hoots for him, and if he comes, I don't want him let in.

Lady E: That won't make me angry. But do you know what I'd like you to do, please?

Menaechmus II: Just give your order, lady.

Lady E: That dress you gave me . . . well, would you take it to the embroiderer's and have it all fixed up and have some fancywork added that I want?

Menaechmus II: That's a good idea. It will kill two birds with one stone. It will look so different that my wife won't notice it when you're wearing it on the street.

Lady E: Take it with you after you have finished your dinner.

Menaechmus II: Fine.

Lady E: Shall we go in?

(Lady E and Menaechmus II enter the house.)

Messenio: (To the audience.)
That's the end for him, all right. He's the dinghy, and she's the pirate ship. She's dragging him off. But I'm a fool to ask myself to keep my master in line. He wants me to listen to what he says, not to be his commanding officer.

(Exits. Enter Peniculus, very glum.)

Peniculus: (To the audience.)
In all my born days, I've never committed a more downright crime than I did today. I let myself be picked for jury duty. There I sat, yawning my head off, and meanwhile Menaechmus sneaked off from me and probably went to Lady E's house for a delicious dinner. I'll go anyway. Maybe there are some scraps left.

Greek & Roman Plays for the Intermediate Grades © 1993 Fearon Teacher Aids

(Menaechmus II steps out of Lady E's house, carrying the dress. He is tired and not paying attention to what he is doing.) But what's this I see. It's Menaechmus! He's wearing a garland. Dinner must be over. Too late for me to eat! I'll watch what he does. (He hides on one side of the stage.)

Menaechmus II: (Weaving and staggering about and speaking to the house.)
I'll have the dress fixed up nice and pretty and bring it back later. Don't you worry any, my lady.

Peniculus: (To the audience.)
The dress! He's taking it to the embroidery shop. He's cleaned up the dinner. Poor me, his friend, has been shut out. I'll tell you something right now. I'm not the man I am if I don't make him pay for all this. I'll get my revenge! Just watch what I'll give him!

Menaechmus II: (To the audience.)
The gods in heaven certainly have given me good luck today when I had no reason to expect it. That was a most delicious dinner. She says I gave this dress to her after stealing it from my wife. I can see she's making some kind of mistake, but I jumped right in, just as if I did have something to do with it, and started "yessing" her. Whatever she said, I agreed to it.

Peniculus: (To the audience.)
 I'll speak to him. I'm just itching to stir him up a bit. (He walks toward Menaechmus shaking his fist.)

Menaechmus II: (To the audience.)
Who is this? What's he coming at me for?

Peniculus: Well, well, how do you do? Steady as a rock aren't you? Louse! Rat! Traitor! What did I ever do to you that you should treat me this way? Is there any reason why you should spoil everything for me? You ran out on me a while ago downtown, didn't you? Polished off the dinner without me, didn't you? What's the idea of doing that?

Menaechmus II: Please, please, my friend, what have I to do with you? What do you mean by talking to me like that? You don't know me, for I'm a stranger here. On the other hand, how would you like a punch in the nose?

Peniculus: Hah! It looks like you have given me that already.

Greek & Roman Plays for the Intermediate Grades © 1993 Fearon Teacher Aids

Menaechmus II:	Tell me, my friend, if you don't mind, what is your name?
Peniculus:	On top of everything, you're going to make fun of me now? As if you didn't know my name!
Menaechmus II:	But I don't! As far as I know, I have never seen you before. I have never met you. But, anyway, whoever you are, stop bothering me. (He starts to walk away.)
Peniculus:	Don't you know me?
Menaechmus II:	I wouldn't say I didn't, if I did.
Peniculus:	Don't you know your old friend?
Menaechmus II:	Your head isn't screwed on straight, my friend. I can see that!
Peniculus:	Now listen! Didn't you steal that dress you're holding from your wife today and give it to Lady E?
Menaechmus II:	No! I tell you, I don't have a wife. I didn't give it to Lady E, and I didn't steal it. Are you crazy?
Peniculus:	O.K.! Play your game, and I'll play mine. Talk like that to me, will you? Well, all will come home to roost. You'll pay for eating that dinner without me! I'll see to that! (He enters the home of Menaechmus I.)
Menaechmus II:	(To the audience.) What in the world is all this? Everybody I meet talks absolute nonsense to me. Are they trying to make a fool of me?
	(Servant girl comes out of Lady E's house.)
Servant Girl:	Menaechmus, Lady E says pretty please, will you take this bracelet with you to the goldsmith? She would like an ounce of gold added to it and to have it all fixed up new.
Menaechmus II:	Sure, sure! I'll do that. And anything else she wants done, tell her I'll do it. Anything she likes.
Servant Girl:	You know what bracelet this is?
Menaechmus II:	Yes . . . no . . . yes . . . the gold one, I guess.
Servant Girl:	This is the one you stole from your wife's jewel box.

Menaechmus II:	I never did!
Servant Girl:	What, you don't remember? Well then, give me back the bracelet, if you don't remember it.
Menaechmus II:	Wait a minute. Why, yes, of course, I remember. Yes, this is the one I gave to Lady E. Say, where are the armlets that I gave her along with it?
Servant Girl:	You never gave her any armlets.
Menaechmus II:	Ha ha! Yes, you're right. This was all I gave her.
Servant Girl:	Shall I tell Lady E you will take care of it?
Menaechmus II:	Yes, I will. I'll see that she gets the dress and bracelet both back at the same time.
Servant Girl:	Thank you, Menaechmus. (Exits into Lady E's house.)
Menaechmus II:	(To the audience.) Yes, I'll take care of them all right! I'll sell them as quickly as I can for whatever I can get for them. All the gods are helping me, that's a fact. The gods are going to make me rich. The gods love me! I'll take off this garland and throw it over to the left. Then, if they follow me, they will think I went that way. I'll go and find my servant, if I can. I want to tell him myself about the good luck I've had. (Exits. Enter Mrs. Menaechmus and Peniculus from the house.)
Peniculus:	He was taking your dress to the embroidery shop. He had on a garland. Yes, your dress, the one he stole from you earlier today. Look! There's the garland he was wearing. I was right, wasn't I? He went this way, if you want to follow him. (Menaechmus I enters, looking very glum.) Look! What luck! He's coming back. And he doesn't have the dress.
Mrs. Menaechmus:	What shall I do to him now?
Peniculus:	Do the same as you always do—give him a tongue lashing. Let's hide in the background and listen.
Menaechmus I:	(To the audience.) Lady E is waiting for me, I know. The minute I could, I ran away from the court. She's angry at me now, I suppose, for the dinner is cold. Perhaps the dress I gave her that I stole from my wife will have calmed her down.

The Menaechmi Twins

Peniculus:	What do you say to that?
Mrs. Menaechmus:	He's a pretty poor sort of husband, and I made a mistake in marrying him.
	(Menaechmus I starts toward Lady E's door. Peniculus grabs him by the sleeve.)
Peniculus:	Wait a minute!
Mrs. Menaechmus:	Yes, sir. You'll pay plenty for your trickery!
Peniculus:	That's telling him.
Mrs. Menaechmus:	Did you think you could pull dirty tricks like this without getting caught?
Menaechmus I:	What is this all about, my dear? (Puts his arm around his wife.)
Mrs. Menaechmus:	Take your hands off me!
Peniculus:	Go to it!
Menaechmus I:	Are you cross with me?
Mrs. Menaechmus:	You ought to know!
Peniculus:	He knows. He's just pretending he doesn't, the rat!
Menaechmus I:	What is the matter?
Mrs. Menaechmus:	(Bursting into tears.) My dress!
Menaechmus I:	Your dress?
Mrs. Menaechmus:	Yes, my dress.
	(Menaechmus I starts to tremble.)
Peniculus:	What are you so scared of?
Menaechmus I:	Who, me? Why, I'm not scared of anything.
Peniculus:	Nothing but one thing. The dress! That makes you turn pale. Yes, you! You shouldn't have eaten the dinner behind my back. Go after him, Mrs. Menaechmus!
Menaechmus I:	(Whispering to Peniculus.) Keep quiet, won't you?

Greek & Roman Plays for the Intermediate Grades © 1993 Fearon Teacher Aids

Peniculus:	No sir, I won't keep quiet. Now, go on back.
Menaechmus I:	Back where?
Mrs. Menaechmus:	Back to the embroidery shop. Go on! Go pick up the dress.
Menaechmus I:	What is this dress you keep talking about?
Mrs. Menaechmus:	I'm so unhappy!
Menaechmus I:	(Puts his arm around her shoulders.) Why are you so unhappy? Tell me all about it. Has one of the servants been acting up?
Mrs. Menaechmus:	Boo-hoo-hoo.
Menaechmus I:	Has one of the slaves been talking back to you?
Mrs. Menaechmus	Boo-hoo-hoo.
Menaechmus I:	Tell me about it. They won't get away with it.
Mrs. Menaechmus:	(Jerking away from him.) Nonsense!
Menaechmus I:	You're awfully cross. That makes me feel bad. It must be one of the servants you're cross at.
Mrs. Menaechmus:	More nonsense!
Menaechmus I:	You're not cross at me, are you?
Mrs. Menaechmus:	Now, that's not nonsense!
Menaechmus I:	Why, I haven't done anything wrong.
Mrs. Menaechmus:	There you go—nonsense again!
Menaechmus I:	My dear, what's the matter with you?
Peniculus:	He's trying to soft soap you.
Menaechmus I:	Can't you stop bothering me! I'm not talking to you.
Mrs. Menaechmus:	Go away from me!
Peniculus:	That's telling him! (Whispering to Menaechmus I.) Eat the dinner while I'm not there, eh? Then afterwards, come out with your garland on and make fun of me, eh?

Greek & Roman Plays for the Intermediate Grades © 1993 Fearon Teacher Aids

The Menaechmi Twins

Menaechmus I:	Now look here! I tell you I haven't had any dinner and I haven't set foot inside that house today.
Peniculus:	Oh you haven't, eh?
Menaechmus I:	I most certainly haven't.
Peniculus:	Of all the nerve! I've never seen anything like it! Didn't I see you awhile, ago right here in front of the house with your garland on, saying my head wasn't screwed on straight? Saying you didn't know me and insisting you were a stranger here?
Menaechmus I:	(Sincerely puzzled.) Why . . . why, no! This is the first time I've been home since I left you downtown.
Peniculus:	Yes, I know you! You didn't think I had any way to get back at you, did you? Well, I've told your wife everything.
Menaechmus I:	What did you tell her?
Peniculus:	Ask her yourself.
Menaechmus I:	What in the world has he been telling you, my dear? Why don't you say something? Won't you tell me what it is?
Mrs. Menaechmus:	As if you didn't <u>know</u>! Asking me, indeed!
Peniculus:	(To the audience.) Fine fellow he is! Look at him pretending he doesn't know. (To Menaechmus I.) You can't keep it quiet. She knows all about it. Yes sir, I told her the whole story.
Menaechmus I:	What is this?
Mrs. Menaechmus:	Since you haven't any sense of decency at all and aren't willing to confess what you did, just be quiet and listen. You'll find out why I'm cross and what he's been telling me. Somebody stole a dress from me.
Menaechmus I:	Somebody stole a dress from me?
Peniculus:	See! He's trying to confuse you. The rat! It was stolen from her, not from you. If it had been stolen from you, we wouldn't know where it was.

Greek & Roman Plays for the Intermediate Grades © 1993 Fearon Teacher Aids

Menaechmus I:	Mind your own business. Now, dear, what were you saying?
Mrs. Menaechmus:	My dress, I tell you, it's gone!
Menaechmus I:	Who stole it?
Mrs. Menaechmus:	Hah! The one who stole it can tell you that.
Menaechmus I:	Who was it?
Mrs. Menaechmus:	A fellow called Menaechmus.
Menaechmus I:	Well! That was a mean thing to do. Who is this Menaechmus?
Mrs. Menaechmus:	You are "this Menaechmus!"
Menaechmus I:	Who, me?
Mrs. Menaechmus:	Yes, you!
Menaechmus I:	Who says so?
Mrs. Menaechmus:	I do!
Peniculus:	And so do I! And you gave the dress to Lady E.
Menaechmus I:	I did that?
Mrs. Menaechmus:	Yes, you, you, you!
Menaechmus I:	By Jupiter and all the gods, I swear my dear that . . .
Peniculus:	No, no, no, no, no! We are speaking the truth.
Menaechmus I:	Well, but I didn't exactly give it to her. I just . . . well . . . I, uh . . . well, you know, I just lent it to her.
Mrs. Menaechmus:	Well, I don't lend your clothes to anybody. Women should lend women's clothes, and men lend men's. Now you go bring that dress back.
Menaechmus I:	I'll see that it's brought back.
Mrs. Menaechmus:	Well, you'd better. You'll not come back in the house unless you have the dress with you. I'm going in. (Starts toward the house.)
Peniculus:	Hey! What about me? I put in a lot of time on this for you.

Greek & Roman Plays for the Intermediate Grades © 1993 Pearon Teacher Aids

Mrs. Menaechmus:	You'll be paid back for your time when somebody steals something of yours. (Exits.)
Peniculus:	(To the audience.) Humph! That never will happen. I haven't anything anybody would want to steal. I'm going downtown. I can see quite clearly that I've lost my place in this house. (Exits.)
Menaechmus I:	(To the audience.) Now, I'll go and ask Lady E to give me back the dress. I'll buy her another one, even nicer. (He knocks on Lady E's door.)
Lady E:	Why Menaechmus, why are you waiting out here? Come on in.
Menaechmus I:	No, no. Say . . . uh . . . that dress . . . please . . . the one I just gave you . . . uh . . . will you give it back to me? My wife has found out what I did. I'll buy you another one worth twice as much. You can pick it out.
Lady E:	Why, I gave you that dress to take to the embroidery shop just a few minutes ago. Yes, and the bracelet, too, to take to the goldsmith's.
Menaechmus I:	To me? You gave the dress and the bracelet to me? No, you didn't, and I can prove it. I gave it to you before I went downtown? Well, I've just come back now, and this is the first I've seen you since then.
Lady E:	I see what you're up to! Just because I trusted you, you're cooking up a scheme to cheat me.
Menaechmus I:	No, really. I'm not asking for the dress because I want to cheat you. No! I tell you, my wife's found out about it.
Lady E:	Well, I didn't ask you to give it to me. You brought it to me yourself . . . you gave it to me. You said it was a gift. Now you want it back. All right . . . keep it! Take it! Wear it! You or your wife, either one! Put it away in your cedar chest, for all I care!
Menaechmus I:	Oh, now, wait! Don't be so cross. Let me explain. (She slams the door in his face.) Please come back. Just for my sake? (To the audience.) I heard her bolt the door. Now, I am locked out. Nobody believes a word I say, either at home or next door. (Exits.)

(Enter Menaechmus II.)

Menaechmus II: (To the audience.)
I was foolish when I gave the purse and the money to Messenio. I suppose he's gone by now.

(Mrs. Menaechmus enters from her house.)

Mrs. Menaechmus: I'll just stand out here to see how soon my husband returns. Oh look! I see him. Thank heaven, he has my dress!

Menaechmus II: (To the audience.)
I wonder where Messenio is wandering about now?

Mrs. Menaechmus: (To the audience.)
I'll go to him and give him the reception he deserves. (To Menaechmus II.) Aren't you ashamed to let me lay eyes on you, you disgraceful man, with that dress?

Menaechmus II: I beg your pardon. What is the matter, madam?

Mrs. Menaechmus: Shame on you! How dare you even whisper? How dare you say a word to me?

Menaechmus II: What have I done? Why shouldn't I dare to say anything?

Mrs. Menaechmus: You ask me that? Of all the boundless nerve. You've insulted me! I will not stand for it! I'd rather get a divorce and live alone the rest of my life than to sit back and let you insult me the way you do!

Menaechmus II: What does it matter to me whether you stick with your marriage or leave your husband? Say, do people always do this sort of thing here? Do they always start telling wild yarns to a stranger the minute he arrives?

Mrs. Menaechmus: What "wild yarns"? No, I tell you I won't stand for it any longer. I'd rather get a divorce than put up with your behavior.

Menaechmus II: As far as I'm concerned, go get a divorce and live by yourself.

Mrs. Menaechmus: Well! But you told me over and over that you didn't steal my dress and now you're holding it right under my nose. Aren't you ashamed?

Greek & Roman Plays for the Intermediate Grades © 1993 Pearon Teacher Aids

Menaechmus II:	Really, madam. You are very impolite, and you're not being fair at all. You say that this dress was stolen from you? I tell you another woman gave it to me to have some alterations made on it.
Mrs. Menaechmus:	Now, by heaven that's the limit. All right! I'm going to tell my father the terrible things you've been saying and doing. (Calling into the house.) Decio! Decio! (Decio enters.)
Decio:	Yes, madam?
Mrs. Menaechmus:	Go find my father, (the mediator), and tell him to come back to my house with you. Tell him there's a dreadful mess.
Decio:	Yes, madam. (Exits on the run.)
Mrs. Menaechmus:	When he gets here, I'm going to tell him everything you've done!
Menaechmus II:	Are you crazy! What have I done?
Mrs. Menaechmus:	You stole my dress and took it to that woman! Your own wife's property! Is my story right or isn't it?
Menaechmus II:	Oh, come now, madam. Please tell me, if you can, what is your favorite prescription for nerve strain? I need a little of it.
Mrs. Menaechmus:	You can laugh me off, but you can't laugh off my father. Here he comes! Do you know him?
Menaechmus II:	This is the first time I've ever seen him or you.
Mrs. Menaechmus:	You say you don't know me? And you don't know my father?
Menaechmus II:	Yes, and I'll say I don't know your grandfather either, if you care to send for him.
Mrs. Menaechmus:	Oh, you! You're acting, just the way you always do!
	(Enter Senex, assisted by Decio.)
Senex:	(To the audience.) I'm a very old man, but this seems to be important, so I'll come along and hurry as fast as I can. But at my age, it isn't easy. I'm not as spry as I used to be. I'm so full of

Greek & Roman Plays for the Intermediate Grades © 1993 Fearon Teacher Aids

years that I can feel them pressing down on me. This cane doesn't seem to be holding me up anymore. Is there an extra chair or stool in the audience that I might use? (Sits on stool handed to him.) Bad business, being old. Yes, very bad. Troubles, troubles, troubles. Why if I should list them all . . . . (Begins to count on his fingers.) No . . . no . . . it would make my speech too long. But this business has me worried. What in the world do you suppose it is? Why should my daughter ask me to come to her house all of a sudden? I expect she and her husband have been having a little argument. My daughter doesn't ever invite me to her house, unless she has a reason . . . her husband's done something or they've had a spat. Well, whatever it is, I'll soon find out. Thank you for the use of the stool. (He hands back the stool.) Oh! There she is . . . standing in front of her house. And there's her husband, too. Grim! It's just what I suspected.

Mrs. Menaechmus: Hello, father. How are you?

Senex: I'm all right. How are you?

Mrs. Menaechmus: (Bursting into tears.)
Boo-hoo-hoo!

Senex: I hope you're not having any trouble.

Mrs. Menaechmus: Boo-hoo-hoo!

Senex: What are you crying about? Why is he angry? What is he doing way over there? Had a little skirmish, the two of you, haven't you? Come now, tell me which of you started it. And make it brief. No long orations, please.

Mrs. Menaechmus: I never did anything wrong at all. You can put that out of your mind right now, father. But I just can't stay on here. I can't stand it, not in any way, shape, or fashion.

Senex: What is all this about?

Mrs. Menaechmus: I'm just a laughingstock, father. That's what I'm being made into.

Senex: By whom?

The Menaechmi Twins

Greek & Roman Plays for the Intermediate Grades © 1993 Pearon Teacher Aids

Mrs. Menaechmus:	By him, my husband!
Senex:	How many times have I told you not to come to me with your accusations?
Mrs. Menaechmus:	How can I help it, father!
Senex:	How many times have I told you that you should be nice to your husband.
Mrs. Menaechmus:	But he has done something awful!
Senex:	If he's done anything wrong, I'll take him to task.
Mrs. Menaechmus:	He has been stealing my jewelry and dresses. He robs me! He takes my pretty things when I'm not looking and gives them to Lady E.
Senex:	He's in the wrong if he does what you say. But if he doesn't, then you are in the wrong for accusing an innocent man of something he didn't do.
Mrs. Menaechmus:	He has the dress right now, father, and the bracelet. He's bringing them back because I accused him.
Senex:	I'm going to ask him what happened. (To Menaechmus II.) Tell me, what's the trouble Menaechmus? What are you two quarreling about? I'd like to know. What are you cross about? Why is she angry? What is the trouble here?
Menaechmus II:	I don't know who you are or what your name is, sir, but I swear by Jupiter on high and all the gods that . . .
Senex:	Swear? About what? Swear to what?
Menaechmus II:	That I've done absolutely nothing to this lady who's accusing me of stealing this dress!
Mrs. Menaechmus:	Perjurer!
Menaechmus II:	If I ever set foot inside the house where she lives, I'll be the unluckiest of all the unlucky men in the world!
Senex:	What do you mean, you'll never set foot inside the house where you live? You must be insane!

Greek & Roman Plays for the Intermediate Grades © 1993 Fearon Teacher Aids

Menaechmus II:	Do you, sir, say that I live in that house?
Senex:	Do you say you don't.
Menaechmus II:	I do indeed say I don't.
Senex:	How can you say you don't, unless you moved out last night? (Whispering to his daughter.) What about this? You didn't move out of here, did you?
Mrs. Menaechmus:	Now where would we go? Why would we do a thing like that?
Senex:	I'm sure I don't know.
Mrs. Menaechmus:	It's perfectly plain, he's making a fool of you. Don't you see?
Senex:	All right, all right, Menaechmus. You've had your fun. Now let's get down to business.
Menaechmus II:	Pardon me, but what have I to do with you? Where did you come from? Who are you? What obligation have I to you or to her, either? She is certainly causing me trouble.
Mrs. Menaechmus:	(Whispering to her father.) Look! Don't his eyes look funny? He does seem a bit green around the gills, too. His eyes are unnaturally bright. Look!
Menaechmus II:	(To the audience.) What could be better? They are saying I'm insane. Why don't I pretend to be insane? That will scare them away. (He lets his arms droop, and his jaw falls open.)
Mrs. Menaechmus:	See the way his arms hang. Look at his mouth. (Runs to her father.) What will I do now, father?
Senex:	Let's move away from him. (He pushes his daughter behind him and stands firm, brandishing his cane at Menaechmus II.)

Greek & Roman Plays for the Intermediate Grades © 1993 Fearon Teacher Aids

Menaechmus II:	(Charging between them and pretending to be insane.) YAHOO! YAHOO! YAHOO! Oh god Bacchus, I hear you calling me! Are you calling me to the wildwood and to the hunt? (Senex and Mrs. Menaechmus run to opposite sides of the stage.) I hear you, but from these purlieus I cannot depart, for on my left a rabid female hound keeps watch upon me, and behind my back a stinking goat looks at me.
Senex:	Why, you . . .
Menaechmus II:	(Rushing toward Senex and brandishing his fists under his face.) Lo, Apollo bids me strike you upon the head!
Mrs. Menaechmus:	(Rushing to her father's arms.) Oh, father! He's threatening to strike you!
Menaechmus II:	(Chases Mrs. Menaechmus about the stage until he sees that she is not going to leave. To the audience.) Ah, me! They say I'm crazy, when they are the ones who are crazy!
Senex:	What should we do? Do you think I should call the servants? Yes, I will. I'll go and get some men to take him away and tie him up inside before he makes any more trouble.
Menaechmus II:	(To the audience.) Oh, oh . . . I'm stuck! If I don't figure out something, they'll take me into their house. (Pretending again to be insane.) Yes, god Apollo, I hear you! At the count of three, you bid me strike my fists against my face until she departs from my sight! One . . . two . . . two and a half . . .
Senex:	Run in the house quickly.
Mrs. Menaechmus:	I'm running. (At the door.) You keep an eye on him, father. Don't let him get away. To think I should live to see a thing like this! (Exits.)

211

Menaechmus II:	(To the audience.) That got her out of the way all right! Now to get rid of the old man. (Pretending to be insane.) Yes, Apollo . . . now you wish me to strike him with the very staff he holds in his hands? Your wish is my command, Apollo! (He jumps for the old man's stick, but Senex holds his cane firm.)
Senex:	You'll get into trouble if you touch me or come one step closer!
Menaechmus II:	(Facing audience and pretending he is speaking to Apollo.) Get an ax you say? Chip, chop, chip! (With an imaginary ax, he starts slowly toward Senex.)
Senex:	(To the audience.) Well, now, I'll have to watch out and be careful. Yes! I'm beginning to be a little uneasy about him, the way he's acting. He may really hurt me! (He stands firm, cane upraised.)
Menaechmus II:	Many are your commands, Apollo! Now you bid me take a team of horses, wild unbroken horses, climb into my chariot, and run down this little old, toothless lion! Now I'm in my chariot! Now I have the reins! Now the whip's in my hand! Get up, steeds! Let's hear the clatter of your hoofs! (He gallops about the stage in his imaginary chariot, coming closer and closer to Senex.)
Senex:	(To the audience.) Ye gods, the fellow is in a bad way. Why, he's completely insane—and just a little while ago, he was perfectly well! It's a terrible attack he's had, and so sudden, too. I'll go and get a doctor as fast as I can. (Exits.)
Menaechmus II:	(To the audience.) At last, they are finally out of my sight. But what am I waiting for? Why don't I go off to the ship while I still can safely? Please, all of you, if the old gentleman comes back, don't tell him which way I went. (Exits. Senex reenters.)

Greek & Roman Plays for the Intermediate Grades © 1993 Fearon Teacher Aids

The Menaechmi Twins

Senex: (To the audience.)
My backside aches from sitting, my eyes ache from looking, both from waiting for the doctor to return from his house calls. Ah, here he comes now. Can't you walk faster than a snail?

(Enter Doctor.)

Doctor: What did you say was wrong with him? Tell me, sir, is he suffering from hallucinations? Would you say that he had comatose hysteria? Or perhaps acromegalic hydrocephaly?

Senex: Now see here, I asked you to come so that you could tell me and would cure him.

Doctor: Oh, that's no problem. He'll be all right. I give you my word of honor on that.

Senex: Well, you take care of him—and care about it, too.

Doctor: Care about it? Why, I'll pace the floor and tear my hair all day long! That will show you how much I care about taking care of him. I always take good care of my patients.

(Menaechmus I enters.)

Senex: Well, there he is. Let's watch what he does.

Menaechmus I: (To the audience.)
Good grief, what a run of bad luck I've had today. I thought I'd kept everything quiet, and then my pal, Peniculus, spilled the whole story and disgraced me. He sure is Mr. Fix-it! All the trouble he made for me, his old friend. I swear, I'll have his life for this! And Lady E acted just as you might expect. I certainly am miserable!

Senex: Do you hear what he's saying?

Doctor: Yes. He says he's miserable.

Senex: Would you talk to him, please.

Doctor: Good afternoon, Menaechmus.

Menaechmus I: Oh go jump in a lake, will you!

Greek & Roman Plays for the Intermediate Grades © 1993 Fearon Teacher Aids

Senex:	(Whispering to Doctor.) Notice anything?
Doctor:	(Whispering back.) Why, a dozen bottles of my own special medicine won't be able to help him. Pardon me, Menaechmus.
Menaechmus I:	What d'ya want?
Doctor:	Would you mind answering a question or two?
Menaechmus I:	Go away, will you!
Doctor:	See! There's the first, tiny indication of psychosis. Won't you please answer the question I asked?
Menaechmus I:	Why don't you ask me whether I eat purple bread, or red, or yellow? Or whether I like scaly birds and feathered fish?
Senex:	Oh, my! Hear that? He doesn't make sense at all. Why don't you hurry up and give him something before it's too late?
Doctor:	No, wait a minute. I have a few more questions to ask.
Senex:	You'll kill the man with all your talky-talk.
Doctor:	Now, tell me, do your eyes often seem fixed and staring?
Menaechmus I:	What? What do you think I am, a lobster? Of all the nerve.
Doctor:	Tell me, does your stomach ever rumble?
Menaechmus I:	When I've had plenty to eat, it doesn't, but when I'm hungry, it does.
Doctor:	Do you sleep soundly? Have any trouble going to sleep?
Menaechmus I:	I sleep soundly, if I've paid my debts. By Jupiter and all the gods, why all these questions?
Doctor:	(Whispering to Senex.) He's beginning to show the first signs of insanity. Better watch out!

Greek & Roman Plays for the Intermediate Grades © 1993 Fearon Teacher Aids

The Menaechmi Twins

Senex:	Insanity! Why he's wisdom personified compared to what he was a while ago.
Menaechmus I:	(Overhearing.) What did you say?
Senex:	You're a sick man, I tell you.
Menaechmus I:	Who? Me?
Senex:	Yes, you! You threatened to run me down with your chariot. Oh yes you did! I saw you do it myself. Yes you did!
Menaechmus I:	(Furious.) Yes, and you stole Jupiter's holy crown! And you murdered your father and sold your mother into servanthood. Accuse me of things, will you? How do you like my answers? Do they sound sane or not?
Senex:	For heaven's sake, doctor, hurry, please! Whatever you're going to do, do it! Don't you see the man's delirious?
Doctor:	You know what I think you'd better do? Have him brought to my clinic.
Senex:	Is that your opinion?
Doctor:	Of course, it is. When he's there, I'll be able to take care of him the way I think best.
Senex:	All right, just as you like.
Doctor:	(To Menaechmus.) Now, now don't you worry about a thing. I'll give you my twenty-day treatment. It always works.
Menaechmus I:	Oh, you will, eh? Well, I'll give you a thirty-day treatment with my fist!
Doctor:	(To Senex.) Take him to my clinic.

Greek & Roman Plays for the Intermediate Grades © 1993 Fearon Teacher Aids

Senex: I'll have him there right away.

Doctor: I'll go along, so I can prepare what I need.

Senex: I'll get him there right away.

(Senex enters the house of Menaechmus I, and Doctor exits.)

Menaechmus I: (To the audience.)
Alone at last! Ye gods, what does this mean, these fellows saying I'm crazy? Why, I haven't been sick a single day since I was born. I'm not crazy! I don't start any fights or quarrels. I'm perfectly sane. I recognize and talk to people. Maybe they are the ones who are crazy? Oh well, what am I going to do now? I'd like to go home, but my wife won't let me in, and certainly Lady E won't let me in. What a mess this has turned out to be! I'll just sit near my door, and perhaps when it gets dark my wife will let me in.

(Enter Messenio.)

Messenio: (To the audience.)
I took the baggage to the rooming house as my master told me, and now I'm coming to meet him. I'll go knock on the door and see if my master is here. (Sees Menaechmus I.) But I'm afraid I've come too late. It looks as if the battle's over.

(Senex comes out of the house with several servants.)

Senex: Now do exactly what I tell you. Pick that man up and take him to the clinic. Don't pay attention to anything he says. I'm going to the clinic myself and will be waiting there for you. (Exits.)

Menaechmus I: Hey! What's all this? (To the audience.) What are these fellows coming after me for? What do they want? What are they after? What's the idea? (They seize him and hoist him to their shoulders.) Where are you taking me? Where are you going with me? Help! Help, oh gods! Help! Help! Let me go!

Greek & Roman Plays for the Intermediate Grades © 1993 Fearon Teacher Aids

The Menaechmi Twins

Messenio:	(To the audience.) What is this? Of all the nerve! Some men are picking my master up and carrying him off!
Menaechmus I:	Won't anybody please help me?
Messenio:	I will, master, I'm not afraid. (To the audience.) What a shame! What a disgrace! My master's being kidnapped in broad daylight right on the open street, in a peaceful, law-abiding town. He's a free man coming here of his own free will. Let him go! Let him go! Robbers! Kidnappers! Gangsters! Let him go, then! (The men drop Menaechmus and run off.) Well, well, sir, I certainly got here just in time to help you.
Menaechmus I:	Yes, my friend, whoever you are, may the gods bless you! If it hadn't been for you, I'd never have seen the sun set today.
Messenio:	Well, sir, if you'd like to do the right thing, how about setting me free?
Menaechmus I:	Set you free? Me?
Messenio:	Yes, sir. After all, I did save your life.
Menaechmus I:	You're making a mistake somewhere, my friend.
Messenio:	A mistake? What do you mean?
Menaechmus I:	I give you my word, I'm not your master.
Messenio:	Don't talk like that, master. Stop joking.
Menaechmus I:	No, I mean it. No servant of mine ever did anything like that for me.
Messenio:	Well, then, sir, since you say I'm "not yours," let me go free.
Menaechmus I:	Why certainly. As far as I'm concerned, consider yourself free! Go anywhere you like.
Messenio:	You really mean it?
Menaechmus I:	Of course I mean it, as far as I have any rights over you.

Greek & Roman Plays for the Intermediate Grades © 1993 Fearon Teacher Aids

Messenio:	That makes it "patron" now, instead of "master," doesn't it? (He shakes hands with himself.) Congratulations, Messenio! But patron, sir, please remember I'm at your orders just as much as when I was your servant. I'll live at your house and go home with you, when you go.
Menaechmus I:	Not at all.
Messenio:	I'll go to the rooming house now and get the baggage and the money for you. I'll bring it right here to you.
Menaechmus I:	Well, sure . . . go ahead.
Messenio:	I'll give it back to you, exactly what you gave to me. You just wait here. (Exits.)
Menaechmus I:	(To the audience.) This is the doggonedest business! The funniest things are happening to me today. Here these folks say I'm not who I am and shut me out. Now on top of that this fellow says he is my servant, and I set him free. He says he's going to bring me a purse and some money. If he does that, I'll tell him he's free to go anywhere he wants, so that when he gets his wits back, he won't be asking me for the money. My father-in-law and that doctor say I am insane. What does it all mean, I wonder? Perhaps it's a dream. I think I'll go into Lady E's house, even though she is angry at me. Maybe, somehow, I can persuade her to give me back the dress so that I can take it home. (Exits into Lady E's house.) (Enter Menaechmus II and Messenio.)
Menaechmus II:	The nerve of you!
Messenio:	Why, yes, yes! Not more than a few minutes ago, I hauled some fellows off you who were kidnapping you, four of them! Right in front of this house. You were shouting to high heaven, and I ran up and saved you. I beat them off by sheer brute force. And because I saved your life, you set me free. When I said I was going after the money and the baggage, you must have run around ahead of me as fast as you could to meet me, so that you could say you didn't mean what you said.

Greek & Roman Plays for the Intermediate Grades © 1993 Fearon Teacher Aids

Menaechmus II:	I told you to go free?
Messenio:	Certainly.
Menaechmus II:	Oh, no, I didn't. You can be perfectly sure of that. I'll turn servant myself before I'll ever set you free.
	(Enter Menaechmus I from Lady E's house.)
Menaechmus I:	(Yelling at Lady E's door.) You can swear to it all you like, but that won't make it any more true that I took the dress and the bracelet from you earlier today.
Messenio:	For heaven's sake! What do I see? Your spitting image!
Menaechmus II:	What sort of gag is this?
Messenio:	It's your own image!
Menaechmus II:	Why yes, it is kind of like me, when I stop to think what I look like.
Menaechmus I:	(Sees Messenio.) Oh, there you are, my friend, who saved my life.
Messenio:	Excuse me, please sir, but would you mind telling me your name?
Menaechmus I:	Not at all. After what you did for me, I'd hardly mind doing anything for you. My name is Menaechmus.
Menaechmus II:	Oh, no! That's my name!
Menaechmus I:	I'm a Sicilian, from Syracuse.
Menaechmus II:	That's my home town and my home country, too.
Menaechmus I:	What did you say?
Menaechmus II:	Nothing but the truth.
Messenio:	(Turns to Menaechmus I.) Well, I know this man. He's my master. I thought you (indicates Menaechmus II) were he. I'm afraid I even made some trouble for you. Please excuse me, if I said anything silly or stupid to you.

Greek & Roman Plays for the Intermediate Grades © 1993 Fearon Teacher Aids

Menaechmus II:	What's the matter with you? Don't you remember that you came off the ship with me this morning?
Messenio:	Why, of course! That's perfectly right. (To Menaechmus II.) You are my master. (To Menaechmus I.) You'll have to find another servant. (To Menaechmus II.) Hello to you! (To Menaechmus I.) Good-bye to you! I say that he (pointing to Menaechmus II) is Menaechmus.
Menaechmus I:	But I say I am!
Menaechmus II:	What is this? (To Menaechmus I.) You are Menaechmus?
Menaechmus I:	Indeed I am! And my father's name was Moschus.
Menaechmus II:	You are my father's son?
Menaechmus I:	No, no, my friend, my father's! I have no desire to grab your father or take him away from you.
Messenio:	Ye gods in heaven, fulfill this hope for me! (To the audience.) I never thought it would come true, but I have a suspicion now it might. If I'm not completely mistaken, these are the twin brothers. They both say they come from the same place. I'll ask my master to step forward. Menaechmus!
Menaechmus I and II:	Yes?
Messenio:	I don't want both of you. Just the one who came on ship with me.
Menaechmus II:	I did.
Messenio:	You're the one I want, then. Come over here.
Menaechmus II:	What do you want?
Messenio:	(Whispering.) That man is either a crook or your own twin brother. I've never seen two men who looked more like another. Water's not more like water, nor milk like milk, believe me! He's like you, and you're like him! Besides, he says his father had the same name as yours, and he says he came from the same place as you. I think we'd better go and ask him some questions.

Greek & Roman Plays for the Intermediate Grades © 1993 Fearon Teacher Aids

The Menaechmi Twins

Menaechmus II:	Good advice. Thanks a lot. Go to it. You're a free man if you can prove that he's my twin brother.
Messenio:	I hope I can.
Menaechmus II:	So do I.
Messenio:	(To Menaechmus I.) I beg your pardon. I think you said your name was Menaechmus?
Menaechmus I:	That's right.
Messenio:	Well, his name is Menaechmus also. You said you were born in Syracuse in Sicily, and that's where he was born. You said your father's name was Moschus, and so was his. Now, you can both help me and yourselves at the same time.
Menaechmus I:	After what you did for me, you couldn't ask anything that I wouldn't be glad to do.
Messenio:	I'm hoping that I can prove that you are twin brothers, born of one mother and one father on the same day.
Menaechmus I:	Remarkable idea! I hope you can do what you say you can.
Messenio:	I can. But come now, both of you, tell me what I ask you.
Menaechmus I:	Anytime you like, just ask. I'll answer. I won't keep anything back that I know about.
Messenio:	(To Menaechmus I.) What's the earliest memory you have of your home? Tell me!
Menaechmus I:	I remember I went to Tarentum with father on business, and that later I lost my father and was taken from there.
Menaechmus II:	God bless me!
Messenio:	(To Menaechmus I.) How old were you when your father took you on that trip?
Menaechmus I:	Seven years old. Yes, I was starting to lose my baby teeth. And I've never seen my father since then.

Greek & Roman Plays for the Intermediate Grades © 1993 Fearon Teacher Aids

Messenio:	How many sons did your father have then?
Menaechmus I:	The best I remember, two.
Messenio:	Which was the older, you or he?
Menaechmus I:	We were exactly the same age.
Messenio:	How is that possible?
Menaechmus I:	We were twins.
Menaechmus II:	The gods are answering my prayers!
Messenio:	Did you both have the same name?
Menaechmus I:	Of course not. I had the name I still have, Menaechmus. The other twin was always called Sosicles.
Menaechmus II:	Everything points to it! I can't hold back any longer. (To Menaechmus I.) You're my twin brother! (Holds out his hand.) I'm so glad to see you. I'm Sosicles!
Menaechmus I:	(Holding back.) Well, why do you have the name Menaechmus, then?
Menaechmus II:	After we heard the news that you had wandered away from father and had been kidnapped by some stranger, father died, and our grandfather changed my name. He gave me the name you had.
Menaechmus I:	That must have been what happened. But tell me one more thing.
Menaechmus II:	What?
Menaechmus I:	What was mother's name?
Menaechmus II:	I believe we called her Mommy.
Menaechmus I:	That's it! My, I'm glad to see you. I'd given up all hope after all these years!
Menaechmus II:	I'm glad, too. I've been looking for you for a long time and have been through a lot of misery and trouble. I'm delighted I've found you at last!

Greek & Roman Plays for the Intermediate Grades © 1993 Pearon Teacher Aids

The Menaechmi Twins

Messenio:	(To Menaechmus II.) This is why that woman called you by his name. She must have thought you were he, when she invited you to dinner.
Menaechmus I:	That's right! I did order a dinner for myself at Lady E's house today. My wife didn't know anything about it. (Chuckles.) I swiped a dress from her, I did, and gave it to Lady E.
Menaechmus II:	(Holding out the dress.) You mean this dress, brother?
Menaechmus I:	That's the one! How did you get it?
Menaechmus II:	Why, that woman took me into her house for dinner and said I'd given it to her. I had a fine dinner! And I took this dress and this piece of jewelry (holds out the bracelet) away with me.
Menaechmus I:	I'm really glad if you've had some good luck because of me.
Messenio:	There isn't going to be any delay, is there, about my being free?
Menaechmus I:	He's quite right. That's perfectly fair, brother. Set him free for my sake.
Menaechmus II:	Messenio, I declare you a free man!
Menaechmus I:	Congratulations on your emancipation, Messenio.
Menaechmus II:	Since everything has turned out as we wanted, let's go back to Sicily, brother.
Menaechmus I:	I'll do just as you like. I'll hold an auction here and sell everything I own. Meanwhile let's go in the house, brother.
Messenio:	May I ask you something?
Menaechmus I:	What is it?
Messenio:	Let me be auctioneer.
Menaechmus I:	All right.
Messenio:	Would you like me to announce the auction right now?

Greek & Roman Plays for the Intermediate Grades © 1993 Fearon Teacher Aids

Menaechmus I: Yes, say that we will hold the auction a week from today.

(The Menaechmi twins enter the house.)

Messenio: (To the audience.)
May I have your attention, please, Menaechmus will hold an action a week from today in this auditorium. He will sell his land, his house, everything. He will sell them for what they will bring. Please tell the children who are absent today about the auction. And now, my friends, I bid you farewell. How about giving us a good loud hand?

(Curtain closes.)

Greek & Roman Plays for the Intermediate Grades © 1993 Fearon Teacher Aids

The Menaechmi Twins

POT OF GOLD

By Plautus

INTRODUCTION

Even though *Pot of Gold* was written centuries ago by the Roman playwright, Plautus, it still survives today as a side-splitting comedy. Its action centers around a man who is in love. He is not in love with a woman, or a pet, or himself, but with a pot of gold. There's never a dull moment!

In a comedy like this, reality is not necessary. The chief concern is to keep the action and the dialogue of the play flowing. The only factor that might slow down the pace is the hilarious laughter of the audience. It is important that the cast stay in character at all times, no matter how loud or long the audience laughs. Many of the characters frequently must speak directly to the audience. When this occurs, have the characters go right to the edge of the stage and truly speak to the audience.

STAGING

Three houses need to be represented on the stage. This can be done by using three wooden doors held upright by frames. Or, represent the three houses by stretching a large piece of cloth or paper across the stage and cutting out three openings.

COSTUMES

Euclio, the miser, should be simply dressed. The servants wear tunics down to their knees. All noblemen should wear loose flowing togas.

VOCABULARY

absolutely	benefit	disaster
accomplice	character	distracted
ails	chores	distribute
anticipate	compliments	donation
associated	constantly	doom
aware	contentment	dowry
barnacle	convince	entitled
bedlam	crockery	exhale

exterminate
fate
festival
fickle
gesture
hesitation
hysterical
impression
incense
influence
intense
intention
involved
iota

loitering
magnanimous
miser
miserly
misfortune
muttering
noggin
pauper
possessions
poverty
prologue
propose
provisions
pumice

raving
reptile
rumor
scamper
scheduled
scheme
slightest
stark
thrifty
tortoise
utensils
utterly
villainy

CHARACTERS

Narrator
Euclio, a miser
Staphyla, Euclio's housekeeper
Phaedria, Euclio's daughter
Megadorus, Euclio's rich neighbor
Lyconides, Megadorus' nephew
Eumonia, Lyconides' mother and Megadorus' sister
Strobilus, Megadorus' servant
Congrio, cook
Anthrax, cook
Servant of Lyconides
Servants
Flute girls

POT OF GOLD

Narrator: Hello, boys and girls! Today, I am the prologue. As the prologue, I will tell you something about the play you are going to see. It is entitled *Pot of Gold* and was written by the Roman playwright, Plautus. It is a comedy. The play is about the stingiest man in the world, the miser Euclio. He's so stingy that when he sleeps, he places a balloon over his mouth to catch and save the air he exhales. And believe it or not, he weeps when he washes his hands for he hates to waste a drop of water. These are just two examples of how stingy he is! Now Euclio has a pot of gold in his house, and he protects it every moment of the day. Of course he trusts no one and checks constantly to see that the gold is safely hidden. Things happen to his pot of gold, so enjoy this Roman comedy!

(The curtain opens, and three doors are seen on an empty stage. The center door is the home of the miser Euclio, the door on the left is the home of his neighbor, and the door on the right is an empty, deserted house. Euclio appears at his doorway, pushing his housekeeper out of the house.)

Euclio: You snooping, evil-eyed, old busybody, get out of my house. Get out and stay out!

Staphyla: Why are you pushing me out of your home? I'd like to know what I have done that is wrong?

Euclio: Don't play innocent with me. I'm much too smart for you.

Staphyla: Why are you doing this to me?

Euclio: Why, why, why? You'll get into more trouble if you continue to ask why! Go away from my house.

Staphyla: I am your housekeeper. I have been your housekeeper for years! Why do you now push me out?

Euclio: If you don't keep moving, I'll make you walk a little faster than a tortoise.

Greek & Roman Plays for the Intermediate Grades © 1993 Fearon Teacher Aids

Staphyla: (To the audience.)
I don't know why I put up with this nonsense.

Euclio: (To the audience.)
What is that old hag muttering to herself? (To Staphyla.) Stand exactly where you are and don't you dare move one tiny step. (To the audience.) She's the wickedest old bedlam I've ever seen. This, I'm sure of! She has eyes in the back of her head. She's a sly one, always trying to sniff out the hiding place of my gold. Now, I must go in to see if my gold is safe. (Enters his door.)

Staphyla: (To the audience.)
I think my master is cracking up. Why, some days he pushes me out of the house ten times . . . ten different times in one day! Sometimes he stays awake all night. He has such a lovely daughter, but she's sad, for she is in love, but she can't get married, for the old miser says weddings and festivals cost too much.

(Euclio appears at his doorway.)

Euclio: (To the audience.)
All is safe, and I do feel a bit better. (To Staphyla.) Now you, get back into the house and do your chores. Keep an eye on things!

Staphyla: Why should I keep an eye on things? There's nothing to steal in your house, but cobwebs. You have nothing worth stealing.

Euclio: Yes, I'm a poor man . . . a very poor man, and don't you forget it. And, yes, I want my cobwebs kept safe. Yes, I'm a poor man and content to be poor. Now go inside and lock the door, and, by Jupiter, don't you dare allow any strangers to enter. Somebody might come by asking for a light, so put the fire out so they won't ask for a light. Do you hear me? If every fire is not put out by the time I return, I'll put you out. If someone comes by asking for water, tell them the well has gone dry. If a neighbor comes by to borrow some utensils, tell them that everything has been stolen. I don't want a single soul entering my house while I'm away. Even if Dame Fortune should want to enter, say no!

Staphyla: I don't think you have a worry about Dame Fortune entering this house. No sir!

Greek & Roman Plays for the Intermediate Grades © 1993 Fearon Teacher Aids

Euclio: Oh be quiet! Now go inside. (Staphyla enters the house.) Now bolt the door . . . I'll be back soon. (To the audience.) Oh, how I wish I didn't have to leave my house, but I simply can't avoid it. The mayor of the city has a donation to distribute to the citizens of the town, and if I don't show up, all my neighbors will suspect that I have some gold hidden away. It wouldn't look right, would it, if a poor man didn't show up for a free handout? Well, I must be going so I'll get back soon. (Exits on the run. Enter from the door on the left Eumonia and Megadorus.)

Eumonia: I'm only speaking to you as a sister has a right to speak. You are my brother, and I should like to see you married. You certainly are old enough.

Megadorus: Help! Help!

Eumonia: Why are you screaming so?

Megadorus: Help! Help!

Eumonia: What ails you?

Megadorus: Every time you visit me, you speak of my getting married. Well, let me tell you, you might as well hit me over the head with a huge club, for I'm not getting married.

Eumonia: You're talking plain nonsense. You should be married.

Megadorus: Tell me something to do that's pleasant.

Eumonia: Getting married is for your own good.

Megadorus: O ye gods, will you ever stop talking about my getting married? All right, I will get married, but on the following terms—she comes into my house tomorrow and gets out the day after.

Eumonia: Stop talking nonsense. I know I can find you a girl with a rich dowry. I'll even propose for you.

Megadorus: Come to think of it, there is one girl I would like to marry.

Eumonia: Well, do tell. Who is she?

Greek & Roman Plays for the Intermediate Grades © 1993 Fearon Teacher Aids

Megadorus:	Do you know the old gentleman who lives next door called Euclio? Well, he's quite a poor man, and . . . and, and, well I . . .
Eumonia:	Well, spit it out. What are you attempting to say?
Megadorus:	I want to marry the poor old man's daughter. Now don't start screaming at me! I know she's a pauper, but pauper or not, I like her.
Eumonia:	May the gods be with you. (Exits into house.)
Megadorus:	(To the audience.) I'll go and see the old man now. I hope he's home. (Enter Euclio in a bad temper.) Why here he comes now.
Euclio:	(To the audience.) I had a strange feeling that things were going to go wrong today. The mayor didn't show up to distribute the money. I must hurry into my house to see if all is in place. Something might have happened while I was gone.
Megadorus:	Euclio, just a moment. I hope all goes well with you and your family.
Euclio:	Thank you, Megadorus. May the gods be with you, too. (Starts to enter his house.)
Megadorus:	I hope you are enjoying good health, Euclio.
Euclio:	(To the audience.) Why is a rich man like Megadorus paying such compliments to a poor man like me? Perhaps he knows about my pot of gold? That's why he's being so friendly.
Megadorus:	You are well, I trust?
Euclio:	Not as well off as I should like to be.
Megadorus:	Ah, but to be contented as you are is the thing. You're a happy man, and that's the main thing for a good life.
Euclio:	(To the audience.) I have a feeling that my housekeeper has told him about my pot of gold.
Megadorus:	You seem to be talking to yourself. Is something bothering you?

Euclio: Just worried about being so poor. You probably know that I have an unmarried daughter, but I'm much, much too poor to give her a dowry so she can get married.

Megadorus: Don't worry too much about your daughter. We will find someone to marry her. I'll help you as best I can. If there's anything I can do, just ask. I give you my word.

Euclio: (To the audience.)
He seems to have his mouth wide open, ready to swallow my gold. I don't trust him one single inch. He's not fooling me by holding out the hand of friendship, when all the time he's ready to smite me with it! I know his type. He's like a barnacle, clinging to anything he touches. (Starts to enter his house.)

Megadorus: Just a moment, Euclio. I have something to say to you that concerns us both.

Euclio: (To the audience.)
He's still trying to get his hands on my pot of gold. He's trying to make a deal with me. Of all things! I'm going inside to see that all is well with you know what! (He enters his house.)

Megadorus: (To the audience.)
That Euclio is certainly more thrifty with his poverty than any man I ever knew. I'm afraid that if I ask him for permission to marry his daughter, he will think I'm making fun of him.

(Euclio reenters in a better mood.)

Euclio: (To the audience.)
The gold is safe, thank the gods! I was truly worried for awhile. I was nearly out of my mind with worry! (To Megadorus.) Now, sir, what is it you wanted to discuss with me?

Megadorus: I want to ask you something, and I hope that you will answer freely. Do you think that I come from a good family?

Euclio: I'm sure that your family background is excellent.

Megadorus: Do you think I'm of good character?

Greek & Roman Plays for the Intermediate Grades © 1993 Fearon Teacher Aids

Pot of Gold

Euclio: Excellent character.

Megadorus: And my record?

Euclio: Excellent record.

Megadorus: Since you approve of me so highly, I would like your permission to marry your daughter. Please say you agree.

Euclio: Are you making fun of me, a poor old man?

Megadorus: Heavens, no! I have no intention of making fun of you.

Euclio: Then why are you asking for my daughter's hand in marriage?

Megadorus: I thought that you might benefit being associated with my family, as I would be by being associated with yours.

Euclio: You must be aware of the fact that you are a very rich man with much influence, while I am a very, very, very, poor man, the poorest of the poor! It would be most foolish of you to associate your family with such a poor family as mine.

Megadorus: You are talking nonsense, sheer nonsense! Please accept my offer to marry your daughter.

Euclio: I warn you, I don't even have a penny to give her for her dowry.

Megadorus: I don't care if you have absolutely nothing to give her. Marrying her will be reward enough.

Euclio: I tell you all this to be sure that you are not under the impression that I have some gold hidden away.

Megadorus: I know you are the poorest soul in town, and I don't care.

Euclio: What's that noise? Jupiter, almighty! I'm ruined!

Megadorus: What's wrong?

Euclio: I think I hear a shovel digging! (He dashes into his house.)

Greek & Roman Plays for the Intermediate Grades © 1993 Fearon Teacher Aids

Megadorus:	(To the audience.) Where has he dashed off to? Without a word of explana-tion, he dashes away. Perhaps he has taken an intense dislike to me? Most strange behavior. (Euclio reenters from his house.) Are you trying to make a fool of me by playing games?
Euclio:	I'm sorry, Megadorus.
Megadorus:	Well, what is your answer? Do I or do I not receive your permission to marry your young daughter?
Euclio:	You may marry her, but remember she receives no dowry from me. (They shake hands.)
Megadorus:	May the gods smile favorably on this marriage.
Euclio:	I hope they will. However, don't forget that you agreed to no dowry.
Megadorus:	I won't forget.
Euclio:	Sometimes you gentlemen get agreements all tangled up.
Megadorus:	Yes, yes, definitely no dowry. I agree! Now, is there any reason why the wedding can't take place today?
Euclio:	Excellent idea.
Megadorus:	Good! Then I'll go and make all the preparations.
Euclio:	Certainly. Good day to you, Megadorus.
Megadorus:	Strobilus! (Strobilus enters from Megadorus' house.)
Strobilus:	Yes, master.
Megadorus:	Come with me to the market. (They exit.)
Euclio:	(To the audience.) He's not fooling me one iota! I'm willing to wager that he's heard a rumor about my having a pot of gold buried away. And, my friends, that's why he's so anx-ious to marry my daughter. Staphyla! Staphyla!

Greek & Roman Plays for the Intermediate Grades © 1993 Fearon Teacher Aids

Staphyla, come out here. Can't you hear me? I'm calling you to come out here!

(Staphyla enters.)

Staphyla: I came out as fast as I could.

Euclio: Quickly, clean up all the crockery. My daughter is going to marry the rich Megadorus today.

Staphyla: Today? That's impossible! She can't get married all of a sudden just like that!

Euclio: Be quiet. You better have everything ready by the time I return. I'm going to the market. Be sure to keep the house locked. (Exits.)

Staphyla: This is impossible. My word, I don't see how I can get everything ready on such short notice. (She enters the house. Enter narrator.)

Narrator: Now, my dear audience, do you believe that Euclio is the most miserly old man in the whole wide world? And you are right! It is now an hour later and down the road I see Strobilus, the servant of rich Megadorus, returning with much food, some hired cooks, and some flute girls to entertain at the wedding feast. (Exits. Enter Strobilus and a group of servants.)

Strobilus: Well, here we are. Here's the place! My master Megadorus wants me to split the whole lot into two parts.

Anthrax: By Hercules, no one's going to split me in two! I'll go where I have to go, but all in one piece

Strobilus: That's not what I meant. Now listen carefully. My master Megadorus is marrying today the daughter of that poor, poor old man Euclio, and half the servants and half the food are to go into the house of Euclio and the rest into my master's house.

Congrio: Couldn't the old man even afford a wedding dinner for his daughter? It doesn't cost that much.

Strobilus: Hah!

Congrio: What do you mean by "hah"?

Greek & Roman Plays for the Intermediate Grades © 1993 Fearon Teacher Aids

Strobilus:	You'd get more from squeezing a pumice stone than you would from that old beggar. I tell you, he becomes hysterical if he sees a puff of smoke escaping from his chimney. And if he loses just a grain of salt, he screams bloody murder!
Anthrax:	Are you serious?
Strobilus:	Why just the other day when the barber finished trimming his toenails, he took all the clippings home.
Congrio:	What a miserable, mean old creature.
Strobilus:	There are many tales I could tell you about him, but we have work to do. Now, Congrio, you and a servant and a flute girl go into Euclio's house, and the rest come with me to the house of my master.
Congrio:	That's not fair! It's a dirty trick, Strobilus, to make me go work for that old cheap skate!
Strobilus:	I'm doing you a great favor!
Congrio:	A favor? Make sense!
Strobilus:	Look, in that house nothing will get in your way, for it's practically empty. While in my master's house, there will be much hustle and bustle with guests getting in your way, gold and silver plates to wash, all types of cloths to place on tables. In Euclio's house, you certainly won't be tempted to steal anything, for there's nothing to steal, and in this way, you won't end up in a dungeon.
Congrio:	All right.
	(Strobilus knocks on Euclio's door.)
Strobilus:	Staphyla, open the bolted door.
Staphyla:	(From within.) Who is knocking?
Strobilus:	Me, Strobilus, servant of rich Megadorus.
	(Staphyla comes out.)
Staphyla:	Well, what is it?

Greek & Roman Plays for the Intermediate Grades © 1993 Fearon Teacher Aids

Strobilus: I've brought you a cook, a servant, a flute girl, and some provisions for the wedding. All of these come with the compliments of my rich master. Show them the way in.

Staphyla: Come with me.

(All enter the house, except Strobilus and his crew.)

Strobilus: Now, let us get to work in the house of Megadorus. (They all enter Megadorus' house. Euclio returns from market.)

Euclio: (To the audience.)
Everything was too expensive at the market. The meat was a terrible price, and the same with the fish and vegetables—all much too expensive. And anyway, if you cast your money away foolishly on special occasions, you won't have any for ordinary days. So I bought my daughter some incense and these few flowers. (He starts to enter his house and notices that his door is open.) Oh may the gods help me! What's this? The door is open! Listen to all that noise inside. I think I'm being robbed . . . I know I'm being robbed!

Congrio: (From within.)
I can't fit everything into this small pot. It's much, much too small. Let's hunt for a bigger pot.

Euclio: (To the audience.)
He's got the gold. He's got my precious gold! Oh, I'm ruined! Oh Apollo, come to my aid! Apollo, slay with your arrows these gold robbers! Oh, I can't wait for Apollo, I had better do something myself. I had better do something now or I shall be ruined utterly.

(Euclio rushes into the house as Anthrax comes from the house of Megadorus.)

Anthrax: (To the audience.)
I need another pot. I'll borrow one from Congrio next door. But what's all that noise coming from the old man's house? I had better get back to my house where it's safe and forget about borrowing another pot. (He goes back in. Congrio and servants rush out of Euclio's house.)

Greek & Roman Plays for the Intermediate Grades © 1993 Fearon Teacher Aids

Congrio: (To the audience.)
Help! Help me! Help me! Oh people, help a poor cook! It's a real madhouse in there. The old man has used me as a punching bag. I have bumps all over me! Oh, he's coming out. I'm a dead cook for sure! (He jumps off the stage into the audience. Euclio runs out of his house.)

Euclio: Come back here! Come back, I say! Stop him! Somebody stop him!

Congrio: What do you want with me?

Euclio: I'm going to report you to the police.

Congrio: What for?

Euclio: For carrying a knife!

Congrio: A cook has to use a knife to cook!

Euclio: What were you doing in my house, eh? What were you doing in my house without permission? Answer that!

Congrio: I was preparing food for your daughter's wedding, what else?

Euclio: And is it any business of yours. What if I prefer to eat my food raw? It saves money that way.

Congrio: I'm all confused. Am I or am I not supposed to prepare the food for the wedding?

Euclio: And all I want to know is, will belongings be safe while you're in my house? Tell me that!

Congrio: What have we said and done to offend you?

Euclio: I know what you have done. You went through all the rooms in my house instead of staying in the kitchen where you belong! And if you ever come close to this house again, you'll have more than a bruised noggin! (He goes back into the house.)

Congrio: Come back, you mean old thing! Give me back my pots that I brought with me, or I'll stay here all night and scream that you are a thief! (To the audience.) This was not my lucky day to land this job! Instead of earning

Greek & Roman Plays for the Intermediate Grades © 1993 Pearon Teacher Aids

some money, I'll be spending money at the doctor's
office to heal my broken bones! Poor me! (He returns to
the stage. Euclio appears from the house with the pot of
gold partly hidden under his arm.)

Euclio: (To the audience.)
Oh, I'm so happy, for I have my pot of gold safely
tucked under my arm. I'll never let it out of my sight
again! (He kisses the pot of gold.) No, I'll never, never
leave it alone again! It's much too dangerous a thing to
do. Now, cook and servants and flute girls, go inside the
house and go on preparing for the wedding. Work fast!

Congrio: Well, it's about time.

Euclio: You were hired to work, not to talk, so stop your muttering and go inside. (Congrio and the servants enter
the house. To the audience.) Well, I got rid of them.
Getting ready for this wedding is giving me a nervous
breakdown, and when I think of the money I spent for
the incense and the flowers! Oh, here comes my future
son-in-law, Megadorus. I suppose I'll have to speak to
him.

(Enter Megadorus.)

Megadorus: Hello, future father-in-law. Don't you think you ought
to spruce up for the wedding? Don't you have some
better clothes to wear?

Euclio: My dear Megadorus, people who dress up are only
showing off. They are only showing off their
possessions.

Megadorus: Just as you say, future father-in law. We must have a
drink of wine together today.

Euclio: No, I'm not drinking.

Megadorus: I'm having a cask of wine sent to your home.

Euclio: No thank you. I drink nothing but water.

Megadorus: Nonsense! We will drink together, and I'll see you
under the table.

Euclio: (To the audience.)
Now I see his scheme. He's out to get me dizzy from wine and then he'll steal my pot of gold! I'll fool him though and hide it someplace outside the house. He will have wasted his time, as well as his wine.

Megadorus: Now it's time for me to get ready for the wedding. Excuse me, Euclio. (He enters his home.)

Euclio: Oh, my poor precious pot of gold, you are always in such danger of being stolen from me. But have no fear, I'll protect you! I'll hide you in the empty, deserted house. People are afraid to enter this house, for they think it is haunted. You will be safe there, my little precious pot of gold. (He enters the third door on the stage.)

(A servant enters.)

Servant: (To the audience.)
Hello! A good servant should always serve his master without any hesitation, and that's me. I'm a very good servant. My master's good always comes first! Even when I'm asleep, I always think of what would be the best way to please my master. I always anticipate my master's orders. Now for the reason why I am here. My young master is in love with old Euclio's young daughter and he has just heard that she's going to be married to his rich uncle, Megadorus . . . so, I'm here to see exactly what's going on so I can report everything to my master. If you don't mind, I'll just sit down quietly here in the corner to keep an eye on things. Nice meeting such a friendly audience. (He sits in the corner of the stage. Euclio comes halfway out the door of the empty house.)

Euclio: Now, my good haunted, deserted house, don't tell a soul about my beautiful pot of gold. I'm sure no one will find it by mere accident. If anyone did find it, they would have a tidy haul, but please don't let anyone find it. I beseech you, empty house, don't let anyone enter. Scare them away. Now I leave you so I can wash up a little for the wedding. I want Megadorus to take Phaedria away as soon as possible, for then there will be one less mouth to feed. Once again, empty house, I put you in charge of my pot of gold. I trust you with it. (He enters his own house.)

Pot of Gold

Servant: (To the audience.)
Goodness gracious! What have I overheard? He has hidden a pot of gold in the empty, haunted house! I'm going to search the house to see if I can find his treasure. (He enters the empty house. Euclio appears from his house.)

Euclio: I feel there is something wrong. I heard a raven croak, and that's a bad sign. I had better check my gold! (He enters the empty house. There are yells and screams. Then Euclio drags out the servant.) You reptile! What did you do, crawl out of the earth? I didn't see you around before. Now that I have you, I'm going to exterminate you. I'll give you something to remember! (He starts hitting the servant.)

Servant: Why are you hitting me? Why did you drag me out of the empty house?

Euclio: You're a thief. Thief! Thief! Thief!

Servant: Tell me, what I have stolen.

Euclio: Give it back to me you beast!

Servant: Give what back?

Euclio: You know what I'm talking about!

Servant: Please listen, I have not stolen anything of yours.

Euclio: Then you give me back what you have not stolen!

Servant: Honestly, I don't know what you're talking about.

Euclio: Show me your hands, you robber.

Servant: (Extends his open hands.)
Here, look!

Euclio: Is that all the hands you've got?

Servant: (To the audience.)
This old man is stark raving mad!

Euclio: Tell me, what have you stolen from the empty house?

Servant: May the gods punish me if I have stolen anything of yours.

Euclio: What do you have under your shirt?

Servant: Nothing.

Euclio: Show me your hands again . . . all three of them!

Servant: Here, look again.

Euclio: You are wasting my important time, and time should never be wasted. I know you've got it!

Servant: Got what?

Euclio: You're not going to trick me into telling you. Give me back whatever you've got that is mine!

Servant: You have searched me all over and have found nothing.

Euclio: I thought I heard someone else in the empty house. Who is your accomplice? Speak! Yes, there is someone else in there. All right, you can go. Now, I'm going in to catch your accomplice. Don't let me catch you loitering about this empty house again! (He enters the empty house.)

Servant: (To the audience.)
Now, he'll never dare leave the gold in the empty deserted house. He will find a new hiding place, and I will follow him. Ssshhh! Quiet! I'll hide in the corner.

(Enter Euclio from the house.)

Euclio: This old house nearly ruined me. Fortunately I heard a raven croak, or I never would have suspected anything to be wrong! I'd like to meet that raven to give him a gift . . . well, on second thought, I would only compliment him. Now, my job is to find another hiding place for my beautiful pot of gold. I know! There's a lonely grove just outside the city wall, overgrown with weeds. That's where I'll hide my precious pot of gold. (Exits with the pot of gold.)

Servant: (To the audience.)
Hurrah! The gods are on my side. I'll follow him on tiptoe and watch where he buries his gold. Even though my master told me to wait for him at this exact spot, I'm not going to lose my chance of getting my hands on a pot of gold! (He follows Euclio.)

Greek & Roman Plays for the Intermediate Grades © 1993 Fearon Teacher Aids

(Enter narrator.)

Narrator: (To the audience.)
Poor old miser! I think his pot of gold is in danger of being stolen. Now you shall meet for the first time Lyconides. He is in love with Euclio's young daughter, Phaedria, and she is in love with him, but, as you know, she is slated to marry rich Megadorus. Here comes Lyconides with his mother Eumonia, Megadorus' sister. (Narrator exits. Enter Lyconides and Eumonia.)

Lyconides: Yes, mother, I can't live without Euclio's young daughter. She loves me and I love her, and we want to get married. Please convince my uncle Megadorus not to marry her. Please!

Eumonia: I will do everything I can, but it is very close to the time of the wedding.

Phaedria: (From within Euclio's house.)
Oh Lyconides, I love you so. Save me from this marriage!

Lyconides: You hear, mother, how she weeps for me.

Eumonia: Come into the house and we shall speak to Megadorus! (She enters the house of Megadorus.)

Lyconides: (To the audience.)
My servant was supposed to have met me here. I wonder where he is? Well, I must go in to hear my fate decided! (He enters the house of Megadorus. The servant returns with the pot of gold.)

Servant: (To the audience.)
Look. Look. Look at me! I'm rich. I'm stinking rich! I'm richer than a King! Isn't this a glorious day, my friends? Oh, oh! Here he comes. I am going to scamper away with my newly found pot of gold. (Exits. Enter Euclio.)

Euclio: (To the audience.)
Poor, poor me . . . poor me! I'm all mixed up and don't know which way to run. Don't just sit there. Somebody stop the thief who stole my buried pot of gold! But who is he? I'm afraid that I don't have the slightest idea. I'm so mixed up that I don't even know who I am. Help me, my good audience, show me the man who has stolen my pot

of gold. You, in the third row, you seem to have an honest face, tell me the one who has my gold. So, you're laughing at me. I'll fix you! This audience is probably full of thieves, too! All of you, sitting there in your nice clean clothes. You, in the last row back there . . . do you have my pot of gold? Oh, I'm a ruined man! Doom and disaster fall upon me. I'm the most unhappy man in the world. I guarded my pot of gold with my life, and now it's gone. There is nothing left for me, but to weep! I can't stand it! I can't bear it! (He begins to wail. Enter Lyconides.)

Lyconides: Why are you howling and moaning so loudly Euclio?

Euclio: I am completely ruined. Ruined, do you hear? My pot of gold has been stolen.

Lyconides: Perhaps I can help you find your pot of gold?

Euclio: Fat chance! Say, did you steal my pot of gold?

Lyconides: On my honor as a gentlemen, I did not.

Euclio: But you know who did?

Lyconides: On my honor, I do not know!

Euclio: If you found out, would you tell me who did?

Lyconides: Yes, I would tell you.

Euclio: And you wouldn't grab a share for yourself and let the robber go free?

Lyconides: If I did such a thing, may Jupiter punish me. But let me make a bargain with you.

Euclio: You don't expect to receive a reward do you?

Lyconides: Relax. There is no money involved with my request from you.

Euclio: Good enough.

Lyconides: In case you don't know who I am, I'm Lyconides, nephew of your next door neighbor, the rich Megadorus. And my mother is Eumonia.

Euclio: So . . . what do you want?

Pot of Gold

Greek & Roman Plays for the Intermediate Grades © 1993 Fearon Teacher Aids

Lyconides:	I believe you have a daughter?
Euclio:	Of course I have a daughter, and she's at home where she belongs.
Lyconides:	Rumor has it that you promised her to my uncle, the rich Megadorus.
Euclio:	Yes, I have.
Lyconides:	I believe he has changed his mind.
Euclio:	Changed his mind? It's because of him I took my beautiful pot of gold out of the house and lost it.
Lyconides:	(Out of the corner of his eye, he sees his servant entering with a pot of gold.) If I find your pot of gold and return it untouched, will you give your daughter to me in marriage?
Euclio:	What a silly question. Of course I will! Just find that gold! (He enters his house moaning.)
Lyconides:	Come out of the shadows, servant, and show me what you carry. What have you found?
Servant:	Something very important. A pot full of gold!
Lyconides:	What villainy have you been up to now?
Servant:	I stole it from old Euclio.
Lyconides:	Give it to me, and I'll return it to its rightful owner.
Servant:	Give it back? You must be crazy!
Lyconides:	Give it to me, servant.
Servant:	No!
	(Lyconides lunges for the pot of gold, but the servant jumps into the audience and escapes. Megadorus enters from his house.)
Megadorus:	(To the audience.) That sister of mine is slightly batty. Just this morning she was practically forcing me to get married . . . married to anybody. Now when I decide to marry

Greek & Roman Plays for the Intermediate Grades © 1993 Fearon Teacher Aids

Euclio's young daughter, she tells me that Phaedria is in love with her son, my nephew, and would I please pick someone else. She certainly changes her mind quickly.

Lyconides: Hello, Uncle Megadorus.

Megadorus: Why Lyconides, you don't look too happy. Have you spoken to Euclio about marrying his daughter?

Lyconides: I'm afraid the old man is much more interested in regaining his gold than being concerned with the happiness of his daughter. He is so distracted about having lost his gold, that he can't think of anything else but that. Oh yes, he'll allow me to marry his daughter, but only if I find his pot of gold.

Megadorus: This poses quite a problem.

Lyconides: A strange problem. I know who has the gold . . . my servant, but he just escaped from me. Now I'll search for that little stinker! (Exits. Euclio enters from his house.)

Euclio: And you, my dear Megadorus, get your cook, servants, and flute girls out of my house.

Megadorus: Is there something wrong, Euclio?

Euclio: Something wrong? Something wrong? Something wrong? Yes, there is something wrong! Very wrong! My whole misfortune began when I ran into you earlier today and made arrangements for a wedding. I have been robbed of my pot of gold. That's what's wrong!

(Congrio, servants, and flute girls enter from Euclio's house.)

Congrio: We have done as you ordered, Euclio. The fire is out, the food is put away, and we are ready to leave.

Euclio: Good, and good riddance!

Congrio: What about our pay?

Euclio: What?

Congrio: I said, what about our pay for working a whole day?

Greek & Roman Plays for the Intermediate Grades © 1993 Fearon Teacher Aids

Euclio:	Pay? I'm not paying anybody. All you did was upset my whole house, waste my firewood, and put your nose in my private business. Pay indeed!
Megadorus:	Don't worry about getting paid, Congrio. You'll be well paid, but first you must complete your day's work. Go back into the house and get ready for a wedding feast.
Congrio:	(To the audience.) Everybody is nuts around here. Go away! Stay! Go away! Stay! Cook the dinner! Don't cook the dinner! What orders am I to obey?
Megadorus:	My orders. I hired you, and you will obey my orders.
Congrio:	This is a true madhouse!
	(Congrio and his group enter Euclio's house.)
Euclio:	A fine state of affairs. I don't even give the orders in my own home any more. Nothing but disaster surrounds me.
Megadorus:	Cheer up, my old stingy friend. Things might turn for the better. (Enter Lyconides with the pot of gold, followed by the servant.) I believe Lyconides is here to speak to you, Euclio.
Euclio:	(His face covered by his hands and weeping.) Oh send him away. I don't want to speak to anyone.
Megadorus:	Euclio, I think my nephew has something that belongs to you.
Euclio:	What do you say? It's my pot of gold! (He grabs the pot of gold from Lyconides.) Oh mighty Jupiter, you have returned my beautiful pot of gold! (He kisses the pot of gold.) Oh, thank you, Megadorus.
Megadorus:	It is Lyconides you should thank.
Euclio:	Oh, I do bless you, my noble Lyconides.
Lyconides:	The real credit for the recovery of your gold belongs to my servant.
Euclio:	You don't say. Well done, servant. And I shall reward you with one golden coin. On second thought, a greater reward for you would be to shake your hand.

Greek & Roman Plays for the Intermediate Grades © 1993 Fearon Teacher Aids

Lyconides: I have already rewarded my servant. I have given him his freedom for giving me the pot of gold to give to you.

Megadorus: And now, Euclio, since you are happy again holding your precious pot of gold, what about the matter of my nephew marrying your beautiful young daughter?

Euclio: Yes, yes, by all means. Let's have a wedding.

Lyconides: Thank you, sir, for being so generous.

Euclio: Wait a moment. Now I have the problem of hiding the pot of gold in a very safe place. Where shall I hide my beautiful pot? Where? Where? Where? What a problem! (Long pause.) Here, Lyconides, you take it.

Lyconides: What? You're giving it to me?

Euclio: Yes! You take it, keep it, and spend it all on my daughter. It will be her dowry.

Megadorus: What a magnanimous gesture, Euclio!

Euclio: Day and night, I haven't had a moment's peace protecting my pot of gold. Everyday, I would change its hiding place at least a dozen times. Each little noise worried me. Now you keep it, Lyconides, and do with it what you will. Now, at last, I'll be able to sleep at night peacefully!

Megadorus: You are truly a wise man, Euclio. You have finally realized that contentment, peace of mind, and sound sleep at night are worth more than a hundred pots of beautiful, shining gold. And now, let's celebrate the wedding of Lyconides and Phaedria.

Euclio: Yes, by all means, let us celebrate. (They all start to enter the home of Euclio.) But, wait, Megadorus, aren't you forgetting something?

Megadorus: I don't think so. (Euclio whispers in his ear. Megadorus turns to the audience.) To our friends, the audience, we extend an invitation for you to join us at the wedding banquet.

(They enter the house, and the curtain closes.)

Greek & Roman Plays for the Intermediate Grades © 1993 Fearon Teacher Aids

Pot of Gold

AMPHITRYO

By Plautus

INTRODUCTION

Jupiter, the most powerful Roman god, decided to have some fun and visit the earth, bringing his son, Mercury, with him. Poor mortals became thoroughly confused by the gods masquerading as real people, but as in all Roman comedies written by Plautus, everything is neatly solved and all ends well.

The tricks the gods play on the people are so humorous that both cast and audience will have fun, but as always, it is essential that the cast stay in character and keep straight faces no matter how much the audience laughs.

STAGING

One house should be represented by a door. When Mercury sits on top of the house and pours water on Amphitryo, a ladder next to the door with Mercury on the top step can indicate that he is on the rooftop. The thunder and lightning at the end of the play can be simulated by shaking a large piece of tin or aluminum offstage and turning a bright spotlight on and off.

COSTUMES

When the gods come to earth, they impersonate everyday people and dress accordingly. Jupiter is impersonating Amphitryo, the general, so both are dressed alike. Mercury is impersonating the servant Sosia, so he is dressed as a servant. Remember that Jupiter has a golden tassel in his cap and Mercury has a feather in his cap to distinguish them in the play.

VOCABULARY

approaching	exploits	libation
bolt	greet	mistress
coax	imitation	moods
deny	impersonating	mortals
devoted	impostor	muddled
distinguish	impudence	nonsensical
dwells	investigate	opportunity

prank	rogues	task
ravenous	scamper	temporary
revenge	scoundrel	
ridiculous	soul	

CHARACTERS

Amphitryo, the general of the army
Alcmena, Amphitryo's wife
Sosia, Amphitryo's servant
Jupiter, a god impersonating Amphitryo
Mercury, a god impersonating Sosia
Blepharo, captain of the ship
Bromia, servant
Thessala, servant

AMPHITRYO

Mercury: (To the audience.)
Hello! . . . Isn't anyone going to say "Hello"? Thank you! My name is Mercury, and I am an immortal god. My father is the almighty Jupiter. I know you're scared to death of him, for he is a powerful god, but you have nothing to worry about today. I'm only here to do an errand for him. Today my father, Jupiter, is in a playful mood. As you see, I'm not dressed as I usually am in my wonderful god costume, but instead am dressed as a servant. You see that house . . . well, in that house dwells Amphitryo and his wife, Alcmena. Amphitryo is off to war and Alcmena is home alone . . . well, not quite alone! You see, my father, Jupiter, is visiting her, pretending he is her husband, Amphitryo, who has supposedly just returned from the war. Why is Jupiter doing all this mischief? I'll tell you if you pay close attention. Jupiter's father and mother were mortals like you, and every so often, he has a strong desire to eat some mortal food. Jupiter is dressed exactly as Amphitryo would be dressed, and therefore Alcmena suspects nothing. She is busy preparing a delicious dinner for him, thinking he is her husband. And what am I doing here? Pay close attention, and I'll tell you more. I'm dressed as Sosia, the servant of Amphitryo, and my job is to keep people away from the house while my father is eating his delicious dinner as he impersonates Amphitryo. It's a rather dull task, but my father is powerful, so I must do as he says. The feather in my cap will help you distinguish me from the real servant Sosia, and the golden tassel in my father's cap will distinguish him from the real Amphitryo. Don't look now, but trouble for me seems to be heading this way. The person approaching seems to be the real Sosia. My job is to keep him away from the house. I'll hide to one side to see what he is thinking.

(Mercury hides. Sosia enters.)

Sosia: Here I am, all alone on a dark, dark night. (To the audience.) Don't you think I'm a very brave soul? I

Greek & Roman Plays for the Intermediate Grades © 1993 Fearon Teacher Aids

certainly am! It's dangerous walking on such a dark street with only a lantern to guide my way. With all these wild teenagers roaming about, one never knows what may happen. Let me tell you something . . . it's no fun being a servant to a rich man. My name is Sosia, and I'm the servant of Amphitryo. My master's ship just arrived in the harbor, and he has sent me into town to prepare a hero's celebration for him. Now wouldn't you think he could have waited until morning? I truly lead a dog's life. All I do is work, work, work, and work! Sometimes I don't even have a chance to get a bit of sleep. Well, anyway we're back from the war safe and sound, and my master is a hero. It will be my honor to announce to his wife, Alcmena, that her hero husband is back. I have just enough energy to give her the news and then to sleep.

Mercury: (To the audience.)
Good grief! He's heading toward the house. I must stop him! You with the lantern, get away from that door!

Sosia: What did you say?

Mercury: What is your business at this door?

Sosia: My business is my master's business.

Mercury: How do I know you have business at this door?

Sosia: Whoever you are, I live here. I'm a servant of this house.

Mercury: Go away!

Sosia: Why can't a servant go into his own master's house?

Mercury: Who is your master?

Sosia: My master is the now-famous war hero, Amphitryo, who just arrived at the harbor and in the morning will come to see his wife, Alcmena.

Mercury: Very, very funny! A pack of lies!

Sosia: My errand is a true one. I am Sosia, his servant.

Mercury: Ha, ha, ha! How dare you have the nerve to say you are Sosia, when I am Sosia! (He starts chasing Sosia.)

Sosia: Help! Help!

Mercury: Again I ask you . . . whose servant are you?

Sosia: I am the servant of Amphitryo!

(Mercury starts chasing him again.)

Mercury: More lies you tell me! Again I ask, who are you servant to?

Sosia: You tell me.

Mercury: And what's your name?

Sosia: Any name you like.

Mercury: Now you are making sense. I knew I was the only servant in this house who is named Sosia. Now scamper home like a good little servant . . . home is back to the ship in the harbor! (Sosia begins to sneak near the door of the house.) Home to the harbor, I said!

Sosia: Can't I just tell my mistress that her master has returned?

Mercury: Home, I said. Home to the harbor! (He raises his hand.)

Sosia: O.K.! O.K.! I'm going home to the harbor, even though that really isn't my home. (To the audience.) This fellow really does look like me. Strange. Very strange. Where did I shed my skin? Strange! (Exits bewildered.)

Mercury: (To the audience.)
            A very good beginning, my friends, a very good beginning indeed. This gives my father at least another few moments to enjoy his dinner of mortal food. There will be an amusing situation at the harbor when the real Sosia attempts to explain what happened to his master. Of course, Amphitryo will call him a liar, and everything will be quite muddled. Quiet . . . I think my father, the imitation Amphitryo, is about to come out of the house.

(Jupiter and Alcmena enter.)

Jupiter: My beloved wife, the dinner was delicious. You outdid yourself! Please forgive my sudden departure, but a war hero like myself has many things to do.

Greek & Roman Plays for the Intermediate Grades © 1993 Pearon Teacher Aids

Amphitryo

Alcmena:	But Amphitryo, you just returned after such a long time. Must you eat and run so soon?
Jupiter:	My men are awaiting commands from me. They are lost souls without me. Of course, I would rather stay with you, my beloved wife, but duty calls.
Mercury:	(To the audience.) Isn't my father a crafty one?
Alcmena:	You make it sound as if your wife isn't very important to you.
Jupiter:	That's not so. You are the most important woman in the world to me.
Alcmena:	Your conduct is very strange, dear husband. You no sooner arrive than you have to leave.
Mercury:	He speaks the truth, madam. A more devoted husband does not exist.
Jupiter:	Be quiet, Sosia! Who asked you to interfere?
Alcmena:	Be gentle, Amphitryo.
Jupiter:	Don't be angry with me, dear wife. I sneaked away from my men to tell you of my exploits . . . you were the first to know. Doesn't that prove how much I think of you?
Mercury:	(To the audience.) See how clever my father is.
Jupiter:	Now, dear wife, I truly must be going back to my men.
Alcmena:	I think I'm going to cry!
Jupiter:	Don't spoil your beautiful eyes, dear wife. I'll be back very, very soon . . . sooner than you think.
Alcmena:	Boo-hoo-hoo! Boo-hoo-hoo!
	(Jupiter begins to leave, but Alcmena restrains him.)
Jupiter:	Darling, you must let me go! I must, must go! Look . . . here's a present I forgot to give you. I personally defeated my enemy, and here's his drinking bowl, just for you.

Alcmena:	It's lovely . . . a lovely present from a lovely man.
Mercury:	Now, dear master, you should say, "No, a lovely present for a lovely lady."
Jupiter:	I though I told you to keep quiet!
Alcmena:	Please, my dear Amphitryo, be gentle with our Sosia, for he's just trying to be kind to me.
Jupiter:	Just as you say, dear wife.
Mercury:	The dawn will soon be here, master. Time to leave.
Jupiter:	You start down the path, Sosia. I'll soon follow.
	(Mercury exits.)
Alcmena:	Please come back very, very soon.
Jupiter:	Sweetheart, I'll be back sooner than you think.
	(Alcmena enters her house.)
Mercury:	(Off stage.) Master, you had better move along.
Jupiter:	Let the dawn come up.
	(The whole stage bursts into light. Jupiter exits. Enter Amphitryo and Sosia.)
Amphitryo:	Get a move on with you, Sosia.
Sosia:	(Carrying a very heavy bag.) I'm moving sir, I'm moving.
Amphitryo:	The very idea of telling me such a crazy story! How did you expect me to believe such a tall tale?
Sosia:	Everything I told you did happen, master.
Amphitryo:	I find it very hard to believe that you are telling me the truth.
Sosia:	It did happen, master. I bumped into myself!
Amphitryo:	You are a fool.
Sosia:	No, master, I'm not a fool. I'm in the house and I'm out here with you.

Greek & Roman Plays for the Intermediate Grades © 1993 Fearon Teacher Aids

Amphitryo

Amphitryo: (To the audience.)
             Obviously he is out of his mind!

Sosia: Me, Sosia, out here . . . me, Sosia in the house. I can't
             make it more plain than that!

Amphitryo: You're trying to make a fool of me.

Sosia: Why would I not tell the truth?

Amphitryo: Prove it to me. How can you be inside the house and
             outside the house at the same time?

Sosia: It's difficult to explain, master, but he convinced me he
             was me. We are like two drops of milk!

Amphitryo: You're still speaking nonsense! (To the audience.)
             Something terrible has happened to his brain.

Sosia: He stopped me from going into the house.

Amphitryo: You must have dreamt you saw another you.

Sosia: You'll believe me as soon as you meet the other Sosia.

Amphitryo: You are very difficult to understand. Now to surprise
             my wife! (He knocks on the door. Alcmena appears.)

Alcmena: Husband!

Amphitryo: With joy your Amphitryo greets you! You are the no-
             blest wife in all of Thebes. You are without equal. Have
             you been in good health? Are you glad to see me?

Alcmena: Why such a long speech when you just said good-bye a
             few moments ago? Are you joking with me?

Amphitryo: I don't understand. I haven't seen you today.

Alcmena: What? Are you denying that you saw me earlier?

Amphitryo: I'm not in the habit of telling lies.

Alcmena: Just a few moments ago, you said that since you were a
             war hero you had to return to your men. Why were you
             able to return so soon? What happened?

Amphitryo: Alcmena, what are you talking about?

Alcmena: As if you didn't know.

Amphitryo: (To the audience.)
Has my wife gone mad?

Sosia: Perhaps it's the shock of seeing you after such a long time.

Amphitryo: (To the audience.)
Perhaps she is walking in her sleep.

Alcmena: All I know is what I saw this morning. I saw both of you earlier today.

Amphitryo: Impossible!

Alcmena: I know I saw you in this house.

Amphitryo: Impossible!

Sosia: Wait a minute, sir. Perhaps the ship sailed up the street while we were sleeping in our bunks.

Amphitryo: Be quiet! You certainly don't believe her story, do you? Alcmena dear . . .

Alcmena: Yes, dear?

Amphitryo: Is this a sweet silly prank you are playing?

Alcmena: What a nonsensical question!

Amphitryo: Every other time I returned home, you always welcomed me with much joy. Today you seem to be in a very strange mood.

Alcmena: For heaven's sake. I welcomed you home earlier today with open arms! And you were there too, Sosia.

Sosia: (Whispering to Amphitryo.)
She's off her rocker.

Alcmena: I heard that! And I'm nothing of the sort.

Sosia: Think carefully, my dear. You say you saw me earlier today in this house?

Alcmena: Yes! Yes, yes, yes, yes, yes, yes, yes!

Amphitryo: Perhaps in your dreams?

Alcmena: No, not in my dreams! I was wide awake.

Greek & Roman Plays for the Intermediate Grades © 1993 Pearon Teacher Aids

Amphitryo

Amphitryo:	(Whispering to Sosia.) I think my wife has gone insane!
Alcmena:	Perhaps it's just temporary.
Amphitryo:	When did you first feel your dizzy spells coming on?
Alcmena:	I am perfectly sane. I don't have dizzy spells.
Amphitryo:	Then why do you keep on insisting that you saw me in this house earlier today? I had dinner on my ship.
Alcmena:	What are you saying? You had dinner with me!
Amphitryo:	What! I had dinner with you?
Alcmena:	I speak the truth. After dinner, you kissed me good-bye and went back to the ship.
Amphitryo:	I did?
Sosia:	Madam, are you sure you weren't dreaming?
Alcmena:	Go soak your head!
Sosia:	I think it would be better for you to soak your head.
Alcmena:	Are you going to let a servant talk to me like that?
Amphitryo:	Be quiet, Sosia! I left you this morning, you say?
Alcmena:	Yes!
Amphitryo:	Do you still insist I was here this morning?
Alcmena:	Do you still deny you were here this morning?
Amphitryo:	Yes, I deny it! I haven't been home until this very minute.
Alcmena:	And do you deny giving me a bowl?
Amphitryo:	May the gods help us! I never gave you a bowl!
Alcmena:	Yes, you did . . . with your own two hands you gave me a bowl!
Amphitryo:	You say I gave you a bowl?
Alcmena:	Yes, you gave me a bowl. Would you like to see it?

Greek & Roman Plays for the Intermediate Grades © 1983 Fearon Teacher Aids

Alcmena:	(Calling to her servant within.) Thessala, bring me the bowl my husband gave to me this morning.
Amphitryo:	(Dragging Sosia to a corner of the stage.) If she has the bowl, then what she says is true.
Sosia:	Impossible. The bowl is in the box with your seal upon it . . . unbroken.
	(Thessala appears with the bowl.)
Alcmena:	Now, are you satisfied?
Amphitryo:	Sosia, I believe I'm going mad. Mad! MAD! Sosia . . . open the box.
Sosia:	Master, that's ridiculous! The seal is unbroken, so the bowl must be within.
Amphitryo:	OPEN THE BOX, NOW!
Alcmena:	I don't think you are well. Where did the bowl come from if it didn't come from you?
Sosia:	(Opening the box.) It's gone!
Amphitryo:	IT'S WHAT?
Sosia:	It's gone! Gone! GONE!
Alcmena:	It's not gone. It's here.
Amphitryo:	O.K. . . . O.K. . . . Now, who gave you the bowl?
Alcmena:	The man who is looking at me right now gave me the bowl.
Amphitryo:	You without doubt are crazy!
Alcmena:	You gave me the bowl just before you returned to your ship.
Amphitryo:	Go on!
Alcmena:	That's it!
Amphitryo:	Sosia, just don't stand there. Speak!
Sosia:	I feel something strange is happening here.

Greek & Roman Plays for the Intermediate Grades © 1993 Pearon Teacher Aids

Amphitryo:	Yes, you are right, I'm going to investigate this whole matter. Sosia, I'm going to find a lawyer. (Exits.)
Sosia:	Mistress, now that we are alone, tell me, have I a double and is he in the house?
Alcmena:	You'll see double if I hit you in the eye! Get out of my sight!
	(Sosia enters the house. Alcmena follows. Jupiter enters.)
Jupiter:	(To the audience.) Now, which Amphitryo am I? Do you remember? I'm the Amphitryo whose servant Sosia is also Mercury. Remember now? Good! When I live up in the clouds, I am the god Jupiter, but on earth with you mortals, I am Amphitryo. Well, one of the Amphitryos. Mercury has strict orders to be on hand as soon as I need him. I believe Alcmena comes.
	(Alcmena enters from the house.)
Alcmena:	(To the audience.) It's impossible for me to live in this house with my husband accusing me of deceiving him and not believing anything I tell him. He even said I was crazy. Imagine that!
Jupiter:	Alcmena, my dear wife . . . here I am.
Alcmena:	Go away!
Jupiter:	Go away? You don't really mean that, do you?
Alcmena:	You heard correctly!
Jupiter:	You are upset.
Alcmena:	Don't you think I have a right to be upset after all the things you said to me?
Jupiter:	Send Sosia out here.
Alcmena:	Sosia, come out.
	(Sosia comes out of the house.)
Sosia:	You want me, master?

Jupiter: Yes, I want you.

Sosia: I hope you and the mistress made up.

Jupiter: How silly of you to think so. Everything has been settled.

Sosia: Great!

Jupiter: Run and tell the captain of the ship to come to my house for lunch.

(Sosia exits.)

Alcmena: I'll go prepare the luncheon. (Exits.)

Jupiter: (To the audience.)
I have them both fooled. They both think I'm the real Amphitryo. Mercury! Mercury! Mercury! Hear me wherever you are. When the real Amphitryo returns, think of something to keep him away from the house . . . keep him away while I'm eating my lunch. (He enters the house. Mercury enters from the audience.)

Mercury: Out of the way everybody. Move I say! I have urgent business for my father, Jupiter. I am a god, so you must obey. Yes, my father is the great god Jupiter, so beware. If he wants something, he gets it. Here's what I am going to do. Listen carefully, dear audience. I'm going to place a garland upon my head and then sit on the roof of the house and pretend I'm crazy. The real Sosia, of course, will be blamed for all that goes wrong. I must obey my father, the great Jupiter. Here comes the real Amphitryo now. Up onto the roof I go.

(Enter Amphitryo.)

Amphitryo: Couldn't find a lawyer anywhere. (To the audience.) I'm going into the house now to ask my wife a few direct questions. (He attempts to open the door, but it is locked.) Well, this is a fine situation . . . my own front door is locked! (Bangs on the door.) Open this door! I insist you open this door!

Mercury: (From the roof.)
Who is knocking, please?

Amphitryo: I am.

Greek & Roman Plays for the Intermediate Grades © 1993 Fearon Teacher Aids

Amphitryo

Mercury:	And pray tell, who is "I am"?
Amphitryo:	I am is me! Open this door!
Mercury:	You mustn't knock on doors, my friend.
Amphitryo:	What are you doing on my roof? Is that you, Sosia?
Mercury:	Yes, it's your Sosia. What do you want.
Amphitryo:	What do I want? What do I want?
Mercury:	That's what I said . . . what do you want?
Amphitryo:	I'll tan your hide for this impudence!
Mercury:	Allow me to pour you a libation.
Amphitryo:	What did you say?
Mercury:	To your very bad health! (He pours a bucket of water on Amphitryo.)
Amphitryo:	May the gods strike you dead! Come down here, you little monkey!
Mercury:	Don't go away. I'll be right down.
Amphitryo:	(To the audience.) He is really crazy! I never should have left him out of my sight. (Mercury appears.) Now, what do you have to say for yourself?
Mercury:	What do you have to say for yourself? I'll see if my master wished you to enter his house.
Amphitryo:	Sosia! Are you completely batty? Who do you think your master is?
Mercury:	What a silly question! Amphitryo is my master, of course.
Amphitryo:	I should hope so! And now your master has come home and wishes to enter his house.
Mercury:	I know that. My master came home last night and is already within.

Greek & Roman Plays for the Intermediate Grades © 1993 Fearon Teacher Aids

Amphitryo:	Is that so? Kindly ask your master if he would please come out to speak with me.
Mercury:	As you wish, sir. (He enters the house.)
Amphitryo:	Now, I'll grab the scoundrel! I'll catch him eating my food in my house.
	(Mercury returns from the house.)
Mercury:	I regret to inform you that my master can't see you now. He said for you to return in a few days.
Amphitryo:	Is my wife at home?
Mercury:	How can I tell you where your wife is, if I don't know who you are.
Amphitryo:	Very well, I'll rephrase my question. Is your master's wife at home?
Mercury:	Oh yes, she's at home.
Amphitryo:	Help! Help! Help! Merciful gods, help!
	(Alcmena enters.)
Alcmena:	Who is causing such a racket? Husband! Why have you left the house again? We were just ready to sit down for lunch! What is wrong, Amphitryo? Remember you said it was all a joke.
Amphitryo:	A joke? A JOKE? A joke to be shut out of my own house? To have a crazy servant dump ice water on me!
Alcmena:	I truly think you're mad!
Mercury:	I agree, madam. Shall I fetch a doctor, or shall I dump more water on his head?
Amphitryo:	Get away from here, you beast!
Alcmena:	(To the audience.) I think he is mad! Truly mad! I'll try to coax him back into the house and then send for a doctor.
	(Alcmena attempts to coax Amphitryo into the house, but just then, the captain of the ship, Blepharo, enters.)
Blepharo:	Greetings to you, Alcmena . . . I know you must be happy to welcome back your war hero husband. It's

Greek & Roman Plays for the Intermediate Grades © 1993 Fearon Teacher Aids

Amphitryo

most pleasant to see you two reunited. Well, Sosia, you returned from the ship much faster than I did.

Mercury: I came on winged feet, captain.

Blepharo: I'm ready, Amphitryo, for the luncheon you invited me to. I'm most ravenous.

(Sosia enters very tired.)

Amphitryo: I can't believe my eyes. Two Sosias! Who are you? And who are you?

Mercury: We are twin brothers.

(Sosia attempts to speak, but Mercury covers his mouth with his hand.)

Amphitryo: I think you're a couple of rogues! Now dear, dear wife . . . who is the man in my house? Who are you entertaining?

Alcmena: For the millionth time, no man is in my house. No man has entered my house, but you!

Amphitryo: But . . . but . . . but . . . you said that . . .

(Jupiter enters from the house.)

Jupiter: Alcmena, dear wife, why have you left the house?

Alcmena: Two husbands before me . . . two Amphitryos . . . I don't believe my eyes! (She faints.)

Jupiter: Look after her.

(Mercury and Sosia carry her into the house.)

Amphitryo: This is an impostor, Blepharo! Grab him!

Jupiter: Just a moment. How can you be sure, Blepharo, who is the impostor? I say he is!

Amphitryo: He is!

Jupiter: He is!

Amphitryo: He's the impostor!

Jupiter: He's the impostor!

Amphitryo: He is!

Greek & Roman Plays for the Intermediate Grades © 1993 Fearon Teacher Aids

Jupiter: He is!

Blepharo: This is too much for me to decide! (He runs away.)

Jupiter: Now I shall go in to comfort my wife. (He enters the house.)

Amphitryo: (To the audience.)
Whatever shall I do? I must get my revenge! I'll go directly to the King, that's what I'll do! No, I'll go inside my house and straighten the whole affair!

(Amphitryo attempts to enter the house, but a bolt of lightning knocks him down. Bromia enters from the house.)

Bromia: Master, are you all right?

Amphitryo: I think I'm dead!

Bromia: Do you think you can stand up?

Amphitryo: Just tell me one thing. Who am I?

Bromia: Why you are my master, Amphitryo.

Amphitryo: Bromia, you are the only sane person around here.

(A crash of thunder and flashes of lightning.)

Bromia: Merciful heavens, help!

Amphitryo: Not another bolt of lightning for me?

(Jupiter appears dressed as the god Jupiter.)

Jupiter: Have no fear, Amphitryo . . . I am on your side. Yes, it was I who visited your faithful wife. I had myself invited to dinner and lunch. Blame not Alcmena, for she thought I was you! Even the gods have their playful moods! Now I go back into the clouds . . . good luck, Amphitryo!

(Jupiter exits, Mercury enters. More thunder and lightning.)

Mercury: (To the audience.)
You had better clap very loudly, or Jupiter will strike you with a bolt of lightning, too!

(The curtain closes.)

Greek & Roman Plays for the Intermediate Grades © 1993 Fearon Teacher Aids

Amphitryo

A THREE DOLLAR DAY

By Plautus

INTRODUCTION

This Roman comedy has an impostor, and impostors almost always are unmasked. There are other interesting characters, too, such as the ones representing Luxury and her daughter, Poverty. There is also a very, very lazy son named Lesbonicus. Much fun can be had with him. Luxury, Poverty, and others often speak to the audience, and when they do, they should speak sincerely and directly.

All comedies should be brightly lighted. Mood is not important—action and directness are the key elements in producing Roman comedies.

STAGING

As is typical of Roman comedies, the stage has houses. Here two houses and an annex are called for. The center and left doors represent homes of wealth, while the door to the annex on the right represents poverty. The wealthy doors can be draped with bright cloth, a large bow, a large flower, or some other colorful decoration. The annex door can consist of rags and perhaps be smaller in size. To clearly show ownership of the houses, tack large signs above the doorways. For example, the name of Charmides, the original owner of the center door, can be crossed off and Callicles' name written underneath it.

COSTUMES

The parents and elderly characters wear floor-length togas, while the teenagers can wear shorter garments. Much imagination can be used in designing the costumes for Luxury and Poverty. When given plenty of freedom, students never fail to develop a creative approach to these characters.

VOCABULARY

advantage
annex
associate
assure
avoid
berserk
concerns
concur
confide
confidential
conscience
consent
consumes
contemporary
contract
critical
deeds
deficit
destitute
determined
disaster
dowry
eavesdrop
elderly
entrusted
extravagant
extremely
financial
flaunting
foreigner
generation
gossip
guardian
hoard
impostor
ingenious
intention
irresponsible
knowledge
luxuriously
mongers
obnoxious
opinion
pauper
personality
poverty
propose
prosperity
prudent
rash
regard
represents
reputation
ruination
scoundrel
severely
spirit
squandered
status
swindle
trustworthy

CHARACTERS

Luxury
Poverty, Luxury's daughter
Megaronides, an elderly gentleman
Callicles, Megaronides' neighbor
Lesbonicus, Charmides' son
Charmides, Lesbonicus' father
Lysiteles, Lesbonicus' best friend
Philto, Lysiteles' father
Stasimus, servant of Charmides and Lesbonicus
An Impostor

A THREE DOLLAR DAY

Luxury: Come this way, my daughter. Come with me and play your role.

Poverty: I'm coming, mother, but I'd like to know what I am supposed to do.

Luxury: Do you see that house over there? (Points to the annex.) That is where you are going. I want you to go in there right now. Yes, now. (Poverty slowly enters the annex.) Well, my dear audience, I see you are confused. You are wondering what all of this is about. Pay attention, and I will make things crystal clear to you. According to Plautus, who wrote this comedy, I am playing the role of Luxury. You can see by how luxuriously I am dressed that I'm very rich. That other girl who entered the house is playing the part of Poverty. She is very poorly dressed. Now I will tell you the reason for sending her into the annex of that house. Listen carefully. . . . In that house lives a young man who has foolishly squandered all his money. Since I represent luxury, I no longer associate with that person or house, but my daughter, who represents poverty, will fit in nicely. As the spirit of the rich, I associate with the rich, but my daughter, who is the spirit of the poor, associates with the poor. She is in rags as you saw, and the poor young man has no money left. To make things clearer for you, two old gentlemen will soon be having a conversation. Why don't you eavesdrop and find out more? Be silent and use your ears. (Exits. Enter Megaronides from his house.)

Megaronides: (To the audience.)
I now must do a very difficult thing. I must be critical of a friend, and you know how hard that is. This is what I have to do today. (Enter Callicles from his house.) See that man? He is the friend with whom I must find fault. He has been acting poorly and deserves punishment. I will speak to him about the matter that concerns me, but first I will make polite conversation. Good day, Callicles.

Greek & Roman Plays for the Intermediate Grades © 1993 Fearon Teacher Aids

Callicles:	Oh, it's you my old friend and contemporary. I trust you are enjoying good health?
Megaronides:	Thank you, I am. And the same with you, I trust?
Callicles:	And your wife?
Megaronides:	Fine! She's fine. But enough of this nonsense . . . I have something very urgent and important to discuss with you.
Callicles:	What is it?
Megaronides:	I'm afraid I have something most unpleasant to say to you. Actually, I plan to scold you severely.
Callicles:	Me?
Megaronides:	Is there anyone else here but us?
Callicles:	No.
Megaronides:	Then why do you ask if it is you? You don't think I want to scold myself, do you?
Callicles:	What do all your words mean, friend Megaronides?
Megaronides:	First of all, you are the target of much ugly gossip in the city. The citizens are calling you a money grabber, and some have even gone so far as to call you a vulture.
Callicles:	I can't stop people from speaking evil of me, but I can assure you they have no reason to speak of me in such a fashion.
Megaronides:	Answer me this . . . was my neighbor, Charmides, a friend of yours?
Callicles:	Certainly he was and still is. I'll even give you the facts to prove it. Remember when his wife died, and he had his grown daughter to look after as well as his son who was squandering the family fortune? Well, Charmides had to take a long business trip to make some money. Charmides realized I was a trustworthy friend of his, so he asked me to keep an eye on his daughter, his property, and his irresponsible son. Now I ask you, Charmides wouldn't have asked me to do this if he didn't think I was a true friend, would he?

Greek & Roman Plays for the Intermediate Grades © 1993 Fearon Teacher Aids

Megaronides: I still say you have been acting like a scoundrel!

Callicles: You are speaking in riddles, my friend.

Megaronides: The house you just came out of belonged to your friend Charmides, but didn't you just buy the house from his son? Answer that if you can!

Callicles: Yes, you are correct, but I paid him good money for it.

Megaronides: That's exactly my point. You actually gave his son, Lesbonicus, the money?

Callicles: Yes, I did.

Megaronides: My dear Callicles, to place money in that boy's hand is like giving him a sword to kill himself. You know he has no self-control. You are sending him to his ruination!

Callicles: Are you trying to say that I shouldn't have paid him what I owed him?

Megaronides: You should definitely not have paid him! His father named you the guardian of his home, son, and daughter, and you have bought the house and turned everything to your advantage.

Callicles: Those are harsh words coming from you, Megaronides. And now I will confide in you and tell you the secret behind all this affair. Charmides, before he left, entrusted me with a very important secret, swearing me to silence.

Megaronides: You can trust me, Callicles. The secret will be completely safe with me.

Callicles: You check that side, and I'll check this side to be sure no one is listening. We must be extremely careful.

(They look around the stage carefully.)

Megaronides: I didn't find a soul around. Speak forth the secret. I'm sure we can trust our good friends in the audience not to tell. Speak freely, Callicles.

Callicles: (Whispering into Megaronides' ear.)
All right, listen. Just before Charmides left on his trip, he showed me a certain room in his house, and in that

Greek & Roman Plays for the Intermediate Grades © 1993 Fearon Teacher Aids

A Three Dollar Day

room, was a hoard of money. Quick, look around before I continue with my story.

(They both look about the stage again.)

Megaronides: I can assure you no one is listening.

Callicles: With tears in his eyes, Charmides pleaded with me to keep the secret of this room to myself and to be sure his son never discovered the gold in it. The money was to be kept safe until Charmides returned from his business trip. It was to be a dowry for his daughter when she married.

Megaronides: These few words have changed my opinion of you.

Callicles: That young rascal, Lesbonicus, has made things difficult for me.

Megaronides: What has he done now?

Callicles: While I was away for a few days, that young whipper-snapper put up the house for sale. He did all this without my knowledge or consent. By selling the house, he would get money to spend foolishly.

Megaronides: Poor Charmides, to have such a son.

Callicles: You see the position I was in. I couldn't let him sell the house with the secret room full of gold. I couldn't tell him about the treasure, so all I could do was buy the house myself. That is why I handed Lesbonicus a fist of money for the house, but at least the secret room full of gold is still safe waiting for Charmides to return. Right or wrong, Megaronides, that is what I did.

Megaronides: You have silenced me, Callicles. Where is the young rascal living now?

Callicles: He is living in that (pointing) small annex behind the house, which was not included in the sale.

Megaronides: And Charmides' daughter?

Callicles: She is living with my family, safe and sound. Any other questions before I leave?

Greek & Roman Plays for the Intermediate Grades © 1993 Fearon Teacher Aids

Megaronides:	Thank you, Callicles, for sharing the secret with me. (Callicles exits. To the audience.) You see how evil and wicked gossip is? Some people who think they know everything cause much trouble. They nearly ruined my friendship with Callicles. Those gossip mongers should be punished. I realize I'm wasting your time lecturing you about gossip, for I know you people don't gossip. (Exits. Enter Lysiteles.)
Lysiteles:	(To the audience.) My name is Lysiteles, and I am a friend of Lesbonicus, the young chap who spends money freely. Ah, but here comes my father. (Enter Philto.) Greetings father. What can I do for you? I am at your service. I am not attempting to avoid you.
Philto:	I hope not! A well-behaved son should have constant regard for his father. And you are a good son. I hope you never associate with bad company. I know what young people are like these days. The young generation today is hopeless. I'm sorry to have lived to have seen such times. Always do as I tell you, my son. Listen to all my advice, and you will always have a clear conscience.
Lysiteles:	I have always been obedient, father, and I shall continue to be so. Your word is my law. Haven't I always dressed neatly? I don't steal. I come home early at night.
Philto:	All I tell you is for your own good.
Lysiteles:	Father, I have a favor to ask of you.
Philto:	What is it?
Lysiteles:	I have a friend named Lesbonicus who lives in that house, and he has been having problems of late. Father, I would like to give him a helping hand. Will you permit me to assist him?
Philto:	I suppose you wish to lend him some money?
Lysiteles:	Yes, he's broke.
Philto:	I suppose at one time he had plenty of money?

Greek & Roman Plays for the Intermediate Grades © 1993 Fearon Teacher Aids

A Three Dollar Day

Lysiteles: Yes.

Philto: And pray tell, how did he lose all his money?

Lysiteles: He was a bit too extravagant with his money, and I'm afraid he spent it foolishly.

Philto: Well, I must say, that's a fine friend you have . . . a beggar who is broke! I tell you, Lysiteles, I won't have you associating with that kind of person.

Lysiteles: But father, I assure you he's a good fellow.

Philto: You're only throwing your money away, helping such a person.

Lysiteles: Father, I would be ashamed to desert a friend in trouble.

Philto: I'd rather have you ashamed than sorry.

Lysiteles: But father, we have so much money, thanks to the gods. We have so much money that it would take two lifetimes to spend it all.

Philto: My dear boy, do you think great wealth grows greater if you subtract it?

Lysiteles: But father. Please!

Philto: All right! All right! Who is your friend who is so destitute that needs your help?

Lysiteles: He is the son of Charmides, Lesbonicus, who lives in that house.

Philto: That one! Oh, no! Not him! He consumes everything near him. Money is like water to him.

Lysiteles: Don't blame him completely, father. Lesbonicus is only a youth.

Philto: So are you only a youth, but you don't act like he does.

Lysiteles: Perhaps the gods smile more upon me.

Philto: Very well. How much do you want to give him?

Lysiteles: Father, I don't want to give him anything. My request is for you to forbid me to accept something from him.

Philto: Accept something from him? Please explain more clearly what you are attempting to say.

Lysiteles: Do you know his family, father?

Philto: Yes, an excellent family. His father, Charmides, is a most upright citizen.

Lysiteles: Well, Lesbonicus has a sister, and I want to marry her, even though she has no dowry.

Philto: What? Marry a wife without a dowry?

Lysiteles: Please don't refuse.

Philto: I can't believe my ears . . . a wife without a dowry?

Lysiteles: Yes.

Philto: I could lecture you for hours about how wrong you are wishing such disaster upon yourself, but I will not oppose you. Have it your way.

Lysiteles: May I ask you for one more favor?

Philto: You mean there's more to all of this?

Lysiteles: Would you go to Lesbonicus yourself and do the asking?

Philto: This is what I get giving in to you . . . more trouble! All right, I'll do it.

Lysiteles: You're a real father! I'll wait for you at home.

(Exits.)

Philto: (To the audience.)
My poor son! What a mess he is inflicting upon himself. Well, that's the way he wants it, and that's the way he will have it! (Enter Lesbonicus with Stasimus.) Well, well, here comes Lesbonicus with his servant.

Lesbonicus: Tell me, Stasimus, where has all the money gone?

Stasimus: The baker, the butcher, the grocer. Money soon disappears, master, when you give party after party.

Lesbonicus: Did everything cost that much?

Stasimus: Money doesn't last forever, master, when you spend it freely.

Greek & Roman Plays for the Intermediate Grades © 1993 Fearon Teacher Aids

A Three Dollar Day

Philto:	(To the audience.) A very rash young man!
Lesbonicus:	What a deficit! What a mess!
Stasimus:	You have spent all the money you received from Callicles when he purchased your house.
Lesbonicus:	I'm afraid you're right.
Philto:	(To the audience.) Good grief! When his poor father Charmides returns, what a blow this will be to him. Poor old man! He will find himself so poor that he will have to become a beggar at the city gate.
Stasimus:	And remember you owe the bank quite a bit, too!
Lesbonicus:	Right again.
Philto:	(To the audience.) I will speak to him. Greetings Lesbonicus and Stasimus.
Lesbonicus:	Greetings to you, sir, and how is your son, Lysiteles?
Philto:	He sends you his very best wishes.
Stasimus:	(To the audience.) Good wishes aren't very much without good deeds attached. I wish to be free, but what good does my wish do me? My master wishes to be more prudent with his money, but he might as well wish for the moon.
Philto:	I am now speaking for my son. He wishes to marry your sister, and I concur with his wish.
Lesbonicus:	Are you flaunting your prosperity in my face? Are you insulting my poverty?
Philto:	My dear, Lesbonicus, son of Charmides, I have no intention of insulting you. I repeat, my son, Lysiteles, sincerely wishes to marry your sister.
Lesbonicus:	I'm sorry, sir, but my family does not have the same status as yours. We are poor. Look somewhere else for a match for your son.

Stasimus:	(Whispering to Lesbonicus.) Are you cuckoo or something? How can you refuse such a splendid offer from such a rich person? He will help your financial difficulties.
Philto:	I will not allow you to make such a foolish decision.
Stasimus:	Hear, hear!
Lesbonicus:	If you don't stay out of my business, I'll knock off one of your ears!
Stasimus:	(To the audience.) I can listen with one ear as well as two.
Philto:	I propose to accept your sister as a bride for my son without any dowry. You see, it is not a question of status. Well . . . say something. Give me an answer.
Lesbonicus:	I agree, sir, but I insist on making our farm, not far from the city, my sister's dowry.
Philto:	I just told you that I want no dowry.
Lesbonicus:	And I say I insist upon one.
Stasimus:	(Whispering to Lesbonicus.) Are you mad? The farm is the only good possession we have left. You have spent or sold everything else.
Lesbonicus:	Will you be quiet. I don't have to explain things to you.
Stasimus:	(To the audience.) It looks like the bitter end for all of us. I must think of something. (To Philto.) Sir, may I speak to you way over here? (They move to the far side of the stage.)
Philto:	What do you wish to speak to me about, Stasimus?
Stasimus:	This is most confidential, so keep your mouth closed about it.
Philto:	I give you my word.
Stasimus:	I'm doing you a great favor by telling you this, sir . . . don't accept the farm as the dowry. First of all, the land is so infested with sickness that the oxen drop dead whenever the land is ploughed.
Philto:	Really?

Greek & Roman Plays for the Intermediate Grades © 1993 Fearon Teacher Aids

A Three Dollar Day

Stasimus:	And furthermore, the grapes are bitter and nasty tasting.
Philto:	Is that so?
Stasimus:	Everyone who has owned that land has had nothing but bad fortune. One owner of that farm even killed himself, he became so discouraged.
Philto:	Really?
Stasimus:	And the slaves drop like flies from farm fever. If you're looking for trouble and headaches, you'll find it on that farm.
Philto:	Thank you, Stasimus, for all the inside information. Your secret is safe with me.
Lesbonicus:	What has my servant been telling you, sir?
Philto:	Oh, what all servants talk about . . . their freedom. Since we can't come to an agreement about the dowry, why don't you settle that with my son, Lysiteles? But what is your answer about your sister marrying Lysiteles?
Lesbonicus:	I give my consent.
Stasimus:	Good!
Philto:	And I say good, too!
Lesbonicus:	Stasimus, run to the house of Callicles and tell my sister what we have arranged.
Stasimus:	Yes sir!
Lesbonicus:	And offer her my warmest congratulations.
Stasimus:	Yes sir!
Philto:	Now off to my house to draw up the wedding contract and pick the wedding day. (Exits.)
Lesbonicus:	Stasimus, do as I tell you.
Stasimus:	Are you going to Philto's house?
Lesbonicus:	First I must see how I can settle the dowry business.
Stasimus:	But are you going to Philto's house?

Greek & Roman Plays for the Intermediate Grades © 1993 Fearon Teacher Aids

Lesbonicus:	I'm determined not to have her marry without a proper dowry.
Stasimus:	But are you . . .
Lesbonicus:	I don't intend to embarrass my sister for . . .
Stasimus:	Are you going . . .
Lesbonicus:	My own stupidity, of course . . .
Stasimus:	But . . .
Lesbonicus:	It's only fair that she should . . .
Stasimus:	Sir, are you . . .
Lesbonicus:	. . . have a decent dowry.
Stasimus:	Go, sir, go.
Lesbonicus:	I'm going. (Exits.)
Stasimus:	(To the audience.) Finally, I made him move. . . . Well, at least I saved the farm for us. Now to carry out my master's orders. I can't stand the sight of this house since we were turned out of it. (He enters the house of Callicles. Luxury enters.)
Luxury:	(To the audience.) You see how nicely the characters are helping you to understand the plot? Keep listening carefully, and you'll discover more. My poor daughter, Poverty, is still hanging on to Lesbonicus. Poor Poverty. The characters are ready to speak again, so I shall leave. (Exits. Enter Callicles and Stasimus.)
Callicles:	What are you so excited about Stasimus?
Stasimus:	My young master, Lesbonicus, has made arrangements for his sister to marry the son of Philto without a dowry.
Callicles:	I don't believe it! Marry her into a wealthy family like that without a dowry? Unthinkable!
Stasimus:	Philto does not want a dowry.

Greek & Roman Plays for the Intermediate Grades © 1993 Pearon Teacher Aids

Callicles: That poor girl. It will be most embarrassing for her to marry without a dowry. Something must be done about this. I'll visit Megaronides to see what advice he can offer. (He enters the house of Megaronides.)

Stasimus: (To the audience.)
That greedy old Callicles. I know what he's after! He is going to try to buy the farm from my master, just as he bought the house. Poor Charmides, all your property will be gone by the time you return from your trip. Here comes Lesbonicus and Lysiteles . . . they don't look too happy. I must hear what they have to say to one another . . . I'll go over to the side and listen to every word.

(Enter Lysiteles and Lesbonicus.)

Lysiteles: Lesbonicus, please don't run away from me. Don't try to avoid me.

Lesbonicus: Please don't bother me. I have things to do.

Lysiteles: I'm trying to help you.

Lesbonicus: The way I see it, you're playing a dirty trick on me.

Lysiteles: I am?

Lesbonicus: Yes, you are!

Lysiteles: Only a fool would refuse an honest favor from a friend.

Lesbonicus: You're not doing me a favor. I know what the citizens of the city will say. And I would be disgracing my sister to allow her to marry you without a suitable dowry.

Lysiteles: But if you give me your farm as the dowry, then you will live in poverty forever.

Lesbonicus: Why don't you stop worrying about my living in poverty and be more concerned with my reputation.

Lysiteles: Oh no, you're not trapping me. As soon as the wedding is over and you have given me the farm as the dowry, you will be a pauper, and you won't associate with your friends, and then the citizens of the city will blame me. They will say that my stingy personality drove you away. Oh, no! Oh no you don't!

Greek & Roman Plays for the Intermediate Grades © 1993 Fearon Teacher Aids

Stasimus:	(Jumping out.) Three cheers for Lysiteles. Bravo! Bravo!
Lesbonicus:	Who asked you to put in your two cents' worth?
Stasimus:	I'm going. (Hides again in the corner.)
Lesbonicus:	Come into the house, and we will continue our conversation.
Lysiteles:	No! Here is my final offer to you. Let me marry your sister without a dowry, and you remain in the city and share all my wealth. If that offer is not satisfactory to you, then I can no longer be your friend. These are my last words to you!
	(Lysiteles exits and Lesbonicus enters his annex.)
Stasimus:	(To the audience.) Well, that was a fast exit by those two. Where does that leave me? Now I suppose my young master will join the army, and I will have to go along as his servant. Oh, what a miserable life that will be! Oooohhh! Poor me! (Exits. Megaronides comes out of his house with Callicles.)
Megaronides:	I agree that the girl should have a dowry.
Callicles:	How can I allow her to be married when I have her father's money hidden in the secret room?
Megaronides:	You are right! The dowry is right there waiting for her. And you can't wait for her father, Charmides, to return, for that might mean waiting forever.
Callicles:	What a mess! I simply can't trust Lesbonicus with the secret of all that money in the hidden room. Why he would go absolutely berserk and spend it all in two weeks!
Megaronides:	Wait! I just had a brilliant idea!
Callicles:	Yes? Yes? What?
Megaronides:	Yes, my idea is brilliant. It's an ingenious plan!
Callicles:	Yes? Yes?

Greek & Roman Plays for the Intermediate Grades © 1993 Fearon Teacher Aids

A Three Dollar Day

Megaronides:	We will have to hire some fellow who looks like a foreigner.
Callicles:	I don't understand.
Megaronides:	He will have to be a very good liar.
Callicles:	I still don't understand.
Megaronides:	This person we shall hire will go to Lesbonicus pretending that he is a messenger from his father. He will have two letters with him. One letter for Lesbonicus will say he is well and in good health, and the other letter will be for you saying that he has sent with the messenger a bag of gold for his daughter's dowry, in case she plans to be married. Get the idea, now?
Callicles:	Yes. Excellent!
Megaronides:	When you dig up the hidden treasure in the secret room, Lesbonicus won't suspect a thing. Now go along quickly to get some of the gold out of the room. Take care that no one sees you.
Callicles:	Immediately.
Megaronides:	Don't let anyone in on the plan. I'll go find a suitable impostor for the job.
Callicles:	Fine!
	(Callicles enters his house. Megaronides exits. Enter Charmides, back from his long business trip.)
Charmides:	Back at last to my own native land! I thank you, Neptune, for guiding me safely home! (To the audience.) Yes, I am Charmides, father of Lesbonicus. I have been away on a long business trip. Yes, I made a great deal of money, and now I can rest. Someone is coming, dressed in a very strange manner. I'll step to one side to hear what he has to say.
	(Enter the Impostor hired by Callicles and Megaronides.)
Impostor:	Well, this is my three dollar day! (To the audience.) That's how much I'm earning today. I'm supposed to pretend that I've come from a far away land with some letters. But three dollars is three dollars! Right?

Greek & Roman Plays for the Intermediate Grades ©1993 Fearon Teacher Aids

Charmides:	(To the audience.) He looks like some kind of a nut! I'm going to keep an eye on him, for I believe he's up to no good.
Impostor:	(To the audience.) Ah! There's the house where I'm supposed to knock!
Charmides:	Heaven help me! He's heading right for my door!
Impostor:	(Knocking on the door.) Open up!
Charmides:	Why are you knocking on that door?
Impostor:	I'm looking for a young chap named Lesbonicus and an old man called Callicles.
Charmides:	(To the audience.) Why that sounds like he's looking for my son, Lesbonicus, and my good friend, Callicles. What do you want of them?
Impostor:	Why do you want to know?
Charmides:	Just answer my question. What do you want with those two people?
Impostor:	The father of young Lesbonicus gave me two letters to deliver.
Charmides:	(To the audience.) I never gave him any letters.
Impostor:	This letter is for Lesbonicus, and this letter is for Callicles. The gentleman I met made me promise to deliver them in person.
Charmides:	(To the audience.) Now, I'm going to have a bit of fun. (To the impostor.) Can you describe the man who gave you these letters to deliver?
Impostor:	Certainly! He was much taller than you . . . oh, at least twelve inches taller.
Charmides:	(To the audience.) Strange that I'm taller in one country and shorter in my own. Are you sure you know this man who gave you the letters?

Greek & Roman Plays for the Intermediate Grades © 1993 Pearon Teacher Aids

Impostor:	What a silly question! Of course I know him. How else did I come by the letters?
Charmides:	What did you say his name was?
Impostor:	Let me see . . . . It's . . . uh . . . uh . . . uh . . .
Charmides:	Are you telling me his name is uh-uh-uh?
Impostor:	It's on the tip of my tongue, but I just can't seem to say it.
Charmides:	(To the audience.) I think I arrived home just in time, don't you?
Impostor:	(To the audience.) I think he has me trapped!
Charmides:	I have a feeling that you don't know this gentleman very well.
Impostor:	But, of course, I know him very well.
Charmides:	Is his name by any chance Charmides?
Impostor:	Yes . . . yes . . . that's it!
Charmides:	(To the audience.) This is really a crazy situation. Would you recognize this man if you saw him?
Impostor:	Of course I would. How ridiculous! I've known him all my life. Why else would he trust me with a bag of gold to deliver? We are best friends.
Charmides:	(To the audience.) What a liar! I never saw him before this very day, and yet he insists that I gave him some gold. Are you sure it was Charmides who gave you this gold?
Impostor:	Sure I'm sure!
Charmides:	Give me the gold!
Impostor:	What gold?

Charmides: The money you said you received from me.

Impostor: Money I received from you?

Charmides: Yes, from me.

Impostor: Who are you, anyway?

Charmides: My name is Charmides, and I'm the man who gave you the gold.

Impostor: Oh no you aren't.

Charmides: Yes I am.

Impostor: You are an impostor! It takes one to know one. You can't swindle me!

Charmides: Listen carefully. I repeat, I am Charmides!

Impostor: Are you really?

Charmides: Yes, really, really!

Impostor: The real Charmides?

Charmides: Yes, the real Charmides!

Impostor: Well, so you finally have returned to your native soil after all these years. Well, well!

Charmides: Yes. Now be gone before I report you to the authorities! (Impostor exits. To the audience.) Now I can relax a bit! What an obnoxious fellow! Well, well, here comes Stasimus, my loyal servant.

(Enter Stasimus.)

Stasimus: (To the audience.)
I suppose nothing has been settled yet about the dowry?

Charmides: My greetings to you, Stasimus.

Stasimus: Can I believe my very own eyes? It is really the master returned? Oh beloved master, welcome, welcome!

Charmides: Tell me, is all well with my son and daughter?

Stasimus: Both alive!

Greek & Roman Plays for the Intermediate Grades © 1993 Fearon Teacher Aids

Charmides:	For that I'm grateful. Now, let us enter the house. (He starts toward the door of his former house.)
Stasimus:	Where do you think you're going, sir?
Charmides:	I'm entering my home, of course.
Stasimus:	Sir, do you think this is your home?
Charmides:	Of course it's my home.
Stasimus:	Sir, I'm afraid that this is no longer your house.
Charmides:	Am I hearing you correctly?
Stasimus:	Sir, your house has been sold.
Charmides:	My house sold?
Stasimus:	Sir, your son has sold your house!
Charmides:	Sold my house?
Stasimus:	Sir, you seem upset.
Charmides:	Who me, upset? Upset? Upset? I'm ruined! Betrayed! I can't breathe . . . help . . . I faint!
	(Charmides falls into the arms of Stasimus. They both fall to the ground.)
Stasimus:	Help! Help! My master is dead!
	(Enter Callicles from the house.)
Callicles:	What is the trouble?
Charmides:	So! You call yourself a friend? Some friend! You certainly took very poor care of my property, friend!
Callicles:	I'll explain everything! Come into the house.
	(They all enter the house. The annex door swings open, and Poverty is kicked out.)
Poverty:	(To the audience.) I'm delighted this comedy has come to an end. Save your pennies, my friends, or I might be visiting your houses!
	(Curtain falls.)

Greek & Roman Plays for the Intermediate Grades © 1993 Fearon Teacher Aids